W9-CJG-951

Accent on Privilege
English Identities and Anglophilia in the U.S.

Accent on Privilege

English Identities and Anglophilia in the U.S.

KATHARINE W. JONES

TEMPLE UNIVERSITY PRESS

Philadelphia

Temple University Press, Philadelphia 19122
Copyright © 2001 by Temple University
All rights reserved
Published 2001
Printed in the United States of America

☉ The paper used in this publication meets the requirements of the American
National Standard for Information Sciences—Permanence of Paper for Printed
Library Materials, ANSI Z39.48-1984

Library of Congress Cataloging-in-Publication Data

Jones, Katharine W., 1967–
   Accent on privilege : English identities and anglophilia in the U.S. /
Katharine W. Jones.
      p.   cm.
   Includes bibliographical references and index.
   ISBN 1-56639-900-9 (alk. paper) — ISBN 1-56639-901-7 (pbk. : alk. paper)
      1. British Americans—Ethnic identity.   2. British Americans—Race
identity.   3. British Americans—Social conditions.   4. United States—
Ethnic relations.   5. United States—Race relations.   6. National character-
istics, British.   7. Great Britain—Foreign public opinion, American.
8. Racism—United States.   9. Social status—United States.   10. Sex role—
United States.   I. Title.

E184.B7 J66 2001
305.821073–dc21   2001027686

Dedicated to my Grandfather,
Dick Orlando Jones, 1903–99.
  By his example, he taught me the joys of
  hearty laughter, attentive listening,
  and lifelong learning.

"Imagine there's no countries
It isn't hard to do
Nothing to kill or die for . . ."
  —*John Lennon,* Imagine,
    EMI Blackwood Music Inc., 1971

Contents

Acknowledgments

I OWE an enormous debt of thanks to many people who have helped to make this book possible. The people who agreed to be interviewed let a stranger into their homes and talked freely and frankly about their experiences in the U.S. Without their honesty, the book would not have been possible.

Friends and colleagues have generously given their time to read drafts of parts or all of the manuscript: Rachel Batch, Jeanne Bowlan, Victoria Heckler, Jennifer Hope, Alistair (Alix) Howard, Julie Kimmel, Vince Mola, Samantha Pinto, and Jessica Stern all provided me with thoughtful, critical, and engaging comments. Judy Gerson and Richard Williams have guided and encouraged me throughout my academic career, and Ruth Frankenberg has inspired me by both her own work on whiteness and her comments on my dissertation. This book was shaped in part by work that I did in graduate school with the assistance of Farid Abdel Nour, Roberto Franzosi, Priti Joshi, Pat Roos, Kim Wittenstrom, and Eviatar Zerubavel. Fellow immigrants who inspired this project are Tina Antill, David Clouston, Siân Davis, Melissa Joralemon, and Ashley Wharton. Paul Bonk, Kathleen Casey, Nicky Isaacson, Norah McCormack, Sue Rovi, Tom Schrand, Sue Schrand, and Susie Sobel have all provided moral support along the way. Others who have helped me to find important pieces of information are Gregg Bucken-Knapp, Clare at the British Tourist Authority in New York, and Louise McShane and Sherri Litweiler at the Gutman Library. The American Association of University Women supported me with a generous fellowship, which enabled me to analyze my data. People at Rutgers University and Philadelphia University have provided me with material and emotional support, particularly Marion Roydhouse, who helped to clear a path to enable me to write. The staff at Temple University Press have been particularly helpful, especially Tamika Hughes, as have Janet Greenwood and Susan Maier of Berliner, Inc. Michael Ames, my acquiring editor, was so committed to the manuscript that I felt strengthened by his unswerving belief in me. Micah Kleit stepped in at a critical moment and guided me through the process of completing the manuscript. Thanks also to Simon Gibbard, Diana Jones, Duncan Pickstock, and Andrew Wilkinson, who helped me to visualize the book and its cover.

My family—Diana Jones, Peter Jones, and Wendy Jones—have not only read parts of the manuscript, but have also supported me with love and good humor on the days when I have doubted myself. Finally, Patty McDaniel has been a pillar of strength throughout the writing process. She has read the manuscript countless times, always providing a fresh perspective, and her steady counsel and wise analyses have been a constant source of inspiration.

To everyone who has helped with the writing of the book, thank you.

1 "I Want to Be Able to Be English When *I* Want to Be"

Identities as Sites of Contestation

I used to find a certain kind of *Englishness* engaging. I don't anymore.

Pat Barker, *The Eye in the Door*

I don't want to change the world
I'm not looking for a new England . . .

Billy Bragg, *A New England*

ENGLISH IDENTITIES

"I WANT TO BE able to be English when *I* want to be." So remarked Ken,[1] who clearly views his national identity as negotiable. His parents were both English; he had been educated at an English "public" school;[2] he thought of England as home; but he had spent the previous six years in the U.S. His status as an English person in the U.S. seemed to give him the sense that he could repudiate or exaggerate his national identity at will. Speaking from a position of relative privilege, this young white man had a sense of control over the degree of Englishness he felt. National identity, for him, was dynamic and contestable.

This book explores the issue of identity construction, using English immigrants in the U.S. as a case study. By interviewing a sample of white English people living on the East Coast of the U.S., I examine how they experience and understand their national, racial, class, and gender identities in a foreign context. My interest is in how individuals contest, reject, or affirm their identities in everyday interactions using particular cultural practices. Because they operate within a context of American Anglophilia, I am also able to analyze the relatively privileged position of English people in the U.S.

Although my focus is on the English in the U.S., the people I spoke to came from a context in which English identity was in a state of flux.

Many of them had moved to the U.S. because of the lack of employment in England, often as part of the so-called brain drain,[3] whereas others had left England because they despised the government and policies of Prime Minister Margaret Thatcher. When I conducted the interviews in the mid-1990s, England seemed to many to be on a road to nowhere—still recovering from the skyrocketing unemployment of the 1970s and 1980s, with a per capita gross domestic product somewhere between Italy's and Greece's;[4] bruised by the handover of its empire; dependent on the U.S. for financial and military aid;[5] warily eyeing the expanding mandate of the European Union; and facing the possibility of the *Break-up of Britain*, the title of Tom Nairn's famous book on the subject,[6] as Scottish, Welsh, and Northern Irish nationalists grew ever more vocal.

Today, with continued concerns about the European Union and the new legislative assemblies in Edinburgh, Cardiff, and Belfast, the English seem to be confronting a new identity crisis, and a growing number of books and articles on England and Britain address this concern.[7] The phenomenon of "Cool Britannia" and the seeming loss of the "stiff-upper-lip" mentality following the death of Princess Diana have added to the debates.[8] The English people I interviewed discussed many of these issues, showing the interest everyday English people have in defining identity. In the chapters that follow, I show how the interviewees attempted to redefine national identity for themselves, rejecting a "Little England"[9] mentality, the image of a stiff upper lip, the heritage industry, the emphasis on the monarchy, and the colonial mind-set. However, although some of the people I spoke with had repudiated England by moving to the U.S., they often seemed to view England through the misty eyes of nostalgia. This book therefore taps into a number of unresolved issues about English national identity.

WHY *ENGLISH* NATIONAL IDENTITY?

I chose to study English, rather than British, national identity for a number of reasons. Although the formal name of the nation-state is the United Kingdom of Great Britain and Northern Ireland, this includes four different nations: Scotland, Wales, Northern Ireland, and England. Much has been written about regional nationalisms in Scotland, Wales, and Northern Ireland, prompted by fears about, or pleas for, a (Dis)United Kingdom.[10] Because each nation within Britain has its own relationship to the whole, there are potentially many different kinds of British national identity. A study of British national identity would have to address the complexities of all the nationalisms within Britain or run the risk of overgeneralization. Although focusing exclusively on England marginalizes the other three nations, by choosing white, upper-middle-class English people, I decided to study members of the most privileged national grouping in Britain.[11]

It is particularly important to investigate this privileged position of England, because England is so often conflated with "Britain"—in the minds of some English people, anyway.[12] While conducting the interviews, I quickly realized that the people I was talking to often disagreed with me about the appropriate terminology to describe the national identity we were discussing. For example, when I asked a question about *England* or *English* culture, many interviewees answered in terms of *Britain* or *British* culture. In most cases, this slippage seemed unconscious, as they used "England" and "Britain" interchangeably. Indeed, some openly admitted that they saw the two as basically the same. Others, however, wished to draw a distinction between the two terms. Some argued strongly that they were English, while others were just as forceful about the fact that they were British. Proponents of the term "English" explained that it was preferable to be specific; and proponents of the term "British" argued that it was better to be inclusive of people from Scotland, Wales, and Northern Ireland, who were also part of the nation. In terms of my own language in this book, I refer to the people I interviewed as "English," and I usually refer to "England" rather than "Britain." However, in cases where the context suggests "British" as a more accurate description (for instance, in discussing statistics about Britain, British imperialism, or the British government), I use "Britain," the more inclusive term.

THE INTERVIEWEES

In order to explore the phenomenon of English national identity abroad, I interviewed thirty-four English people living in the Northeastern U.S. I saw this group as sociological "strangers"[13] in an unfamiliar cultural context, whose experiences of negotiating their "alien" status in the U.S. would yield rich data about their multiple identities. As Stuart Hall (1993) asserts, "You only know who you are when you go somewhere else." This suggests that the English abroad are an appropriate group to examine when analyzing the forms that English national identity can take. In particular, English people's interactions with Americans offer ways for them to talk about their understandings of being English in a context in which English culture is generally valued.

I conducted the interviews from March to October 1995 and traveled up and down the U.S. East Coast to meet with the interviewees. I found these English people using "snowball" sampling, which involves tapping into networks and letting the first interviewees act as guides to the next set of interviewees. For some of my sample, I approached people who worked in international organizations or who attended international groups; I also relied on networks at my university. I was particularly interested in interviewing white, predominantly middle- and upper-class people in order to analyze the effect of privilege on identity construction. I tried to find diversity in terms of age, region of origin in England, number of years lived in the U.S., immigrant status, and reasons for moving to the U.S. I interviewed equal numbers of women and men to explore whether gender had an effect on national identity. I describe the people I talked to in more detail in the appendix at the end of the book.[14]

During the one- to four-hour interviews, I asked people to discuss how they understood what it meant to be English. My questions covered the conditions under which they experienced their identities, the times they downplayed or emphasized them, and the different identity-constructing devices they used. I obtained a mixture of personal revelation and individual anecdotes about being English in the U.S. and reflections on the meanings that different aspects of their identities had for them. I taped all of the interviews, then transcribed and coded them using a computer program before beginning the analysis.[15]

My own identity as an English person living in the U.S. improved my chances of gaining access to the interviewees and may have changed the dynamics of the interviews themselves. The rapport I achieved with the respondents was due partly to our shared identity, at least according to some of the interviewees. (I actually have dual-nationality, but, as I discuss in Chapter 4, I have a fairly un-Americanized English accent.[16]) One respondent, Frances, for instance, claimed, "If you were American, . . . I'd probably be answering the questions differently. [I] wouldn't be so relaxed. [You ask] straightforward questions. There are always nuances to what [Americans] ask you." Her words imply that she thought of me as very different from an American interviewer and that she trusted me in ways that she would not trust an American. Another interviewee, Octavia, commented on the fact that she had curled up on the couch in the den to talk to me: "I don't think I'd be sitting here talking like this if you were American, meeting you for the first time."

Most of the interviews were informal. I was lucky enough to interview many people in their homes, and we usually sat around the kitchen table or made ourselves comfortable in the living room. As I interviewed some people, their children ran in and out. Others invited me to stay for dinner or to return on other occasions (which I did). Some sent me relevant newspapers or books after the interview, or we kept in touch via e-mail. All were extremely willing to let me into their lives and seemed very eager to talk about their experiences.

This comfort level affected the interviews in various ways. The interviewees usually commented on my Englishness and asked where I was from or what I thought of what they had said. At first, these moments made me uncomfortable because I worried that the questions would disrupt the flow of the interview. However, as I interviewed more people, I saw these moments as instances in which the respondents were building a connection and developing a sense of trust in me. I grew less afraid of answering their questions, although I sometimes found myself in difficult positions when I did not agree with their analyses. As feminist researchers have argued, one-sided interviews can be exploitative, and I tried to abide by the principle that an interviewer should give as well as take from the interviewees.[17] Some seemed to find the interview cathartic: A few people said they felt as though they were talking to a therapist, while others obviously relished the memories the questions aroused. The interviews did, however, make some respondents feel homesick and sad.

The interviewees were extremely open and usually answered questions without hesitation. As I explore in Chapter 7, they sometimes thought of Englishness as emerging naturally during their interactions with other English people. Hence, they often seemed to assume that I shared their experiences and feelings about Americans and so did not feel that they had to tailor their responses to fit what they thought I wanted to hear. The disadvantage to this is that their perceptions of my Englishness may have encouraged them to express biases and prejudices against Americans more forcefully than they would have if I had been noticeably American. They seemed to find the experience positive: Some argued that they could get to "deeper issues" quickly with me because I shared their cultural references. However, the flip side is that they may have assumed that I would understand them to such an extent that they did not need to offer much explanation. An interviewer who was not so noticeably English undoubtedly would have obtained a different kind of interview. And as in any interview, I faced moments in which I was conscious of how much we had not talked about—that my incursion into their lives was just the "tip-of-the-iceberg" (Frankenberg 1993: 41). The respondents' perceptions of my Englishness may have exacerbated this. Like all social-scientific work, this study has its biases, and these issues should be borne in mind when reading my analyses.[18]

THE SOCIAL CONSTRUCTION OF IDENTITY

Rather than assuming that people unquestioningly possess a national identity passed on to them from the top down, I use a "bottom-up" approach in this book, asking how that identity is experienced and understood by individuals and focusing on the words they use to describe it.[19] Identity, after all, provides an answer to the perennial human question, "Who am I?"[20] Because nations and identities are social constructions,[21] empirically examining the role that individuals play in constructing national identity makes sense.

Individuals, however, are likely to experience the concepts on which they base their identities as "real," existing "out there." Hence, they tend to see their identities as essential, natural, and unchangeable rather than as constructed by individuals and society.[22] This "natural attitude"[23] obscures the work that individuals do during interactions to "create . . . and sustain [their] reality" (Kessler and McKenna 1978: 5).[24] Therefore, they come to assume that all holders of their identity share essential traits and characteristics.[25] By analyzing how individuals consciously and unconsciously infuse with national symbolism such daily activities as telling jokes and watching television, we learn how national identity is enacted rather than take it for granted. Thus, I explore how national identity is manifested, maintained, rejected, or renewed in individuals' daily lives.

Drawing on insights from ethnomethodology, symbolic interactionism, feminist theories, and analyses of race and ethnicity, I argue that national identities are a product of routine interactions and practices.[26] This scholarship focuses on the ways that individuals participate in the construction of both the social world and their own selves as they interact with others. Presenting themselves almost as if they were actors in a play, individuals hold one another accountable for their behavior; this is how meaning is created in everyday life.[27] Identities emerge as we interact with others through the meanings we create—what we say, what we wear, how we act, and how others interpret our actions.[28] Just as some argue that we "do" gender in our daily lives,[29] I point to the ways in which individuals do work to construct their national identities. "Identity," therefore, can almost be seen more as a verb than as a noun. Indeed, my research shows how we use cultural practices in our daily interactions to negotiate our identities. In the same way that wearing certain clothes or using separate bathrooms reproduces gender identity, so watching particular films or speaking with a particular accent can reproduce national identity.

Focusing on the everyday aspects of identity shows the agency individuals have in constructing and responding to their identities. It also illustrates the situationally specific nature of identities, which wax and wane as individuals assert or downplay them.[30] Identities appear to be dynamic and contested, contingent and provisional, as individuals create, re-create, and challenge them as they live their lives. This quality of dynamism means that individuals have some degree of choice over when to affirm and when to reject their identities, as Ken suggested when he said, "I want to be able to be English when *I* want to be."[31] Identities are not omnirelevant, and people do not have to "do" their identity all the time. In fact, identities vary in salience depending on the person, the interaction, the practice, and the situation. However, identities are usually latent and have the *potential* to be relevant.[32]

In addition, individuals "do" their identities within particular contexts. The work they do on their identities is constrained or facilitated by forces outside their control. These forces—power structures and discourses—consist of economic, political, and social processes experienced as customs, ideals, languages, norms, institutions, and ideologies.[33] However, these structures, in turn, are the result of daily practices that have themselves become routinized and institutionalized over time.[34] Indeed, structures and practices are linked together in a dialectical relationship. While structures constrain or enable individuals' practices, those structures are also composed of practices. Thus, the potential always exists for new structures or new discourses to be formed from practices.[35]

Identities, then, are not free-floating. Rather, they are subject to structural constraints and enablements. Although people may negotiate the meaning of their identities as they act and interact, and may assert or reject parts of their identities at different moments, their actions ultimately are limited by the broader sociohistorical and structural locations within which they operate. Thus, the processes of identity construction are always responsive to cultural and structural factors.

GENDER, RACE, CLASS, AND NATIONAL IDENTITY

Scholars of gender, race, and class have noted the ways in which these kinds of identity intertwine to produce new and compounded forms of experience.[36] Indeed, examining the intersections of different forms of identity enables us to overcome simplistic assumptions about the uniformity and universality of identities. Precisely because identities are constituted at the level of practice, as well as at the level of structure, gender, race, and class will be more or less relevant in different situations and will intersect with one another to produce diverse sets of experience.[37] To these intersections, I add national identity, arguing that forms of nationality are predicated on certain definitions of gender, race, and class.[38]

In the case of people from England, the relationship between whiteness and national identity has a long history.[39] England's colonial expansion (in Wales, Scotland, and Ireland, as well as farther afield) constructed the peoples with whom the English came into contact as "others." Thus, at particular

> historical moments, certain "others" became central to public definitions of Englishness. . . . The Irish labouring man, the South Pacific "savage," the prostitute or the redeemed negro might dominate the hierarchies of English "otherness," either with a fearful demonology or in the spirit of a civilising dream. (C. Hall 1993: 216)

The combined force of the "demonology" and "civilising dream" was partially justified by beliefs in Social Darwinism,[40] which argued that blacks[41] were inferior to whites and hence needed to be civilized. Colonialism thus provided an "other" with which colonizers could contrast themselves.[42] Often this contrast involved projecting devalued traits onto these "others" while constructing oneself as the epitome of all that was civilized and good.[43] However, the discourses used to construct white hegemony in colonies were also used to keep white working-class and female colonials in line.[44] White, male, and upper-middle class identity thus depended on "its others to shore up its sense of security, to reflect back the disowned parts of itself as inferior, contemptible, dependent, frightened or threatening."[45] As they asserted white European hegemony, meanwhile, the colonizers constructed innocent and utopian images of themselves.[46]

As current work in racial and ethnic studies shows, the spirit of the empire lives on, as whiteness is still constructed in opposition to racial and ethnic others.[47] Indeed, the immigration to England of people from formerly colonized countries has thrown the racist discourses embedded in Englishness into sharper relief.[48] The legacy of empire has contributed to the definition of whiteness as the normative, taken-for-granted category in Englishness, as I discuss in detail in Chapters 5 and 6. In addition, because the state and the rights and responsibilities of citizenship are not gender-neutral,[49] it is perhaps unsurprising that women are usually seen as reproducers of the nation and its values and as symbolic markers of boundaries between nations.[50] Indeed, feminist deconstructions of immigration legislation have shown the ways in which gender and race function together to define women immigrants only in terms of their capacity to marry and reproduce rather than as independent entities.[51] Thus, definitions of national identity in England are gendered as well as raced.

IMMIGRANTS OR EXPATRIATES?

There are very few contemporary studies of white English people living the U.S. (Pauline Greenhill studied English immigrants in Canada but was not specific about their race.[52]) There are, however, many historical treatments of immigration from the British Isles to the U.S.[53] The presence of English people in the U.S. has been noted in the media and popular culture (as I show in Chapter 3). In 1995, the year in which I conducted my interviews, 673,832 people who were born in England were living in the U.S.[54] Of these people, 85.98 percent were white,[55] 54 percent were women, and 72.32 percent worked in managerial, professional, technical, sales, or support positions.[56] A large percentage of these English people lived in California (20.83%); however, the percentage was also large (24.53%) in the Northeast, where I did my interviewing (4.86% in Massachusetts; 7.54% in New York; 6.91% in New Jersey; 2.42% in Pennsylvania; 2.46% in Maryland; and 0.34% in the District of Columbia). Other pockets of English people were living in Illinois (6.08%) and Florida (7.52%).

My study investigates the intersections of nation, race, class, and gender at a particular nexus. By interviewing middle- and upper-middle-class white English immigrants, I explore the national identities of those with relative privilege. I focus exclusively on whites to emphasize that whiteness is a racial category that can be analyzed using concepts similar to those used to study other racial categories.[57] The burgeoning literature on whiteness suggests that researchers should interrogate the ways white people experience their racial identities, how whiteness has been constructed historically as a category,[58] and how it is negotiated by whites on a day-to-day basis as it confers "unearned advantage" and "conferred dominance" on its members.[59]

Skin color gives white immigrants in the U.S. privileges that they might otherwise be denied, given their immigrant status. However, the white English people I talked to often did not see themselves as immigrants. As I discuss in detail in Chapter 3, they were apt to distance themselves from immigrants who were not white and not middle class, suggesting the racialized and classed nature of the term "immigrant." For instance, some argued that bureaucratic restrictions that might apply to immigrants from the "Third World" should not apply to them because they were white English professionals. Especially in the U.S., the dominant discourse about immigration is a discourse about particular kinds of immigrants. Although the anti-immigrant legislation of the 1990s applied to white and non-white immigrants alike, anti-immigrant sentiment is usually directed toward people of color, whom Americans seem to see as more "un-American" than white immigrants.[60] "Immigrant" also is often a coded way to refer to people of color. As some of my interviewees pointed out, Americans do not usually see white English people as immigrants. As the scholarship on whiteness suggests, the underlying understandings of the U.S. as a white nation run deep indeed.[61]

Yet there were other reasons that many of the people I spoke to rejected the term "immigrant." Like the Iranian exiles Hamid Naficy (1993: 16) examined in Los Angeles, they are not "native" to either their home or to the host society. They are no longer legally "foreigners," neither are they *bona-fide* "citizens." They are neither openly, nor secretly, nor dually "marginal." They are not merely "strangers" or simply cultural "tourists," and they cannot strictly speaking be considered members of an established "ethnic group." Finally, they cannot be entirely characterized as "sojourners," "refugees," or "homeless." [They are] none of the above entirely but all of them partially.

The people I talked to were "liminal" in that they lived in one country but dreamed of their eventual return to another. Only one had definite plans to return to England, and only two had definite plans to remain in the U.S. Sixteen of the others had vague plans to go back, and fourteen had vague plans to stay. However, these "plans" were unstable enough to vary within the course of an interview.[62] In addition, just under half of the interviewees (sixteen) were British citizens but held green cards that allowed them to work in the U.S.; twelve had British citizenship but no green card: They were waiting for their green cards or held student visas or other kinds of special visas issued for short-term work; and six interviewees were dual-nationals, with British and American citizenship (four of these had obtained U.S. citizenship since arriving in the U.S.).[63]

If, as Naficy argues, exiles by definition dream longingly of their homeland, then these people were exiles, as their nostalgia for England shows.[64] However, they did not define themselves as such. They were more likely to define themselves as "expatriates" (although others wished to distance themselves from the expatriate label), and only a few saw themselves as "immigrants" (as I discuss in Chapter 3). When I began this project, I assumed that "expatriate" referred to people who planned to go "home" one day, while immigrants were those who planned to stay. However, these plans seemed to have little or no correlation with whether people described themselves as immigrants or expatriates.

The term "expatriate," with its affectionate shortened form "expat," suggests more positive connotations than "immigrant." Bearing in mind the status of the U.S. as a former British colony, choosing "expatriate" rather than "immigrant" to describe oneself draws on a legacy of colonizing expatriates traveling the world, perhaps retaining the option of returning "home." However, several of the people I talked to made fun of the expatriate label, situating it within a colonizing context that they found inappropriate to their own experiences. Mike, for instance, chuckled about a program he had heard on the BBC World

Service in which "strange British . . . expats in [places like] Burma" write in to request "jingly-jangly, American, awful popular songs" from the 1950s that the host retrieved from the BBC archive for them. "It's just all a bit weird," he concluded, explicitly distancing himself from the poor souls for whom the BBC archive was a lifeline. Alex was more self-reflective about how the term "expatriate" might actually apply to her: She saw herself as a "ridiculous . . . Brit abroad" because she and her husband belonged to a British group that celebrated Guy Fawkes Night,[65] ate British snacks, and took quizzes about the London Underground, among other things. She laughingly suggested that she felt like "these ladies on the northwest frontier of India . . . in the heat partaking in tea . . . , and I suppose this is the modern-day equivalent."

Alex had obviously found a community of other people from Britain;[66] most, however, wanted to distance themselves from the idea of "expat communities," English "ghettos," and other "Brits abroad."[67] Thus, Harry rejected the idea of "get[ting] too chummy" with other English people, and Ian had no desire to sit around and "eat pork pies" with "expats." Even those who described themselves as having immigrated to the U.S., such as Frank, were likely to claim that they felt "stateless," despite their residence or nationality in the U.S. Thus, neither "immigrant" nor "expatriate" stuck consistently. A set of terms that was popular among some interviewees included "travelers," "citizens of the world," "gypsies," or "roving people" with "wanderlust."[68] When they used these terms, they saw themselves as belonging nowhere, believing that they were definable by the excitement they found in travel.

These semantic debates about the meaning of their move to the U.S. highlight the contradictions under which these people operated. Although they were immigrants in the U.S., with the feelings of alienation and homesickness that this engendered, they were also there under conditions of relative privilege. This was not only because Americans usually did not see them as immigrants (because of their skin color or because of their Englishness), but also because they enjoyed the luxury of choosing whether or not to be immigrants at a time that anti-immigrant sentiment ran high. Immigrants are assumed not to speak English; these immigrants spoke English as their first language (and often believed that they spoke it better than Americans). They also lived under conditions of relative Anglophilia, as particular kinds of English culture appeared to garner social status on the U.S. East Coast.

PRIVILEGE AND ANGLOPHILIA: MAKING USE OF ENGLISH CULTURE

The relationship between English and American culture lies at the heart of the experiences of the people I talked to. Their privileged position as white people is exacerbated by the approbation lavished on English people by Americans. Aside from the political "special relationship" between the two countries (resolidified since the Ronald Reagan–Margaret Thatcher days by Bill Clinton and Tony Blair), American culture itself is particularly Anglophilic. Again and again this phenomenon emerges: in the use of English accents on American television to sell high-quality products, the popularity of *Masterpiece Theatre* and similar British television programming, the influx of British films and actors in the U.S., the extensive interest in Princess Diana and the mourning that accompanied her death, and the fact that Britain is Americans' number-one travel destination in Europe.[69] The people I talked to also experienced Anglophilia from individual Americans in the Northeast in their daily lives, from positive comments about their accents to assumptions that they were intelligent and well educated. In general, they felt that Americans were complimentary about English people and English culture. This Anglophilia can be seen as form of cultural capital on which English people can draw.[70]

The value placed on English culture in the U.S. suggests the incentives these individuals had to "do" their national identities.[71] As individuals interact with others, they use culture to construct their own meanings and understandings of the world. Ann Swidler's conception of culture as a "tool kit," or a repertoire from which people draw as they decide how to act, shows that culture provides social actors with symbols, rituals, stories, habits, worldviews, and guides to action.[72] They use these "material[s] of [their] daily lives, the bricks and mortar of [their] most commonplace understandings" (Willis 1979 [1977]: 184–5) to engage with the world and define it as they see fit. However, in implementing and drawing on these guides, they

> extend and adapt these schemata and rules. Each application involves responding to circumstances which are, in some respects, new. . . . [This] is a creative process which often involves some degree of selection and judgement, and in which the rules and schemata may be modified and transformed in the very process of application. (Thompson 1990: 148–9)

Thus, culture constantly evolves and changes as people use it to live their lives. This dynamism allows for multiple meanings. As Floya Anthias and Nira Yuval Davies (1992: 33) write, "although at certain moments there might be a hegemonic construction of the collectivity's culture and history, its dynamic, evolving, historical nature continuously re-invents, reconstructs, reproduces the cultural inventory of various collectivities."

The English people I interviewed worked with culture to make sense of their various identities. Often they used hegemonic images of Englishness, especially those emanating from media, popular culture, or collective memories or myths. For instance, some used representations of England from films and television programs to argue that England was a beautiful, green, historical theme park. Others responded to questions of imperialism by drawing on hegemonic discourses of power-evasion[73] or by expressing guilt and shame. Still others rejected the representations of Englishness they saw around them, preferring to use their own memories or to avoid generalizing about England at all. In these cases, interviewees engaged in conceptual work as they responded to hegemonic definitions of Englishness, sometimes challenging them, sometimes accepting them unquestioningly, and sometimes reworking them for their own purposes.

In the chapters that follow, I discuss three other instances of identity work[74] that emerged from my interviews as individuals talked about using cultural practices to enhance or downplay their identities as English. I point to the unintentional or habitual ways that they used culture in their daily lives, especially as they negotiated their accents. I also examine the more intentional practices used by these interviewees, particularly those from which they gained material or psychological benefits. Thus, I show how they garnered privileges from acting in "English" ways, most notably by playing up aspects of themselves that others defined as English. Also, they were able to enhance their own self-esteem by distancing themselves from Americans, using forms of culture as diverse as humor, fashion, and accent. In addition, I find evidence of a degree of playfulness in their identity negotiation, as they parodied versions of Englishness, exaggerating their national identity in jest. These cultural practices, together with their interactions with Americans and other English people, suggest the ways in which their identities wax and wane on a routine basis as they live their lives in the U.S.

CHAPTER OVERVIEWS

In Chapter 2, I examine the interrelationships between nostalgia and national pride, showing the ways the people I talked to use discourses of naturalness to negotiate these extreme national sentiments. I show how they do conceptual work using representations of England from the media and popular culture to enhance their self-esteem; however, they also criticize the stereotypes of Englishness embedded in these images so they can retain control of the definition of that identity. Thus, I show how the nostalgia the interviewees felt for particular cultural practices and particular versions of Englishness contributes to the construction of their national identity, despite their oft-stated ambivalence about having a national identity.

The interviewees' understandings of themselves as privileged in the U.S. are the focus of Chapter 3. I examine their responses to their race and class privileges, particularly the extent to which they see themselves as different from other immigrants in the U.S. I also focus on their perceptions of Anglophilia, the love of English culture that they believe Americans have. I note the ways they hold Americans responsible for their Anglophilia, and I show how some critique it while others use it to their advantage. Woven throughout this chapter is the tension between discourses of identity as natural and identity as work. I use two examples of cultural practices—humor and fashion—to show the ways they do work to distinguish themselves from Americans, even though they might believe that there are natural differences between them and their hosts.

In Chapter 4, I further investigate the work that my informants put into their English identities, examining their use of linguistic practices in identity negotiation and construction. I focus on a particular instance in which superiority and privilege become relevant—the English accent. My interviews show how English accents are valued in the U.S. during interactions and the vested interest these English people have in maintaining their accents—and even emphasizing them. I suggest that this is so because they equate their accents with their English identities. I show the different kinds of practice embedded in their accent negotiation, arguing that they work at their accents to distance themselves from Americans or to gain privileges from them, and I use the relationship between accent and identity to refine the concept of practice.

My analysis shows the contradictory nature of identity—that individuals do work to construct something they already believe is core to their being. Again, I consider the tension between believing an identity to be natural and putting work into upholding that identity through practices.

Chapters 5 and 6 explore the intersections of race, gender, and nation in order to elucidate privilege from another angle. I examine the content of the interviewees' national identities, investigating how they do conceptual work to envision England and Englishness. Unsurprisingly, given hegemonic representations of England, they are most likely to imagine ideal-typical English people as white and male. However, in their responses to Britain's imperialist past, they sometimes challenge hegemonic ideals of Englishness. In other instances, I find that they use their national identities to bolster their sense of privilege, notably in their attempts to downplay racial difference in England in comparison to the more "raced" U.S. My work provides evidence for the ways in which racial, gender, and national identities function together, in this case to accentuate these interviewees' sense of themselves as superior.

In my conclusion, I discuss the various ways we have seen these English people doing identity work—that is, treating their identities as if they need to be upheld, maintained, emphasized, or downplayed. I show how the interviewees negotiate their national identities in their daily lives, using discourses of naturalness and culture, accountability (with both Americans and English people), and four different kinds of practices. My evidence refines the theory of identity as work, pointing to the way individuals may deconstruct as well as reconstruct their identities.

2 Avoiding Extremes
Negotiating Nationalism and Nostalgia

I don't want to appear nationalistic.... I should have this constant disclaimer that "nationalism is bad! I don't like it!"

Mike

I travelled among unknown men,
In lands beyond the sea;
Nor, England! did I know 'til then
What love I bore to thee.

William Wordsworth, "I Travelled Among Unknown Men"

In the end, I suppose, anyone with any sense will always find more in their country that embarrasses them than fills them with pride, and England seems a more embarrassing country than many, especially this year, when being English seemed synonymous with being bumptious, arrogant, stupid, bellicose and puerile.

Nick Hornby

IT MIGHT SEEM ODD to begin a chapter on English national identity with an epigraph that suggests that "being English seem[s] synonymous with being bumptious, arrogant, stupid, bellicose and puerile," but I explore here the tension in admitting that one has a national identity, claiming pride in that identity, and expressing discomfort with that identity. Many of the English people I interviewed claimed not to be nationalistic as a way to distance themselves from any kind of national pride. However, they often qualified this statement. Sometimes these qualifications asserted feelings of nostalgic pride in England, especially about its history and geography. Yet some would also qualify their nostalgia as too extreme. Thus, I show how the interviewees negotiated their anxieties about seeming too nationalistic or too nostalgic with their considerable pride in England.

Two themes run through my analysis. The first is the interviewees' understanding of their national identity as natural. Often, I find them

17

using their belief that they are "naturally" English to justify their feelings of national pride and belonging. The second is the use they make of popular culture and the media. The representations of England embedded in these discourses enable them to find safe ways to express their love for England, ways that avoid the necessity of seeing themselves as overly nostalgic or nationalistic.

WORKING AT IDENTITY

Although I focus on the ways identity is experienced on individual levels in this project, the identities on which I focus—race, class, gender, and nation—are all collective identities. These identities are produced on a macrosociological level as well as on the more micro levels of interactions and individual experiences. The term "identity work" is useful in conceptualizing the relationship between these two levels: "identity work [involves] . . . signifying, labeling, and defining" the identity in order to give it meaning (Schwalbe and Mason-Schrock 1996: 115). In later chapters, I will show how the people I spoke to drew on nation, class, gender, and race to define themselves during their interactions with Americans. In this chapter, I focus on the conceptual work they do during the interviews to understand their national identities. Their definitions of English national identity are structured in large part by the collective definitions available to them in England and in the U.S. We see them working with these structural definitions, sometimes challenging them, sometimes accepting them unquestioningly, and sometimes reworking them for their own purposes. In particular, I examine the ways they use or respond to the issue of national pride. They attempt to construct a form of English identity that is viable for them—one that resonates with meaning, yet does not seem politically or culturally problematic to them.

Since the publication of *The Invention of Tradition*,[1] historians and cultural critics alike have become more aware of the ways that "'traditions' which appear or claim to be old are quite often recent in origin and sometimes invented" (Hobsbawm 1983: 1). In particular, the collection details the ways that nations rely on the selective use of "old" traditions and the invention of new traditions in order to construct a past that appears to lead seamlessly and naturally to the present.[2] Traditions are invented, ethnicities constructed, nationalisms created, and communities imagined to enhance a sense of continuity between the past and the present.[3] However, the collective memories of shared pasts are often selective or falsely nostalgic, drawing upon "fantasy, narrative, and myth" (Hall 1990: 226).[4]

Several authors note that the tendency to invent traditions is greatest in periods of rapid social change and upheaval.[5] For example, in the nineteenth century, England suffered the upheavals of the Industrial Revolution and its aftermath, including the depopulation of rural areas and increased rationalization and bureaucratization of everyday life. It also witnessed many changes in the twentieth century; participated in two world wars; suffered from protracted economic depressions; dismantled most of its empire; encouraged and then discouraged immigration from formerly colonized countries; experienced nationalist and separatist movements in Wales, Scotland, and Northern Ireland; questioned its political, judicial, and constitutional systems;[6] and, most recently, began to reevaluate its own national identity in light of European integration. It is not surprising, then, that scholars have found much evidence of the invention of English tradition, harking back to the "good old days" when life was supposedly easier and less complicated.[7] Especially in the Thatcherite 1980s, advertisements, newspapers, television dramas, films, and political pronouncements all made extensive use of invented traditions, imagining history in ways that idealized the nation and romanticized the past.[8] Several authors note the ways that history has been turned into "national heritage," a term that encourages individuals to see themselves as custodians of the past;[9] this extracts history from its context, restaging England as a "museum-land conserved by National Trust, marketed by Heritage, and tailor-made for tourists" (Porter 1992: 2).[10]

The English landscape has played an important role in the invention of an idealized past. A long tradition of myth-making constructs an ideal rural (and often Tudor) version of social life as the epitome of Englishness. This means that English people can conceptualize their history through the landscape, because the past is "there both to be dug up and also to be visited" (Wright 1985: 74). The ideal is rooted in a particular kind of landscape, which is found only in certain parts of the south of England and is of relatively recent origin: A "patchwork of meadow and pasture, the hedgerows and copses, the immaculate villages nestling among small tilled fields" came to stand for the whole of England during the twentieth century (Lowenthal 1991: 213).[11] This, despite the fact that, since 1861, England has been predominantly industrial and urban.[12]

The rural ideal posits a utopian "golden age" when all was well with the world; however, it also means that people can actually visit the countryside and feel themselves to be in touch with and benefiting from England's imagined traditions. As Eric Hobsbawm points out, invented traditions are often used to enhance the superiority of elites,[13] and the class-specific ways that the countryside is maintained is no exception: stewards manage wildlife for hunting; squires keep huge country houses and gardens intact;[14] the National Trust, which is secretive about its holdings, appears to protect tenants and lessees at the expense of the public;[15] and farmers are subsidized to "become scenic stewards for tourism" (Lowenthal 1991: 217).

Despite the public invocations of national identity and tradition in England, people do not simply accept them passively. They use collective traditions and memories to make sense of the world, finding themes, understanding causality, conceptualizing what is possible and probable, and explaining why things happen the way they do.[16] In confronting their feelings about England, and their desires about how they wanted to be English, the people I talked to both drew on and contributed to mythical, invented ideas about Englishness, doing a form of conceptual work as they imagined their nation.[17]

The nostalgic perspective of expatriates and immigrants may be even stronger than that of those who remain, as "rabidly nostalgic heritage magazines" that depend on an "expatriate perspective" show (Wright 1985: 77). Indeed, the experience of leaving one's homeland often produces idealized visions of that homeland.[18] As well as constructing new historical narratives, myth and imagination "help . . . the mind to intensify its own sense of itself by dramatizing the difference between what is close to it and what is far away" (Said 1978: 55). Myths and imagination, then, become a way that immigrants can come to terms with what they left behind.

Immigrants and expatriates construct their identities through this myth-making process so that "identity [becomes] the narrative of the self; it's the story we tell about the self in order to know who we are" (Hall 1989: 16). The process of telling one's identity story involves conceptual work; in my interviews, respondents used popular culture and the media, as well as their experiences in the U.S., to give shape and form to their identities. As they envisioned England, they responded to their perceptions of dominant images of England, cultivated through the media and popular culture in both England and the U.S. They re-created or reshaped these representations, creating their own myths and narratives out of them. They each imagined England differently, perhaps because they were working within different paradigms of Englishness (for instance, based on region, class, or their length of time away) or because they responded to the same paradigms very differently. For example, as will become clear later, the movie *Four Weddings and a Funeral* had very different effects on different people.[19] Some saw the movie as reflecting something essential about Englishness and the way English people operate. Others saw it as unrepresentative of England and argued that it created a parody of England.

Many different ideals of Englishness may thus contribute to the ways that people conceptualize their national identity and national pride. Some are more aware than others that images produced in popular culture often are not simply unrepresentative, but false. Others, though, have a pure ideal of Englishness. Their national feelings take on a normative component. As they describe what England means to them, they may be detailing the ways that England should be and, more often than not, the ways that it is different from the U.S. As they envision versions of Englishness, they are acting to manipulate, exaggerate, destroy, or accept the images already available to them.

In the first half of this chapter, I use two cultural aspects of Englishness—history and geography—to explore the ways that the people I talked to negotiated their feelings of pride with their wish to downplay nationalism. In particular, I find that their pride was accompanied by strong emotions, and by a narcissistic impulse, as they situated themselves in a historical and geographical context. However, a second group found these expressions of cultural pride deeply problematic. This group pointed to the falsity of nostalgia and the ways that media images of England are often unrealistic and unrepresentative. Some of them noted the ways in which elites produce these images for their own benefit, and they were self-critical and sarcastic about their own use of clichés to imagine England. However, even the least nostalgic of the people I spoke to relied on nostalgic and naturalistic images of England as they contemplated whether they would ever return there permanently.

IMAGINING AN IDEAL ENGLAND?

The Impact of History and Geography

Many interviewees focused on the beauty of England as they talked about how they felt about being English. They remembered the prevalence of historically interesting places, and they lovingly described the countryside. When asked to sum up England, they usually conceptualized history as part of the environment. Tara, for instance, said that she missed "the greenness, the beauty of the trees, . . . the age of buildings." History often provided the context for the way they imagined England. Thus, Peter noted that in England, "history [is] on your doorstep. We take it for granted living there, but when it's not there, it's something you miss." Several people commented on England's wartime experiences. Brad remembered seeing "war-damaged property" when he was young, which contributed to his sense that "history comes through the woodwork" in Europe.

Harriet ardently described the ways she saw history imbued on the landscape:

> When tourists come . . . they get what they came for—lovely old buildings and all the heritage. . . . My parents live in this little village . . . , [which] is just so beautiful. . . . It's so archetypally English. . . . There's a tiny tenth-century church and little cottages with roses going up the sides, and they're all thatched and lovely.

Her use of the historical–rural ideal to sum up England is obvious here.[20] Emma also exclaimed that "there's so much history" in the town where her family lives, explaining that the church in which she was married had been built in 1200. Several interviewees were very interested in history. Brad showed me his collection of historical biographies, and Alex admitted that "it fascinates me to think of all the things that have happened in Britain for so long and the age of things and I miss all that."[21] As the literature suggests, these interviewees conceptualized history as part of their environment in England; in their memories, history was all around them and they were part of it. History therefore became an important aspect of their definitions of Englishness.

Many also expressed a nostalgic longing for and pride in an image of England as a place of "rolling hills, beautiful green fields" and "gray days and mists [in] the countryside," as Craig and Peter said. Imogen noted "how sweet and quaint and nice it is, like toytown with all these little painted signs on the roads and . . . little fields with their little hedges," while Lucinda missed "those very cold damp winters, going on a winter walk and seeing rabbits; . . . and in the summertime, the fields of hay and going on walks . . . in the countryside." They made implicit and explicit contrasts with the U.S., complaining about how visually unappealing parts of the East Coast are compared with England.

Some interviewees, such as Lucinda, were quite explicit that they were using "[the stream of] English movies we've been having recently" to reinforce their memories of the countryside in England. She waxed lyrical about the atmosphere of these movies; as she talked, England emerged as a beautiful, sunny place, epitomized by the Merchant–Ivory period pieces that focus lovingly on the green fields and pastoral landscapes. She missed

> that feeling of being in England, being in the countryside and the noises, it's just not the same atmosphere as it is here. And just seeing *The Remains of the Day* and all those [movies]; . . . it's just so England. And I think the most beautiful place in the world is England in the summertime in the countryside, when it's sunny and you've got those colors and those noises.

Lucinda's enthusiasm extends to creating a new adjective out of "England"—"it's just so England"—to describe the beauty and atmosphere of the countryside. Emma, too, used "England" to describe flying over England: "It's very green, . . . and it's wonderful to fly over and look down at it, and you think: Wow, that really looks like England." Both women tautologize England by using the word "England" to describe what England looks like to them; it is as if they cannot imagine or describe England without resorting to stereotypical notions of Englishness. Lucinda's rhapsodical, lingering memories of England are echoed in the countless essays and books written about the beauty of England.[22] She talked at length about her childhood in England, describing the sounds, the smells, and the feeling of walks in the countryside in both summer and winter. Her vivid memories placed a strong emphasis on the emotions evoked by the countryside.

Likewise, Peter and Ian became emotional when talking about the land. Both mentioned *All Creatures Great and Small*, a television show set in Yorkshire that reminded them of home. Ian said it gave him "a warm buzz," while Peter actually began to sniff (half-jokingly) as he described his memories of his mother playing the theme music of this show on the piano. He also described how gray weather reminded him of treks across Dartmoor and Exmoor ... when I was a kid. ... Not because it's depressing as such. Sometimes it's nice to just wallow in your own thoughts and memories ... and watch the sky and feel the mist and the rain and the wind. I think coming from somewhere like Northern Europe—you know how certain songs can remind you of things?—I think weather can just make you remember places, times, when I was a kid.

The extent of Peter's emotion surprised me because he seemed concerned at other points to portray himself as a hegemonically masculine man.[23] He stressed the masculine nature of his workplace (the stock market), telling me that women are physically incapable of working on the floor because they can't shout loudly enough, and he regaled me with stories of his drinking exploits in "down-and-dirty" bars. But when it came to expressing his national identity, he became emotional, pointing to the pictures on the walls of places of interest in England and telling me stories about his childhood experiences in England. Hugh, also a man with traditional gender values, openly talked about the emotions his memories of England brought up. At times, singing in church in the U.S., "there's been a sequence in a verse that has used music that is very poignant, it means a lot, and that's the only time I've really wept over the whole thing, [and] it's not something logical," he told me. "Fortunately, I wear glasses and have a big beard, so no one can tell." (The he cleared his throat.) Hugh maintained his self-image as a masculine man by hiding his tears behind his beard and glasses and by referring to the discourse of logic to downplay his emotions. However, he was also willing to delve into the ways his memories of England appeared in unexpected and poignant ways, aroused through music that helped him to visualize what he had left behind. He explained that at these moments, he felt that "this isn't the right place at all"; his emotions were set off by the disjunction between the music and his present surroundings. Imogen also recounted that she felt strong emotions when she returned to England. She told me about an experience she had had the previous Christmas:

> I rented a car and drove [back home] up the M40 [motorway between London and the Midlands,] with the beautiful rolling hills, and [there was] a hoar-frost, so that everything was white, and ... one of those winter sunsets, so it was all red and everything was going pink, and the radio was on playing King's College Chapel [choir] singing all those hymns. I had to pull over at the side of the road. I was like, "Oh, it's so pretty; oooh, this is nice" [makes crying noises]. [It's not] very sensible, [no]thing that I can put my finger on.

Peter, Hugh, and Imogen reacted to their images of the English countryside and the ways that music evoked these images with extremely
nostalgic and emotional feelings. The music summed up images, or
added poignancy to those images or memories, so that rural England
took on the rosy glow of nostalgic longing. Their emotional responses
illustrate the pull of the countryside and the importance of place to conceptions of identity. The identification of England as a beautiful place
is a way for them to assert their connections with the land.

Situating Themselves Within a Geographical and Historical Context

The English people I talked to worked to forge their connections to the
physical land in other ways. Many of them situated themselves within
geographical and historical dimensions of Englishness to assert their
own status as English, conceptualizing the historical landscape as a
"storied" one (Lowenthal 1991: 216). For instance, as he described pubs
in exquisite detail, Quentin imagined himself as one in a long line of
descendants of male drinkers. He talked about

> the English country pub, where the building has to be three hundred
> years old at least, and there's various historical knickknacks . . . to let you
> know that people have sitting around drinking beer in here for the last
> three hundred years. Somehow that's very stabilizing, to think that you're
> engaging in an age-old tradition, or you're a part of it, which you miss in
> America. . . . And it's good to picture . . . the guys just coming in from
> plowing the field and the whole plowman's lunch thing. Maybe if it's a
> London city pub you can picture Samuel Pepys running around doing his
> London thing.

Here Quentin translates the spatial and temporal dimension of a three-
hundred-year-old pub into a part of his identity. Like those I quoted earlier, Quentin sees the country's age as important to his image of England; he is able to situate himself as a participant in the historical act of
drinking, weaving a thread that stretches out long before him and presumably will continue after him. For Quentin, the continuity between
himself and Samuel Pepys or a plowman, embodied in the age of the
buildings, enables him to use history to construct himself as English. His
"imagined community" is composed of a broad swath of male drinkers
stretching back three hundred years in time.[24]

Other interviewees also situated themselves as English using the
"depth of history," the "sense of history and continuity," the "shared

history," or the ways that "history . . . is so built into us."[25] Frank explained that "centuries of tradition and identity . . . give [English people] the confidence to relax." These words suggest the connections that interviewees forged with other English people, using the idea of "ancestral continuities" (Wright 1985: 84). Vera was even more explicit about how her ideas about history constructed her identity. She argued that her sense of Englishness was a result of

> knowing that all English people are basically descended from Edward III or something. I mean . . . my husband has a family tree that goes back to the 1700s. When I spoke to one man in agriculture, he said his . . . family was here at the Norman conquest and that they've lived in the same place since then. What I'm saying is that whether I like it or not, I'm deeply rooted in England. I can't help not being.

A few minutes later, Vera noted that her mother's side of the family had emigrated to England from Ireland quite recently; her point, however, is that the weight of history behind her "can't help" but make her English. In arguing that all English people are "descended from Edward III," she constructed an imagined community of white, upper-class people who make up the English. Even though she is not part of this unbroken ancestral line, she ignores this to use history to explain her rootedness in England; Englishness for her is based on a mythical version of history, and she uses the idea of "roots" to construct a natural basis for national identity.

The metaphor of roots was an important way for the interviewees to express their sense of connection with other English people and their sense of safety and security in their identity. William, for instance, discussed his pride in English television and film culture this way: "Knowing you're a part of the culture that can produce some of those magnificent things gives you a feeling of being rooted in something. So those roots are important." Alex expressed her feeling of commonality with other English people slightly differently, arguing that Englishness was important to her "because you feel it's your heritage, and you're not going to lose it." Because she knows she will never lose her "heritage," she can feel secure about who she is. Frances contrasted this "feeling of roots and . . . history and continuity" with the U.S.: "Sometimes over here it's very superficial and fragile. People could be up here one day and then right down in the gutter the next day." These comments suggest that the roots metaphor also enabled the interviewees to feel stable and centered in their national identity.

The roots metaphor also implies that the interviewees have a natural connection to the land, as if they are trees that might have been uprooted but whose underpinnings will always be in England. Vera echoed this explanation in discussing her understanding of the relationship between the English and their land: "We English people are an island people. We're never more than about sixty miles from the sea. Everything is colored by the way the wind blows, and the weather is very important to us. Despite the great urbanization, I think the call of the countryside is very strong." In making these comments, she assumes that English people "naturally" have an affinity with the land—the phrases "island people" and "call of the countryside" suggest that the land helps to constitute them as "nationed" beings in some way. Hence, the "call of the countryside" in combination with the pull of history enabled the interviewees to feel essentially and naturally English in a way that no one and nothing (not even moving to or taking out citizenship in another country) could change.

A character in a recent A. S. Byatt novel (1996: 18–9) expresses a similar feeling. Hugh Pink, walking in the woods, becomes aware of the way

> the local earth, . . . in this case England, had become part of the form of the soft pale mass in his skull, part of the active knowledge of his sight and smell and taste. . . . He thinks [this pleasure in living] comes in this sort of landscape . . . because generations of his ancestors thousands and millions of years [ago] . . . have had this sense in this sort of place. The cells remember it, Hugh thinks. Every inch of this turf has absorbed, he supposes, knuckle bones and heart-strings, fur and nails, blood and lymph.

Byatt gives the countryside and its history deeply biological and natural forms. Where Quentin implied that some English people imagine themselves as one in a long line of wanderers in the landscape, Byatt imagines here that England has somehow become imprinted in English people's brains in a transference from countryside to humans. Further, she implies through her character that the linkage works the other way: that because human beings have died and been returned to the earth, and thus become part of the earth, the earth is somehow part of them. This is a powerful image that combines the two ways these interviewees situate themselves within England's environment—through history and ruralism—because it uses these ideals to posit a deep, natural connection with the land. Once one believes that one has a natural bond with the earth, nothing can change that belief. But behind the primal connection expressed here that seems to "touch chords that go back to the beginning of time and the human race" (Baldwin, quoted in Wright 1985: 82) is a narcissistic impulse.[26] If one sees oneself as part of the land and expresses a deep and abiding love for this land, one is clearly loving part of oneself.

We Have So Much History; They Have So Little

This narcissistic impulse also emerged when the interviewees compared themselves with Americans. Several people contrasted their sense of the breadth and depth of English history with what they perceived as a lack of American history. Some, such as Diana and Nigel, qualified this by pointing out that Americans' supposed lack of history was simply a lack of early written history. However, most used the alleged lack of history in the U.S. to enhance their own self-esteem. Although Piers tried to keep his national chauvinism in check, for example, it sometimes got the better of him:

> I sometimes find myself, and I try to stop myself, looking down my nose at a lot of American traditions. I mean, "This is . . . the oldest dorm in service. This was built in the thirties" [*in an American accent*]. My fucking high school was founded in 1382. . . . I laugh at people who live in Tudor homes, and I say, "That's a *mock* Tudor home. I know someone who lives in a Tudor home, and it's a little older than this one."

Likewise, Catriona remembered thinking a sarcastic "So what?" when she heard that a particular American building was two hundred years old, while other interviewees admitted that they had become more aware of England's history since moving to the U.S. Octavia, for instance, claimed to be proud of England's traditions because the U.S. "doesn't really have a lot of traditions."

Andy felt that English people had a stronger sense of historical memory than Americans. The English, he argued, have a "deeper perspective . . . because we have a much longer sense of history of populated and civilized cultures." He used central heating as an example, pointing out that Americans would think "this is what we've got now because we built it." He contrasted this perspective with a European perspective, which, he said, would recognize the evolution of central heating and missed opportunities: "The Romans moved in. We had under-floor central heating, and as soon as the Romans went, we were back to virtually living in caves and mud huts. I mean, how stupid, how naive we were!" His example shows how he values his sense of history and identifies with the experiences of those who lived thousands of years before him. Once again, his words show how these interviewees situated themselves within a broad swath of history, valuing that history and, hence, valuing themselves. As Quentin explained, "I have a longer history that I think I can feel part of. I have a clearer idea of my historical identity. It's one of the things that's kind of noticeably lacking in America—people don't know what it is to be American. They're still discovering it. The American population is still changing so rapidly." He also implied that his "longer history" enabled him to "know what it is to be" English in a way that Americans do not.

This Is Just False Nostalgia

In contrast to these nostalgic longings for England, others with whom I talked were deeply uncomfortable with nostalgia and with how the media and popular culture represent England. As I analyze their words in this and the following sections, their activity in doing conceptual work will become clear: As they criticized images of Englishness and attempted to refute or redefine them, they were grappling with their own images of Englishness. Thus, they used their experiences in the U.S. to criticize an emphasis on history and tradition in England. For instance, by seeing England through American eyes, Antonia pointed out how odd English traditions are. While watching the proceedings of the House of Commons on C-SPAN, she was struck by the fact that "it seems so ... out of date ... [and] old-fashioned, and it must seem so extraordinary for Americans watching this.... Here are [these people who decide our future] exchanging witticisms across [the floor]." She also thought that Americans who had not visited England recently imagined this "incredibly quaint country with great theater and ... beautiful architecture," as opposed to "what it is really like." Antonia identified the falsity of an image of England based on quaintness and nostalgia (although she did not make clear what she thought England was "really like"). Nigel agreed, answering my question, "What does being English mean to you?" this way: "I would like to say we have so many thousand years of culture that no other countries have, but that means shit, really." However, he qualified his dismissive attitude later by pointing out that history was simply something he took for granted: "No it's [not shit]. It's more impressive to other people. You've got so much—they started building the foundations [of Windsor Castle] in 1066 or whatever. . . . It's nice . . . [but] it's something I just really . . . take for granted." Stephen also was very critical of the English "obsession with tradition," about which he felt rather ambivalent:

> Things are very often done for tradition rather than for anything else, [which is] very limiting. . . . Some of the advantages of America [are] a certain flexibility that seems to have come from not having that much recorded history, [so] there's no set ways [*brief pause*]. Like . . . when I was at university in England, [I asked] why something was done this way, and it was like, because it's always been done this way. . . . I think tradition has its place, but I don't believe in keeping it just for the sake of keeping it.

Despite his critique, Stephen could see both sides of the story. When I asked him what England was worst at, he said "change." But when asked what England was best at, he explained that "the flip side of that . . . is not following fashion quite so much."

Several others were even more strident in their critiques of the ways that tradition and nostalgia for the past were used in England. Tara pinpointed "this really annoying tendency to be stuck . . . within the prism of tradition and a class system . . . and a nostalgia for the times when Britain was 'great.'" Ken complained about how newspapers present royal scandals, criticizing the media's obsession with propriety: "Well, this is the 1990s, it will be amazing for some people to find out! I don't think the editor of the *Daily Telegraph* has found out yet, but Queen Victoria has been dead for quite a few years! This is not fucking Victorian England anymore!" His critique points to the ways in which history is used to hold the present to higher standards than he considers necessary. Indeed, Ken was glad to have left behind the "weight and history of English culture, simply by virtue of its having been around for such a long time." Meanwhile, Imogen was happy that the "preposterousness of the . . . monarchy" was being acknowledged, because it gave her more license to criticize tradition.

Harry flatly denied any feelings of nostalgia for the past, passionately distancing himself from England by criticizing the "vestiges of the past that cling to England." He complained about how "English identity is rooted . . . in the Blitz or something. Everything to do with English identity belongs in the past and that to me is the past. Even the Beatles, that's history. Being English nowadays has nothing to do with that stuff." Harry clearly wants to find a new way to be English, a way that doesn't involve nostalgia for events in the past. Citing the Beatles together with the Blitz is a powerful way to distance himself from aspects of England's recent history that have been constructed as ways to be proud of being English. As a man in his early thirties, Harry has chosen examples that have been used by the two generations preceding him to teach his generation how to be proud; both also have been repeatedly repackaged and mythologized as examples of times when "Britain was 'great.'" The fighting spirit of the Blitz has served as a defining moment in which the British showed their courage and mettle. It has not only been recorded in films, novels, television documentaries, and diaries, but has also been passed down through family narratives. And the Beatles, recently remythologized in *The Beatles Anthology*, are regularly held up as the band that "conquered" America. Indeed, every time a new British band hits the charts, it is constructed as the next Beatles. Ken echoed Harry's frustration with this mythologizing by voicing the following criticism:

> England as a mighty power with lots of tradition . . . and the idea of the English gentleman . . . to me is ludicrously out of date. It's sort of *Four Weddings and a Funeral* England, which is probably true for—what—five thousand people in England? The other fifty-five million don't give a fuck about that kind of thing.

Ken, Harry, Tara, Imogen, and the other interviewees who criticized the use of history as producing inaccurate versions of English identity implicitly recognized the ways that the supposed longevity of the identity was produced through the manipulation of images. Ken's comments refer to newspapers and films; others cited English and American tabloids and television shows. Diana recognized the false nostalgia that she gets from reading literature, pointing to the glorification of history: "Things like Dickens and so on, I find really sad 'cause I don't know why English people glorify our history. [It] was so dull and cruel. It was full of torture, and it was horrible." These people note the ways traditions are "invented" to glorify and uphold present-day English national identity in a choke hold of nostalgia.[27]

In addition to being aware of the ways in which the media and popular culture can create falsely nostalgic images of Englishness, some of the interviewees pointed to the role of elites in constructing images of English national identity. Stephen complained about Eurosceptics' reluctance to let go of the British pound. "We've had the decimal system for ... thirty years, and suddenly it's this 'great British institution'?" he asked sarcastically. Gordon criticized the political system in Britain as

> the most antiquated, unreformed structure. [Politics is so] tradition-bound, [not] because that's what people want, [but] because that's what elites decided was convenient. They're the ones who dramatize and who schedule the redramatizations of all this pomp and circumstance and refuse to change the format of Prime Minister's question time, or the layout of the chamber of the House of Commons [so] we can worship the *ancien régime* of a bygone age.

Gordon made a point that is also made by historians—that the deployment of history as tradition often benefits the status quo, stifling dissent and unifying the nation behind a false image of "the way things have always been."[28] He points here to the vested interest that elites have in reinventing traditions and re-reminding people of their history, making change unlikely. In so doing, Gordon, like the others quoted in this section, implicitly questioned the idea that English people are naturally connected to one another because of their history. Indeed, he enables us to see that those in power want English people to believe that this is the case.

MORE FALSE NOSTALGIA

The idea of false nostalgia implies a tension between nostalgic images of England and the reality of the place. The problem with clichés, stereotypes, and other kinds of images or imaginings is that the images sometimes contain a grain of truth. Certainly, it is reasonable to say, for instance, that the greenness of the fields in parts of England is noticeable when one arrives from more industrialized places on the East Coast of the U.S. However, as Alan Howkins[29] pointed out, the rural ideal exists despite the fact that the experiences of the majority of the population in England are urban or suburban and industrialized.

Craig was also ware of the tension between reality and image. He admitted that

> it [was] far easier to come up with criticisms of England while I was there than it is now in retrospect. I know there were issues that I thought about, but I can't remember anymore. But they seemed good reasons to leave at

the time. . . . I could run off a list of things that I didn't like. . . . I can't think of what they were [*both laugh after a brief pause*].

Imagining England in a negative light involved work that he now found hard to do. Although Tara did not "want to be falsely nostalgic . . . about England," she said, "I don't like [it] as much when I am there." The struggle not to be "falsely nostalgic" is so hard because, as Craig noted, ideas of Englishness come to people

> through the media, through fiction, through history—cricket matches, the boat race, . . . this romanticized notion of everyone sitting by the water [on a sunny day in the park] eating out of picnic hampers, which isn't a reality. [You're] more likely to see people, me included, with a couple of cans of beer lying on a T-shirt listening to music. [It's the difference between] what you think of English culture and what it actually is.

Craig thus moved between a nostalgic longing for England so intense that he had forgotten the reasons he wanted to leave and a kind of self-parody, as he recognized how "romanticized" his vision of England had become. Craig attempted to redress the clichéd portrayals of England as an upper-class paradise and playground with an image of himself to produce a more representative picture. Later in the interview, when I jokingly reminded him of his image of picnic hampers and cricket games, he countered with more self-parody: "Even the reality of the cricket game has changed. . . . There's people with cans of Carling Black Label [beer], shouting and jeering with fat bellies hanging out of the top of their shorts. 'It's not the game it was!' [*in a jokey upper-class accent*]." My comment created the conditions for him to laugh at himself even more as he compared his earlier image of idyllic, civilized cricket games with the reality of modern-day cricket. In both cases quoted here, Craig masculinized the image of England and tried to make it much less refined, perhaps even more working-class.[30] He also can be seen, however, as drawing on another image of English people: Cricket fans are now called "the barmy army" by the media, who point to their often rowdy, drunken, and partisan spectatorship. Craig's words suggest that he is working to invoke new images of Englishness that do not often make their way into the consciousness of those in America.[31]

Others were more explicit about how media images construct these false ideals of Englishness and the fact that this happens on an international stage. Frances was aware that she was drawing on archetypes as she summed up England: "It's very clichéd, sort of the green fields bit [*brief pause*], a softer, gentler place." Saying the "green fields bit" illustrates her understanding that she was making a comment that had been made by many others. Gordon, meanwhile, found himself responding to England in terms of clichés: When he visited, he said, he looked at England as a "beautiful experience. . . . It's most vivid in London. . . . It's like being on a [*brief pause*] film set, a historical re-creation. I find that the people are very funny . . . in the way they interact, in the way they walk, what they carry—the grannies with the little hats and the little trolleys they drag behind them." Gordon's enjoyment of England comes from feeling as if he is in a period piece, a result of the prevalence of historical dramas set in England with reconstructed, hyper-realistic settings.[32] He can now marvel at the quaintness of life in England with the eye of an outsider. In contrast, Ken found media images of England unrealistic: "*Four Weddings [and a Funeral]* and *Howard's End.* . . are parodies of what England's like. [They are] not very representative. . . . I feel as though I'm watching a parody of a place that I know very well, and I know perfectly well that it's nothing like that really." He pointed out that these representations of England "are like cartoon England," and he did not "associate them with the place I used to live at all." He was able to distance himself from the images, and his use of the words "parody" and "cartoon" suggested that their attempts to capture or portray any essence of England were laughable. Indeed, one feels that he was concerned that other (non-English?) people would not know "that it's nothing like that really." Tara was more explicit about this:

> I don't like the movies, which I think in part sell on a nostalgic idea of England. I actually disliked [some of the later Merchant–Ivory movies] 'cause I thought they traded in on this existing idea of Britain as this historical theme park. I thought they re-did *Upstairs Downstairs* in movies, and I didn't like that.

Tara's use of the phrase "historical theme park," which other interviewees echoed, suggests the unreality of the images. She also unconsciously pointed to how these representations contribute to the commodification of England: The terms "selling on a nostalgic ideal," "trading in on an existing idea," and "theme park" all suggest the exchange of money. Indeed, it could be argued that some of the period-piece movies can be viewed as advertisements for England's heritage, crude attempts to boost the country's tourist industry.[33]

The interviewees used other methods to relegate their ideas of England to the realm of fantasy or romanticization. Several explicitly criticized the false and sometimes glamorized versions of England they used during their interviews, presumably because they felt that these produced stereotypical images of English people. For instance, Ken told me that his cousin was very English. When I asked him what this meant, he explained that this cousin had

> certain instinctive leanings, I suppose. . . . I mean that I've got notions of what it would mean to be a sort of perfect Englishman, the epitome of an English person . . . stuff like fair play, don't kick a man when he's down, all the sort of clichés. Nothing very edifying, I'm afraid, . . . a collection of nursery-rhyme sort of things.

Ken seems rather embarrassed to be found making stereotypical assumptions about English people, because he quickly devalues his comments by saying that they come out of nursery rhymes. However, at the same time, he points to how these clichés affect his own conceptualizations of Englishness. In addition, he shows a certain amount of gender consciousness that he has defined English people in male terms; he noted later that these clichés are "male-derived and male-oriented. . . . I've never known a woman who blathers on inanely about those things the way men tend to do." This rather dismissive comment is another way to downplay his use of clichés and show that he does not think they are useful, relevant, or important.

Imogen also questioned the ways she had constructed her images of England. She wondered

> how representative of England my little bucolic suburb is. I mean, I know it's not. I've got some Indian friends here who lived in Britain, and we were talking about post offices and how shocked I was that they were all behind bullet-proof glass, and they said, "Well, go to the post offices in Brighton." And I said, "Oh dear, I can't imagine that in Stourbridge!" [*in an upper-class accent*].[34]

Imogen shows that she is aware that she has a romanticized notion of England that is based on her own class and region. Many of the interviewees recognized the element of fantasy in their images of England. In contrast to the expatriate mentality one might expect, they sarcastically saw their imaginings as unreasonable and unrealistic. Thus, Diana recognized that any positive images she had of England were unattainable: "[*Four Weddings and a Funeral*] reminded me of my university days. That's something that by going back to England, I couldn't catch again. Like my childhood, there's a nostalgia, which will stay a dream forever." Adding that England was "like a [lovely little] story book," she explicitly distanced herself from the place by claiming that her nostalgia was unrealistic, something she could never recapture (but that does contain some grain of truth, as she acknowledges that the film reminded her of some aspect of her life in England). Almost every immigrant group keeps some kind of dream alive about their country of origin, a nostalgia that becomes more sentimental as memories fade. These people are self-reflective about this process, distancing themselves from the nostalgia by criticizing the way it is used in films and criticizing their own use of it when they become aware of it.

"You Can't Go Back"

I wondered whether the interviewees' intentions to return played a role in keeping nostalgia alive or in enabling them to critique it. However, no clear pattern emerged among these English people as to whether those who planned to return were more or less nostalgic. Frank's struggles with this issue illustrate the contradictory ways that nostalgia and the falsity of nostalgia are invoked. He talked about the changes that had taken place in the thriving cockney community in which he grew up. Now it is a tourist attraction, and he feels completely distant from those who live there:

> The connections are not there—the places, the people, the atmosphere. . . . Other people have come and replaced it, immigrants have come in . . . and started different kinds of lives. The children have grown up and gone somewhere else. . . . There's an old saying, "You can't go back again." You can't re-create that, and not having been there in the meantime, I haven't changed with it. My experience is still back in those days, and when I go back there, that's what I bring to it, but nobody wants that. That's old-fashioned, . . . the way it used to be. And now [that] my parents have died . . . there's no connections.

Frank's eloquent expression of the idea that one cannot re-create the past recognizes how far removed he is from England now and shows the role of fantasy and dream in the nostalgia of immigrants. As one of those who had been away from England the longest, he was most comfortable calling himself an immigrant and distancing himself from England (at times). At several points in the interview, he discussed how he had lost English traits, had very little family in England, and so had few illusions that he belonged there when he went back. However, he still had periods of homesickness and ultimately believed that he belonged in England:

> When you leave your roots . . . , you're casting yourself adrift. You never really put down emotional roots in a new country. You make [new] ties— family, economic, friends . . .—but your real emotional roots are still there. . . . Although my parents are dead, I'm a product of them and their background, and that's my identity, my real basic identity. I don't want to lose that because . . . I don't have a new one. I don't have an American identity to put on.

Here Frank affirms strongly the idea that he remains rooted in England, and he makes a clear statement that this is his "real basic identity," which will never change. His comments about his old community earlier, however, suggest the ways in which he understands how this feeling of rootedness is based on "old-fashioned" ways.

Despite his homesickness and identification with England, Frank was hesitant about moving back because, he thought, when people return, "they're unhappy because it's not the way they remembered it, the way they want it to be." Like the others I have quoted, Frank recognized the nostalgic quality of his dreams and visions of England, the ways that they are rooted in the past. He would agree with Zoe, who said, "It's not going to be the same. . . . I've expected life to stop because I'm not there." Yet underneath, Frank would prefer to go home: "You always think of ending your days, so to speak, where you started. There's something symmetrical about that. . . . You want something that makes a cycle, and when you break that cycle, . . . as I have, you feel unsure of yourself. You're on quicksand." Frank echoed the feelings of many of the interviewees, some of them much younger than he, who held on to the hope that they would one day return to England. Only one, Mike, had definite plans to return to England, but many of the others toyed with the idea of one day going back. About half of them planned to stay, and half planned to go back one day.[35] As Peter said, "It's nice to know that it's always going to be there. . . . I know that if I really wanted, I [could] go back," and Harry admitted that he was "in love with the place in some ways," although "I don't think I want to go back there until I'm ready to die." Lucinda summed up the sentiments of many interviewees when she said, "I just don't see myself here for the rest of my life. . . . It's just something in me that makes me feel British and not American." In the end, it seems, the nostalgia for England returns in the belief that "something in me" naturally belongs in England.

Keeping Control of National Pride

So far, we have seen the people I spoke to evoking and responding to dominant images of England, especially those of history and the landscape. They have worked with these images, taking pride in them, becoming emotional about them, and using natural and narcissistic discourses to situate themselves within the spatial-temporal context of England. They have created a pure, idealized form of Englishness, remembering England as a mythical land of green countryside and old buildings.

Another group, however, doubled back on these narratives, secondguessing the dominant images of England and pointing out how unreasonable these assumptions about Englishness were. They conceptualized their nostalgia as a fantasy that was both unrealistic and unrepresentative, showing how popular stereotypes of Englishness constructed it as such. Their critiques of this nostalgia helped them retain control of the images. By modifying or refuting the images, they did conceptual work to remain in control of what Englishness is and how it is represented. However, these people, too, used the roots metaphor when they began to talk about returning to England, deploying a natural discourse to explain their feelings of connection with the land.

I turn now to consider the interviewees' use of another cultural stereotype to investigate how they negotiate national pride. This is the "stiff upper lip," or reserve, that the media and popular culture portray English people as having. These interviewees' ideas about the ways that they are or should be reserved provide the context for my discussion of their understandings of national pride. For if they are supposed to act with such reserve, how can they express national pride?

We're Not Proud or Loud

English and Understated

As Alex mused about her experiences in the U.S., she pointed to a stereotype of English people that was important to her life in that country. She wondered aloud whether English people become "cartoon Brit[s] when we're abroad." When I asked her to explain, she continued:

> You get these rather eccentric British people. I do wonder sometimes if
> . . . you become that way for the sheer hell of it. . . . Because you see your-
> self as a non-American, . . . you analyze, "How am I different from Amer-
> icans?" One of these ways is this "over-the-top" attitude they have, so you
> deliberately underplay yourself. So if the weather's bad, you refuse to
> appear [worked up] for the sheer hell of being awkward.

Here Alex eloquently expresses the work she does to construct a calm and unruffled, "English" persona in America. She identifies the way she accentuates a "stiff-upper-lip" attitude identified by many of the interviewees in order to become a "cartoon Brit." Indeed, others believed in the stereotypes Alex alludes to here—that English people are reserved, reticent, and understated compared with "over-the-top" Americans. The phrase itself—"over the top," or "OTT"—is common parlance in England to describe someone or something that is hyperbolic. Some agreed that these characteristics were aspects of Englishness that they valued about themselves or other English people and strove to attain. Tara, for instance, claimed that she aspired to understatement: "If I think I'm losing that modesty, it's when I don't like myself. . . . I really like that about England." Hugh said that he "always tr[ied] to be unflappable, which is something the English are supposed to do." Even Quentin, who joked that he had been forced to leave England because he was "not suitably reserved," prided himself on his unwillingness to complain compared with the overly "emotive" Americans around him.

In contrast to the work that Alex put into maintaining her understated persona, Dorothy believed that her reserve was the natural result of her national identity. She described an interaction during a job interview:

> I said, "I'm English, and we don't tackle things the same way. . . . I won't
> insult anybody, but I'll get results. . . ." It was a classic case of this is an
> American, and I'm an English person, and this is the way we are, and I'm
> not going to budge! . . . We just have this reserve about us, and I said, "I
> won't nosy into other people's business unless I think it's appropriate. . . .
> I can gain respect from people, but not the way you want me to. . . ." It's
> just a basic difference between us. They are very much more aggressive.

Dorothy's refusal here to acquiesce to the demands of the interviewer comes from her belief that her unwillingness to "insult anybody" is a part of her that is inherently English. "They" (i.e., Americans) are conceptualized as "much more aggressive" than English people and as being "nosy" and inappropriate. Dorothy defines her standards of behavior as superior to Americans', attributing the differences she sees to natural national traits. However, Dorothy also works hard to construct herself as naturally different from Americans; in her refusal to change her behavior, she is actively engaged in resisting the interviewer, despite her insistence that her reserve is natural. Others concurred with her that the supposed reserve of English people was positive, arguing that the stereotype of English people as "standoffish" or "cold and reserved" belied a "respect for people." As Tara explained, "[Being] English to me means understatement, modesty, . . . a certain understated consideration for other people which may look like reserve, but I think there is something beneath the politeness. It's not all cold reserve." Here Tara expresses both the importance of reserve for English self-definition and the benefits of this way of behaving. In comparison with this, other interviewees saw Americans as "superficial," loud, pushy, self-promoting, and ambitious, with an "in-your-face-attitude" that is very different from the "genuine" ways in which English people interact.[36] Media images of Englishness reinforced the importance of these contrasts by giving the interviewees concrete examples to use as they explained the differences they perceived. Craig provided an example from the media that encapsulated his understanding of reserve: The film *Four Weddings and a Funeral* made him homesick for his friends in London and for types of behavior that he could not find in the U.S.:

> The close friendships, the taking time to be with each other. There was a certain sort of reserved aspect to it as well [*brief pause*] on an individual level. An acceptance that made the gay relationship between the two men a non-issue, . . . rather than standing up and shouting, "Hey, we're gay and we're—." That understated aspect, . . . that's very much a part of British culture.

Craig makes the film fit with his own memories of England and with his impressions of Englishness as understated and reserved, yet caring. He searches for the nuggets of what he sees as the truth within the stereotypes and argues that he has found something essentially English in the movie. He draws on particular images from the movie—scenes of English friends bantering with one another and his perception of the portrayal of the gay relationship as understated—and finds parallels with his own experiences in England. His memories, then, are thrown into sharper relief by corresponding images he sees on the screen.

Andy agreed with Craig's analysis of friendship in America, explaining his ambivalence and stressing his need to keep behaving in what he perceived as an English way:

> There's this overt friendliness, but it's very superficial, whereas I think in England, ... you tend to be [reticent]. If you want to go and talk to somebody and make friends with them, you do [and] there is something in it. There's a lot less of this very free and easy—oh, how amazing I am—but there's nothing else to it. ... I don't want to become part of that.

Andy's words clearly convey the idea that he perceives Americans as loud and superficial, emphasizing their own achievements at the expense of other people's.

Interviewees contrasted their idea that Americans promote themselves too much with a humbler attitude that they attributed to English people. Alex pointed to Hugh Grant's character in *Four Weddings and a Funeral* to explain that she valued

> [the English] ability to always say that you're never good at anything, to denigrate yourself, to always be apologizing ... [for example,] the quirkiness of Hugh Grant's part. This business of never having any confidence in anything, that's being British. The way you half-apologize. The way we use phrases like, "I may be stupid to ask, but ..."

Andy concurred, explaining that the "typical British man ... won't push himself forward and say, 'Hey, I'm the greatest at ...,' but he may well be the greatest at whatever it is.... I think it's one of our better traits that we don't constantly remind one another how brilliant we are." It is ironic here that, under the guise of telling us that English people are not pushy, Andy reminds us that an English person may well be the best at something. This mirrors the irony of claiming pride in not being proud, as I discuss later. The vehemence with which these English people express their views that Americans are too pushy and brash compared with English people is interesting in light of the fact that they are claiming reserve and the ability to put themselves down.

Andy's words also highlight a complicated negative attitude toward success that commentators have noted about England,[37] that "people in England like to bring down anyone who's suddenly famous or [has] made money." Among the interviewees, Tara and Antonia noted how "difficult [it is] for people to be successful" in England, and Imogen remarked on what she thought was English disdain for the actor Kenneth Branagh, ostensibly because of his success. She laughingly said that one definition of what makes someone English is knowing not to admire the actor because he is "a braggart." Others pointed to the humility of English people, arguing that the English "never admit to being good at anything" compared with Americans, who, as Alex pointed out, put bumper stickers on their cars saying that their children are honor students at particular schools. Others mentioned the stock phrases that epitomize the negativity of English people. Gordon noted English people's use of the phrases "Who do you think you are?" and "He thinks he's bigger than us" as evidence of how English people "keep [people] in their place." Tara pointed to the ways that English people respond to a "Hey, how are you?" greeting as further evidence of their negativity. In England, she said, people were much more likely to say, "'Oh God, I feel terrible' [*in a whiny voice*] . . . or 'Ohhhh, I'm hung over' . . . , [whereas] here if you say, 'I'm having a bit of a bad day,' people think you're having a nervous breakdown. . . . You're expected to be vibrant and alive and positive." She continued by pointing to the phrases "not so bad," "mustn't grumble," and "can't complain" as further evidence of this attitude. "You *can* complain, [and] from the other point [of view], I see that the English are so funny. Everybody complains all the time!"

Another aspect of the English reserve the interviewees identified is the tendency to hide things under a veneer of politeness and civility. Imogen "watching *Sense and Sensibility*, [saw] . . . these ridiculous people doing these ridiculous things and not saying what they really think, [and thought], 'Yup! That's familiar!'" She uses the film as an example of English people's unwillingness to express emotions, an attitude that she finds quite familiar.[38] Ken remarked on the ways in which the mid-1990s crises in the royal family showed how "unpleasant things [such as] . . . dysfunctional families, child abuse, drunkenness, codependents" are often hidden in England, while Emily found *Keeping Up Appearances,* an English comedy televised in the U.S., discomfiting because its characters' tendency to sweep issues under the carpet "is a little bit too true to some of what I saw when I was growing up, I think." The examples chosen by the interviewees suggest that this phenomenon is class-based: Until recently, the royal family was expected to "keep up appearances," just as the heroine of the television show attempts to maintain upper-middle-class pretensions despite her dysfunctional family.

The emphasis on reserve and humility as part of national identity helps to explain my interviewees' attitudes toward nationalism and patriotism. As we have seen, they are very concerned about portraying themselves as calm, quiet, and reserved—yet genuine in their feelings for others—and they note the English habit of putting oneself down. How do people who believe that these are their national characteristics express national pride? The answer, I suggest, is convoluted. Their emphasis on reserve helps to contextualize the attitudes expressed about national identity in the following sections. For instance, Harry described a drunken English skinhead hurling abuse at passersby in a European train station; in response, he commented that "the only time you ever notice people's national identity is when they parade it." Harry's words are apposite because they show how these English people recoil (at least in theory) from parades of national identity. Indeed, Harry points out that the meaning of Englishness for him is the ability to "feel embarrassed for people that embarrass themselves and don't think there's any reason to be embarrassed." Unlike the skinhead, Harry defines "proper" Englishness as a reserved, understated, and embarrassed state, a rather upper-middle-class definition of Englishness. As Nick Hornby (1996: xi), similarly confronted by an English football fan—a flag-waving "nutter" who asked him whether he loved England—opined: "In the end … anyone with any sense will always find more in their country that embarrasses them than fills them with pride, and England seems a more embarrassing country than many." Both Hornby and Harry want English people to conform to upper-middle-class standards of reserve, reticence, and decorum and are embarrassed when they do not. The emphasis on understated reticence among the people I talked to could result from their own positions in the class hierarchy; they define the "proper" ways to be English based on their own stereotypes of upper-middle-class introversion and working-class expressiveness.[39]

Likewise, many of the interviewees deplored the "uninhibited," "outspoken," "extroverted" ways of Americans who, they said, have little regard for "decorum" and whose public and private displays of emotion made them uncomfortable.[40] In contrast to this image of Americans (often conveniently forgetting the English people who "parade" their national identity), the respondents have a vested interest in remaining embarrassed about public displays of pride in their country and in retaining their calm, unemotional exterior to remind themselves that they are English. We see here the distinctions they make between appropriate and inappropriate displays of national identity and pride. Often they distance themselves from Americans, whose national pride to them seems too overt, showy, and open. Seeing ideal English people as understated and humble, they try to find alternatives to American ways of being national subjects.

Nationalism Is Bad

We're Not Nationalistic

Although there is general agreement in the literature that English people prefer to think of themselves as patriotic rather than nationalistic, less agreement exists as to why this may be.[41] Indeed, until recently few scholars had investigated English nationalism as a phenomenon in its own right, conforming instead to the idea that "nationalism is ... a rather vulgar and immature sentiment indulged in by *other people*" (Jackson and Penrose 1993: 9; emphasis in original).[42] The reasons given for this lack of scholarly interest vary: English chauvinism assumes that "the English do not need nationalism [because] ... they are so sure of themselves" (Colls and Dodd 1986: preface); English identity is so taken for granted that it is assumed to be unproblematic (unlike the identities of other nations);[43] "small" nationalisms are more often studied than "big" nationalisms;[44] or the fusion of Englishness and Britishness has left the English confused about what to call themselves, who they are, and their nationalism.[45] As Taylor points out, the English (or, as he calls them, the Anglo-British) have wreaked their brand of nationalism on much of the rest of the world via the British Empire; they are also perceived as the consummate masters of using pomp and circumstance to celebrate their national identity.[46] However, the people I spoke to distanced themselves from nationalism because they found it too overt and expressive. In so doing, they found another way to distance themselves from Americans.

Thus, Craig cited *One Foot in the Grave*, a British television comedy, to define Englishness: "It's [a] very slow, ... subtle, ... dry ... sense of humor. Very much willing ... to make fun of ourselves, a denial of any patriotic experience. ... When we're there, we'd be the first to run down our own country and our own citizens. That's a very English thing." His statement highlights the ambivalence many interviewees felt about their love of English culture and their distrust of expressions of pride in England. As the previous section illustrated, Englishness is something understated for many of the interviewees and involves a degree of negativity and self-deprecation. Craig takes this a step further, conflating the dry wit and slow pace of the television program with a "denial of any patriotic experience": His aim is to distance himself from patriotism and from nationalism by pointing out that English people are willing to make fun of themselves and to "run down" their country.[47] This supposedly "English" trait—the need to distance oneself from any kind of national pride in England—is a theme that runs through much of what the interviewees said about their national identity. However, a counter-theme is also evident in their words—that their national traits and characteristics are natural and, hence, immutable and inherent.

One group of interviewees expressed their ambivalence about nationality by arguing that they found other kinds of identity more important. For these people, agreeing that they had a national identity as English appeared to be tantamount to being nationalistic; thus, they attempted to avoid asserting any national identity at all. By denying a connection with Englishness, they hoped to distance themselves from nationalism completely. Ian, for instance, claimed that his regional identity as a Yorkshireman and his political identity as a Marxist were far more meaningful to him than his Englishness. He cited travel as the way he "had built up resilience to break with all those cultural and nationalistic and ethnic ties," although he added that one can "never break with them completely 'cause you are always still where you came from." Even though he wanted to downplay nationality, he managed to express here the perceived naturalness of this identity, as well. Indeed, one could argue that a "natural" identity represents the ultimate in the kind of understatement the interviewees expressed earlier—one simply *is* English without any thought or effort of will. Harry also claimed an identity as someone who came from Exeter, his hometown in England, decrying nationalism as "a kind of opiate of the masses." Brad also called himself Western European rather than English as a way to distance himself from isolationists in the British Conservative Party. Others claimed other nationalities. William was one of the only interviewees to describe himself as an American, and Emily said that she saw Canada, where she had lived for a number of years before moving to the U.S., as her home rather than England or the States. These people, then, rejected nationalism by downplaying their national identity as English, although William and Emily did this by asserting different nationalities.

These individuals were not alone in expressing ambivalence about nationality by using of the nationalism label. At least two-thirds of the people I spoke to explicitly distanced themselves from nationalism by using some version of an "I'm not nationalistic, but . . ." statement. They usually used the comment to note something that they liked or missed about England, qualifying it with the clause "I'm not nationalistic" in order to downplay any pride they felt in their nation. Thus, they wanted to distinguish national pride from nationalism. Mike, for instance, described his defensiveness about England this way:

> I don't want to come across as being nationalistic, but obviously one does have feelings for one's nation, which become more obvious by not being in one's nation. In fact, I probably know a lot more about Britain now than [I did] before I left, because I'm able . . . to see the good things and the bad things . . . , and there are a lot of bad things about British society, but I'm now far more aware of them.

Mike explained the ambivalence he felt about expressing positive "feelings" for his nation. In his anxiety not to be interpreted as nationalistic, he ended his statements by focusing on the "bad things" about England. His comments show the difficulties the interviewees faced in negotiating their wish to assert pride in their Englishness with their fear that these assertions would be taken as "nationalistic."

I'm Not "Over The Top" About My Nation

Examining the statements of other respondents about their national identity produces a clearer sense of the attitudes from which they wanted to distance themselves. In this section, we see their contempt for public displays of nationality, a version of nationalistic sentiment that they say is flawed. Diana, for instance, expressed how "ridiculous" she thought rituals that celebrated the nation are:

> If you're standing in space, doesn't it seem hilarious that someone can have tears in their eyes while holding their hand on their heart and pledging allegiance to a piece of cloth. I mean, it's so demeaning. . . . And having your coffin draped with a flag—you're a human, and it matters if you

are good or bad. It doesn't matter if you're American or English or something.

Diana is clearly critical of Americans for saying the Pledge of Allegiance; however, she also makes a more general critique of the ways Britain and America honor dead servicewomen and -men. Although some might view these acts as harmless displays of patriotism rather than as nationalism, Diana includes them in her general critique of national boundaries.[48]

Diana also applied her discomfort with what she saw as thoughtless adherence to nationality to her own life:

> If I went to the top of Everest, I'd put my name there. I really would. I'd have a flag saying, ... "Well, Diana got here," because I'd be proud of myself. I wouldn't have a clue what flag to put on the top of Everest, and I [wouldn't] do it on behalf of my [country]. I hate "my country, right or wrong." Isn't that awful? "Britannia rules the waves." "Land of the free and home of the [brave]." I mean, it's ridiculous.

Diana grew up in England but is a dual-national by birth; here, she shows that she is equally horrified by British and American expressions of nationalism by citing both the "Britannia" and "Land of the Free" homilies. Her own experience straddling two nationalities, British and American, has left her unclear about her national status. In arguing that she would not be able to choose which national flag to place at the top of Everest, she illustrates her belief that national identity can obscure individuals: The flag she would use would simply say "Diana." Indeed, by applying her critique of nationality to herself, she points out that we are all human beings beneath patriotic and nationalist rhetoric. This extends her earlier description of the flags on coffins to show her belief that it is one's status as a "good or bad" human, rather than "my country, right or wrong," that is important. The contrast of these two couplets emphasizes her belief that one must be selective in one's identification with people and nations. Others with whom I spoke also cited "my country, right or wrong" as evidence of a mentality they found abhorrent.

But Americans Are "OTT" About Their Nation

Another group of interviewees stated more explicitly that it was American attitudes toward national identity that they despised. They argued that Americans take their national identity far too seriously and are too open about their national pride. The main bone of contention was Americans' attitudes toward their flag. Like Diana, they pointed to the "sacred" nature of the flag in the U.S., perceiving Americans as extremely nationalistic in a way that English people are not. One contrast they drew was between the ubiquity of the Stars and Stripes in the U.S. and the relative absence of the Union Jack or St. George's Cross in England. Harriet, for instance, said, "I always joke, 'Oh look, another American flag, just in case we forgot where we are!' . . . We don't seem to have this need to express ourselves as a united England as much as they like to. . . . Most of them are fiercely, fiercely proud of being American. I don't need to express that. . . . I'm English, and that's that." Her words imply that she doesn't have to work at her Englishness in the way Americans have to work at their national identity by constantly displaying their flag. Yet she also said she argued with her American boyfriend about how "in England, we're innately superior because this, that, and the other. It's a joke, but part of it is true. One somehow feels that with all that history behind one—. It's not me at all, but Englishness . . . somehow makes you superior, which is rubbish. But we play the little games." Here Harriet is clearly uncomfortable with expressing feelings of superiority, as she moves back and forth between claiming that it is a "joke," "rubbish," or a "game," but also that "part of it is true." Obviously, she does feel some sense of superiority because she is English; however, she attempts to separate herself from Englishness so she can downplay the idea that she alone is superior. Rather, it is Englishness that is superior. Her disclaimers seem a little disingenuous, read in the context of her argument that she does not need to express national pride. Joking about one's feelings of superiority is obviously one way to express them, as one affirms and denies them at the same time.

Others enlarged on this critique of the American struggle for a national identity, claiming that feelings of cohesion come much more easily to English people. Piers, Lucinda, and Peter all expressed this, and Gordon's words sum up their sentiments:

> [England is] pretty good at maintaining a national identity, . . . as hard as that is to define. I think that people know what England is even if they're hard pressed to put it into words . . . , whereas in the States I think they really struggle to get that adhesiveness. The flag becomes really impor-

tant . . . , it's all [they've] got, whereas in Britain there's the Queen Mum and eight hundred years of Queen Mums . . . to hold us together.

Gordon uses history and the royal family to argue that England has a strong national identity, even if people cannot put into words exactly what this is. The indefinable quality of Englishness implies once again that Englishness is muted and quiet compared with the "struggl[ing]" that Americans have to do to define themselves. The fact that "people know what England is" implies that this national identity is somehow natural or unchangeable (as it apparently has been the same for eight hundred years[49]). By contrast, Americans struggle over their national identity because the flag "is all [they've] got." Indeed, Piers, Peter, and Nigel all pointed to Americans' "hypenated" ethnic identifications as evidence that the more hybrid U.S. has to work at its national identity in a way that the supposedly homogeneous England does not. Others cited the fact that the U.S. is a nation of immigrants to explain the emphasis Americans put on their flag.[50]

Like Harriet, who said she did not need the same outward expressions of national identity as Americans, Andy claimed not to feel patriotic. However, on the Fourth of July, he said, he hung Union Jack bunting out his window, ostensibly as a joke. He thought that his American neighbors saw the funny side of this, and his actions seem to be designed to poke fun at the patriotic sentiments displayed on Independence Day. Andy's wife, Alex, asked rhetorically, "How many people even own a flag in Britain?" and told me about a story she had read in the local paper in England about a woman who was asked to take her Union Jack down from her house by the town council:

> They refused to let her [fly the flag] because the flagpole was stuck out from her house and it looked like a restaurant sign. They let the Italian restaurant fly an Italian flag, but she couldn't fly a Union Jack. One of those typical British things. I [couldn't] imagine that here. . . . No, being British is fun. Being an American is a very serious business.

By contrasting this incident with their Independence Day prank, Alex maintains that Americans are far more serious in their attitudes toward their national identity than English people are. How her story shows English people's sense of humor, however, is not clear—it seems, rather, that the council took the flag seriously as an inappropriate form of national expression (meanwhile, remember that Andy and Alex's

American neighbors were amused by their Union Jack bunting). Despite their investment in believing in their lack of national pride, Alex and Andy's criticisms of Americans provide a way to assert their own national pride.

Harry also criticized nationalism because it "gets in the way of having a good laugh" in the States. Even though he was as "happy to spit on the flag in England as I am to spit on the flag here," taboos in America prevent him from poking fun at national icons and traditions:

> At least [in England] I can have a good laugh and say what I want to say ... without being accused of being anti-American or anti-English. ... If I upset people in England, say[ing], "Oh, the Queen should hang" or something, people would just say, "Oh, shut up, you silly fuck." They're not going to say, "Oh, you've insulted the flag of my country, and I demand you take that back ... or I'll beat the shit out of you."

It is unclear from these statements whether Harry thinks that his inability to "spit on the flag" in America comes from his alien status in the States or from Americans' propensity to take their national identity too seriously. In some ways, the two are impossible to separate because his experiences as an alien inform his experiences of nationalism in the U.S. The use of physical violence in his example again suggests the seriousness with which these English people believe Americans understand national identity. By contrast, Harry believes that his criticisms of national icons in England are more acceptable than any criticisms he might make in the U.S.—another way to say that Americans are too intense and "over the top" about their national identity.

I Am Naturally English

Despite criticizing what they perceived to be the extent of nationalism in the U.S., some interviewees struggled to find ways to express their own national identity in terms that avoided these inappropriate displays. Ironically, however, their comments sometimes led less to an ardent critique of nationalism than toward a more wholehearted embrace of their Englishness as "natural." As Diana did when talking about the flag she would plant on Mount Everest, Andy and Nigel both asserted their neutral human status as they derided nationalism and patriotism. However, both also combined this neutral stance with the argument that they were not American. In response to a question about whether he would take out U.S. citizenship, for instance, Nigel said:

"You're a person. It doesn't matter whether you're American or English, Australian, Russian, whatever country you live in, or if you have to take out that citizenship, fine. It doesn't bother me. It's not going to change anything. If I was an American citizen, it's not going to stop me being English."

Thus, Nigel starts out by de-emphasizing nationality in favor of personhood, citing a list of nationalities to reduce their significance (much as people sometimes cite a list of colors to de-emphasize racial differences). By the end of his comments, however, he has made clear that he has a much deeper bond with his Englishness than he initially suggested. Again we see the presumption of the "naturalness" of nationality, as Nigel asserts that nothing would stop him from being English underneath (even though "it doesn't matter"). We get the sense from his words that Englishness is important to him in a way that Americanness could never be, even though he also wants to deny the salience of Englishness. Although he tries to downplay his nationality, he actually concludes by asserting that his Englishness is immutable and inherent.

Andy echoed these sentiments, distancing himself from Americans even as he claimed to feel no "great patriotism" toward England: "I don't think I would want to lose being British just because I'm over here. I certainly wouldn't of choice want to say I'm an American." Other interviewees agreed: Zoe, Craig, and Octavia all argued that they would not want to lose their British citizenship, while Vera, Frank, and Gary, all dual-nationals but without valid British passports, claimed that they were still essentially English underneath.

In struggling to find what they consider to be an appropriate discourse to express their feelings for England, these people often rely on the idea of naturalness. This enables them to downplay national sentiment while espousing the idea that they cannot help being English. Again, the idea of naturalness conveniently coincides with the interviewees' attempts to be reserved and understated. Craig pointed to an assumption, common among the interviewees, that England was "part of" them. He believed that England had "shaped who I am and my beliefs, and [my] background's there. So it's obviously a part of me and my outlook. It's something that will always be there, [but] it's not something [about which] I remind everybody." Echoing Ian, many respondents believed that one could not help but be shaped by "where you came from." Antonia, for instance, commented, that, although she despised nationalism, "in the back of my mind, I always know that I'm English really." By believing in the naturalness of their nationality, they could claim to have a national identity while avoiding the pitfalls of nationalism.

Craig also argued that, despite the sentiments he expressed earlier, he would not "stand and wave the Union Jack at every opportunity ... because [England] does have a lot of shortcomings." Crucially, he does not want to "remind" everyone of his nationality, although it is important to the person he is. Although he spent fourteen years as a child in Africa, he believes that he has been shaped by England; he argues, however, that reminding people of this would mean accentuating his nationality too much. His words point to what he considers to be inappropriate displays of nationalism—flag-waving, both literally and metaphorically. In contrast to someone who "remind[s] everybody" about their national pride at every turn, he suggests that an understated and muted approach is more appropriate. Craig's feeling that he is naturally English (despite his childhood abroad) means that he does not have to do anything extra to be English. Because he cannot help it, he can be English with the minimum of fuss and "remind[ers]."

People Should Be Selective in Their Pride

As an alternative to using "naturalness" to claim the unavoidability of national pride, some interviewees were selective about what kind of pride was appropriate. Nigel, for instance, criticized others for their nationalism but denied it in himself. He claimed that Irish Americans who supported the Irish Republican Army (IRA) were inappropriately nationalistic, using a phrase that cropped up at least three times during his interview: "If they're so proud, why don't they go and live in Ireland?" However, he ran into problems when he attempted to delineate the extent of his own pride in England: "I hate that nationalistic fervor. . . . I think it's obscene, so that's why . . . I can't say it bothers me being English over here. If I was that proud of being English—I *am* proud of being English—but if I was that fervent about it, I would still be there. . . . 'I'm proud to be Irish.' Fuck 'em!" For the moment, he resolved the tension by deciding that his departure from England showed that his pride in his nation did not compare to that of the Irish Americans; thus, he could later claim, "It's a shrinking world, unless you're a complete dickhead." However, he had also explained his pride in England earlier by saying, "It's my heritage. There's no reason to be disgusted about it. You are what you are. [You've] got to be proud of a few things." His words imply that he is proud because he cannot help who he is—though he seems unable to apply this idea to the Irish Americans he criticizes.

Others attempted to qualify their national pride by being selective about how they applied it, using English examples rather than American ones. To show why he does not feel allegiance to a flag, for instance, Ken contrasted the pride felt by most Americans toward their flag with the fact that the extreme right-wing, racist National Front uses the Union Jack as its symbol in England. By pointing to the racist connotations of the Union Jack, he is able to assert pride in his nation without being associated with racism or xenophobia; at the same time, he manages to distance himself from Americans' emphasis on their flag. Tara also said that she associated "British pride with football hooligans [and flag-waving], knee-jerk, unthinking patriotism." She implicitly contrasted this "unthinking patriotism" with her own pride in the BBC and more "cultural" forms of Englishness. For Tara, the negative aspects of patriotism lie in knee-jerk reactions of support for one's country. By contrast, she argued, she carefully considers when she can and cannot support England—for instance, by feeling pride in the BBC but not in British policy in Bosnia-Herzegovina in the early 1990s. Tara's examples suggest an upper-middle-class-based critique of "unthinking patriotism."

Others qualified their pride by pointing to the ways in which Englishness was not important to them. Peter, for instance, mused, "What does it mean to me to be English? [*brief pause*] Well, is it something I'm proud of? Yes. But is it something that matters? No." Once pride starts to "matter," his words imply, it becomes something different, perhaps something more dangerous. Yet a few sentences later, he described rising to the occasion when people at work tease him about the scandal-ridden royal family: "I'm not a huge supporter of the royal family. I think it's a wonderful institution, and I'm definitely pro-royalty. [If they criticize the Queen], I'll give them a reaction. You stand up for your country. I definitely defend England. I love England—there's no two ways about it." The contradictions in these statements—that he supports and yet does not support the royal family—echo the contradictions in what being English means to Peter. On the one hand, it doesn't matter, but on the other hand, even lighthearted teasing at work brings out his strong defensive "love" of England. Here Peter grapples with his pride in his nation while feeling the urge to downplay these emotions.

Peter was not alone in having these contradictory feelings. Stephen commented that he was "not big on nationhood" although he wasn't "ashamed to be English." Gary expressed his feelings of national identity by claiming to be "pleased to be English" rather than proud and by pointing out that England has problems: "I feel pleased to be English. Proud to be English if somebody says something particularly good about Britain, but ... there are a lot of negatives about Britain ... I'm not particularly proud to be the carrier of a national flag or the embodiment of a ... nation." Harry went further in his rhetoric, claiming a "deep revulsion for any kind of nationalism. ... I don't think that being English means taking pride in 55 million people" and that even "loving the cultural aspects of your country [is] bullshit."

Even when Americans attacked England, some interviewees claimed, they were happy to admit that the country has problems and to poke fun themselves (in the style that Craig alluded to earlier when referring to the British television program). One archetype they drew on was the sarcastic, ironic sense of humor they thought English people shared (see Chapter 3). Ian, Imogen, and Gary all claimed that they joined in when Americans attacked England, and Tara argued that she criticized England's foreign policy more than her American friends did. Imogen complained that Americans don't "take the piss out of themselves. ... I love people criticizing England. I think it's hilarious! ... Even when they say the most outrageous things! I mean, that's great! Fine! Yeah! We're crap!" However, she then said, "I will defend us or whatever," suggesting that these critiques sometimes result in her own defensiveness.

Catriona, Craig, and Octavia admitted that criticizing England became more difficult after they moved away. Indeed, interviewees noted their defensiveness about topics as diverse as the class system, front-loading washing machines, road maintenance, British policy in Northern Ireland, and English television and movies.[51] Catriona pointed out that "when you're away from your own country, it makes you far more patriotic than you would normally be," and others agreed. Craig cited a line from Wordsworth's poetry to explain his strengthened sense of national identity: "I travelled among foreign men ... , /Nor, England! did I know 'til then /What love I bore to thee."[52] Meanwhile. Frank argued that people "naturally" will "criticize your home country for its politics maybe or its style of living, [or] whatever it does in the international scene," so that one can do little else but defend it. Catriona pointed out that it was fine for her to criticize England, but "woe betide" an American who did so.

Criticizing England

The people I talked to did criticize England during the interviews, however. These critiques were another strategy to distance themselves from forms of national identity with which they were uncomfortable. Just as they argued that many images of England are "falsely nostalgic" or tried not to be nationalistic, they criticized England in order to maintain control over their English identities and to avoid degenerating into "knee-jerk patriotism." In addition, by criticizing England, they could further distance themselves from Americans, either because they perceived Americans as lacking the ability to be self-critical or because they wanted to distance themselves from American Anglophilia. Their critiques enabled them to point to a more sophisticated view of England than Americans have.

Although the interviewees often mentioned that England has "problems," no consensus emerged as to what they thought these problems were. For instance, although some respondents cited recent court cases (such as the Birmingham Six and the Guildford Four) that had rocked the British justice system, others claimed that the British judicial system was one of the best in the world. Many were disgusted with the Conservative Government that was in power in 1995, when the interviews were conducted, and with its economic policies, citing these as reasons they had left or been forced to leave.[53] But while some criticized the British system of government for its lack of constitutional rights and civil liberties,[54] others characterized the British political system as fairer and more tolerant than the American system.[55] And although the majority of interviewees said that English social life—especially its pub culture— was far superior to America's, others criticized England for being "dull" and English people for not being fun-loving enough.[56] Some valued what they saw as a greater propensity for politeness and "civilized behavior" in England, while others cited these as stifling conventions.[57]

More than two-thirds of the interviewees said they missed English newspapers and television news, but a few enjoyed American newspapers and were critical of English tabloid journalism. Relatedly, most felt that the U.S. was too insular, both in its approach to news and in everyday life. In the U.S., Craig said, "I [am] very aware of being out of touch with what is happening in the world, [whereas] at home . . . you were flooded with [news] every day." By contrast, others complained about English xenophobia and insularity, especially English people's negative reactions to Americans and U.S. culture. Brad and his American wife said they noticed "anti-American sentiment" during their stay in England, and Peter and Ian, who had both traveled in Australia and the Far East before coming to the U.S., recounted the blank looks and lack of interest that greeted them when they returned to the United Kingdom. Quentin, Emily, and Diana all saw England as "parochial" in its attitude to outsiders, and others criticized England for its superiority complex (as Chapter 6 discusses in detail).

The interviewees showed great diversity in their attitudes toward class in England: Some were proud of it, but a large number were critical of the workings of the class system. Alex and Anne pointed to the influence of the "old school tie" and "old-boy network," implicitly criticizing the ways that gender and class work together. Some said that class had constrained them as individuals: Mike reported that he had "found it very difficult to do well academically because of my social background." (Mike had gone to a state school before attending Cambridge and, at the time of the interview, was enrolled in a graduate program at an elite East Coast university.) Frank, who grew up in a working-class cockney family, had left England forty years earlier because he believed that

> in England, if you don't have the right school on your résumé, or if you don't have the right family behind you, or . . . if you don't have plenty of money behind you, your . . . horizons are limited . . . by social . . . classification. . . . I didn't want to be on the bottom, and in England, if you're on the bottom, that's your bloody place and you'd better stay there.

Frank suggests his frustrations with the ways in which class in England limits opportunities. Gordon, whose origins were also working class, remarked on the "fluidity of structure" in the U.S. compared with the "integrity to one's station" in England.

Others who had benefited more from the class structure were also critical of it. Lucinda, whose mother came from a wealthy background, noted the "lower standard of living" in England than in the U.S. and the lack of social mobility. Upper-class interviewees noted the pressures that the class system had exerted on them. Ken, whose father had come from a working-class family but whose mother had been presented at court as a debutante, attended one of England's elite public schools; he explained how constraining he had found attitudes about what was "acceptable," saying, "Well, of course you've got to behave in such and such a way—that's what everybody does." Similarly, Peter was glad to have moved away to escape the idea that "it's just not cricket. . . . One has to do the right thing. . . . [Now] I pretty much do my own thing." Harry and Tara both expressed defensiveness about having attended public schools, because this affected the ways that English people interacted with them. Tara said that if she moved back to England, she would need to find ways to "overcome those obstacles that we sometimes have in England, about the code words, about 'Who are you?' Are you someone different from me? Are you snobbish?" Harry concurred, arguing that

> if I could have gone to a boring comprehensive with a respectable achieve-
> ment record and got to university that way, life would be so much easier
> for me. But because I went to a public school and I hated it and rebelled
> against it, I constantly find [with] everybody in England that you meet,
> you have to find out fairly fast what sort of school they went to, and it
> becomes a defining thing.

Harry's insistence that "life would so much easier" if he had gone to a state school is ironic, because he benefited in other ways from his edu-cation (not least of which was his job as a journalist in the U.S.). Zoe, Vera, Mike, and Lucinda criticized the relationship between class and the educational system in England from another perspective, deploring the tracking or streaming of students[58] and pointing out the small per-centage of people who attended universities and colleges in England.

However, others were more positive about the class system. Imogen criticized Americans who make "very simplistic . . . judgments" about class in England, pointing out that social mobility is as prevalent in England as it is in the U.S., and that class "is not this all-defining, all-encompassing, totally rigid thing that everyone says it is." She then cited "the fact that a 'toff' and an 'oick,' or whatever you want to call them, will have a perfectly meaningful and real and genuine conversa-tion in a pub . . . or at a football match" as evidence of the way class works differently in England and America. Choosing class-based epi-thets—"toff" to describe an upper-class person and "oick" to describe a working-class person—undermines somewhat her claim that people can cross class boundaries in England. However, by arguing that these kinds of cross-class conversations do not usually take place in the U.S., she also defends the English class system. Partly, this attitude results from Imogen's own class privilege, but it also stems from the ways in which class is vital to her identity: Seeing how class operates on an everyday basis makes Imogen more aware of its gradations, but it also makes her conscious of the ways in which it affects her life.

Interestingly, interviewees with working-class backgrounds who were critical of class in other ways also defended their own class culture. Mike called his routine as a graduate student obsessive, an approach that originated in his working-class background:

> Before I went to university, I worked in a brick factory . . . and I've always had the ability to switch into that mode very easily and to become hypnotized by factory work and become part of working-class social life as well. [Later] I was teaching in a big, rough comprehensive school. . . . I played bowls and I'd go out drinking with my friends. . . . So it was a very normal working-class routine.

In the interview, Mike repeatedly returned to the theme of his pride in his working-class roots, whether this meant disabusing Americans of the idea that all English people are upper class or "defending class issues, . . . mainly cultural stuff" with Americans. Clearly, he experienced pride in his class status and in the ways that class translated into culture for him.

In qualifying their feelings of pride in England and in criticizing aspects of English culture that they found troubling, the interviewees negotiated the meanings implicit in "I'm not nationalistic, but . . ." They tried to find a way to feel proud of England in ways that were meaningful to them. This involved carefully carving out a space in which they could criticize some English institutions and aspects of English culture and praise others.

CONCLUSION: AVOIDING EXTREMES

The interviews quoted throughout this chapter show the conceptual work that these people do to construct an English identity with which they feel comfortable. Although some of the respondents are very drawn to images of England as old and green, others criticize these ideas as falsely nostalgic and attempt to find other ways to feel positive about their national identity. Both responses, however, draw on two conceptions of identity—identity as natural and identity as work. The theme of naturalness emerges as the interviewees discuss their feelings of being "rooted" in England; however, we also see them working to maintain these roots, most notably by watching television and films and drawing on the images they see therein. Those who criticized nostalgic images of England also drew on popular culture to make their critiques; they, too, however, were likely to fall back on a discourse of naturalness to explain their feelings of connection with England, especially as they contemplated returning there.

In the second half of the chapter, I examined other ways in which the interviewees negotiated their pride in being English. Again, I found them using the idea that their national identity was natural in order to make the negotiation easier. In particular, I noted the role of the stereotype of English people as reserved. Believing that they had a naturally understated and muted style, these interviewees could resolve the dilemma of asserting national pride without being too "over the top" about it. If one is naturally English, then there is no need to engage in public expressions of national pride; it is perhaps the most muted expression of national pride that there is. However, the interviewees also expressed pride in their national identity, despite their desire to steer clear of nationalism—notably, when they compared themselves with Americans. They considered Americans too proud and boastful about their national identity and used them as a foil to show how muted and critical English people could be about England.

The people quoted throughout this chapter struggled to express their national identity in ways that allow them to feel pride without being ashamed of that pride. The tension between their use of discourses of naturalness and the conceptual work they do with cultural images enables them to negotiate this problem. Embracing or denying images of England allows them to retain control over the images, and positing a natural feeling of connection with England—either through the country's land and history or because of their reserve—means that they can abnegate responsibility for the pride and nostalgia that they feel if they want to.

Finally, the interviews show that these English people do not want to be extreme in their national pride or in their nostalgia. In pointing to problems in England, they enhance the idea that they are not nationalistic, and in labeling images of England false, they are able to distance themselves from what they view as overly nostalgic ways to think about England. In their desire to avoid extremes, they contrast themselves with Americans, whom they see as "over the top" about their nation. Also, however, they want to distance themselves from extreme parades of national identity in England, whether they come from "Little Englanders" within the Conservative Party, from football hooligans, or from the makers of Merchant–Ivory-like films.

3   Responding to Privilege

Class, Race, Nation, and Anglophilia

Everything in England . . . comes back to the inextricable links between our
education system [and] privilege, or lack of it.

A. S. Byatt, *Babel Tower*

WHITE IMMIGRANTS in the U.S. occupy a contradictory location,
because their skin color affords them privileges that their immigrant status might otherwise deny them. White women and men from England
are also privileged by the cultural capital[1] that English culture garners
in the Anglophilic U.S. In this chapter, I examine how the people I talked
to define their privileges, noting the ways in which their nationality,
race, and class intersect to produce situations in which they believe they
have advantages. The privileges that they identify are produced in interactions with Americans, and the interviewees generally hold Americans responsible for whatever benefits they accrue.

However, I examine the other side of the coin, as well: What do these
interviewees bring to the interactions? In particular, I focus on their
sense of superiority and how they use cultural practices to construct
themselves as distinct from and superior to Americans. I point out that,
even though they like to define their superiority in natural terms, this
attitude is in fact socially produced as the interviewees "do" identity.
Thus, the production of their privilege is a two-way street. Although
they believe that Americans are responsible for Anglophilia, the interviewees themselves play up the elements of Englishness that they
believe make them superior in an attempt to garner a more complete
sense of superiority.

DEFINING CLASS

I originally intended to sample only middle- and upper-middle-class
English people in order to limit the range of my study to a particularly

privileged version of Englishness. However, the more I found out about my interviewees, the harder it became to assign them to a particular class or socioeconomic status. Traditional Marxist or Weberian definitions of class as relationship to means of production or exchange relationships[2] are complicated by the effects of these English people's move to the U.S., by gender (for instance, whether they should be classified as individuals or as households[3]), their age (especially their student status), and by the impact of their family backgrounds. In addition to collecting socioeconomic indicators of class such as occupation and educational background, I asked the interviewees to self-identify their class. Although he had studied as an undergraduate at Cambridge and was pursuing graduate studies at an elite U.S. university, for instance, Mike defined himself as working class. He explained that he had spent school holidays working in factories and that it was easy for him to settle into a "working-class routine" when he returned to England. Gary, who had a similar educational background, also had a complex attitude toward his class:

> My father is a professional and my mother is a semi-professional [*brief pause*] and I suppose I'm a semi-professional. So by those standards, I would have to say middle class. . . . On the other hand, my father has prolonged periods of unemployment and financial insecurity, so you might say economically lower-middle class or . . . even working class. But since [in England] class is so closely tied with culture, I'd have to say middle class. . . . And I don't earn anything, which I guess makes me working class, right?

As a graduate student in the social sciences, Gary clearly has an understanding of various components that make up class, ranging from occupation to income and culture. His slight discomfort with middle-class status is interesting in light of the "imperial middle" in American class relations, whereby most people classify themselves as middle class.[4]

Others classified their backgrounds as working class—Emily, Gordon, and Frank, for example. By the time the interviews were conducted, however, all three were fairly comfortably middle class. While Emily pointed to the role of the English educational system to account for her social mobility, Gordon and Frank argued that leaving England had enabled them to move up the social ladder. Although Frank had left England thirty years earlier than Gordon, both had felt constrained by the "class-bound" nature of English life. Both men felt that they had been able to mix with social elites in the U.S. in ways they would not have done in England. Their experiences, then, suggest that the classic upward social mobility associated with immigration was a reality for some interviewees, although in their cases it might have also been the result of Anglophilia, as I show later.

By contrast, Nigel, who had been employed as a skilled artisan in England, had become a traveling salesman in the U.S. He seemed to have moved slightly down the social ladder; he classified himself as working class, using the "simple polarization view" (Wright 1996: 390) to argue for a large working class: "I would say working class, the same as 90 percent of the rest of the [population]. Everybody's working class, because everybody has to work, whether it's blue collar or white collar."

Gender also complicated the class positions of the interviewees. Nigel was the only man who had been forced into unemployment as he awaited his green card. Several women, however, were waiting for the right to work in the U.S. At the time of the interviews, both Alex and Zoe were taking care of the house and caring for their children while their husbands worked in the paid labor force, and neither planned to work full time when their green cards came through. Octavia and Vera also did not do paid work in the labor force; the former was about to give birth to her second child, and the latter was very involved with volunteer work. In addition, the two people in my sample who were unemployed during the interviews were women—both Diana and Frances had moved to the U.S. without jobs, Diana on her own, and Frances with her husband. Both had left high-status professional careers and were hoping to find comparable jobs in the U.S., Diana on the basis of her U.S. citizenship, and Frances with her green card.

Despite some of this rather contradictory evidence, the combination of educational background, occupation, estimated total household income, and family background suggests that most of those with whom I spoke were middle or upper-middle class. Where necessary, I refer in my analysis to the ways they self-identified their class backgrounds, but for the most part we can assume that they spoke from positions of relative class privilege.

ESCAPING THE CLASS CONSTRAINTS OF ENGLAND

People who move share the experience of being able to reinvent themselves, whether that involves changing their wardrobe when going away to college, shedding a nickname when changing jobs, or starting a new life when moving to another country. Indeed, all immigrants are able to start again when they arrive in a new country, although some do this under more constraints than others. Many of the people I spoke with expressed a sense of freedom in the anonymity they felt while living in America. For example, Antonia and Harry found being able to "start from scratch" both "liberating" and "refreshing." They relished the fact that they were not defined by their history in the U.S. and often used language that suggested a redefinition of identity that had come with their move. Both Harry and Imogen talked of the "re-invention of self," while Lucinda and Ken echoed an advertising campaign for the U.S. Army by noting the opportunity to "be who you want to be."[5] They argued that their increased feelings of freedom came particularly from having no history in their new home.

However, their experiences had a uniquely English twist: Underlying their ability to reinvent themselves was a perception that they had managed to escape the everyday constraints and expectations of the class system in England. Antonia suggested these implications when she said, "In England, the minute you open your mouth, people are placing you, summing up . . . what kind of school you went to, where you live . . . , whereas here it's nice to have that anonymity that nobody really knows anything about you. You're a bit of a puzzle to them. They know you're from England, but that's about it." As Antonia explains, she has escaped the ways in which class was embedded in her daily life in England. Her feelings of excitement at "being an expat" result from the anonymity of living in a place where people do not pigeonhole her as belonging to a particular class because of her accent and demeanor. Thus, she can define herself the way she wants instead of being defined by those with whom she interacts. Antonia and Tara, both of whom made this point, had the most upper-class accents in my sample.[6]

Other indicators of class also emerged as threatening during interactions with English people. Tara and Harry saw their public-school educations as "obstacles" to "get over" when interacting with other English people, pointing to the "very subtle" methods they used to ascertain one another's background. Tara looked for strategies "to get that out of the way quickly" when she talked to English people, in an effort to "set them at their ease." Although she speaks here from a position of privilege, she sees this privilege as a detriment during interactions. Stephen provided a possible explanation for this: Defining himself as working class, he explained that when he first went to Oxford, he would "make assumptions about" people who had "been to the wealthiest school and [spoke] with highbrow accent[s]" before discovering that they were "basically nice" people. His choice of words suggests that the assumptions he made before he got to know people were not particularly flattering.

Imogen also noted the importance of class during interactions with other English people: Classifying her own class background as "nouv" (short for *nouveau riche*), she watched people "trying to categorize me, and I've seen people do this [*makes 'tick, tick, tick' noise*]. It's not obvious because my accent's posh, but it's got these slightly weird bits in it. . . . I [can] see them thinking, 'Where did you go to school? . . . What does your father do?' [*in an upper-class accent*]." Imogen's experiences as something of an outsider among upper-class people further illustrate the close attention paid to accent as an indicator of class in England. As she described people's attempts to place her in the class system, she screamed in mock horror, suggesting that despite her humor she found this interactive "summarizing" difficult to accept. Diana confirmed this, recognizing the skill that English people have in "identify[ing] anyone in one second by their accent, down to averaging what their parents' income is. . . . Therefore [everyone] knows where he[7] comes from and what he is in relation to the next person." According to the experiences of these people, then, interactions are an arena in which the evidence of class emerges in England; such interactions enable class to become relevant to definitions of others on an everyday, almost ongoing, basis.

By contrast, Harry noted that Americans "[don't] care if I come from a public school," while Tara felt she could be "a complete blank slate . . . without [any] baggage" in the U.S. Despite their class privilege, some of these people were extremely uncomfortable that their class backgrounds were easily ascertained by other English people; they welcomed the relative anonymity of living in America because they could escape any negative feedback associated with their class privilege. Some interviewees suggested that this also applied to people with less-privileged backgrounds. Tara, for example, related a story about a working-class friend of hers from Liverpool who had been a classmate at Cambridge. According to Tara, he still had his Liverpudlian accent, despite his Cambridge education, and was now living and working in the U.S. as a stockbroker. "He liked America," she said, "because . . . his accent never came up. People just assumed it was *the* English accent, [the] same as everybody else's." The implicit comparison here is with England, where his accent and class presumably had "come up" in ways that made him feel constrained. These experiences show that English people from different classes and regions find Americans' lack of knowledge about the class system in England liberating.

This sense of liberation also emerged in contrasts drawn between English tradition and what the interviewees saw as the relative flexibility of the American social system. Some referred to the U.S. as "classless," relishing this despite their own class privilege, while others said that there was more social mobility in the U.S. Ken, who had given up a lucrative job in The City[8] to pursue an acting career in the States, said he had found tradition in England "oppress[ive] . . . [and] constrain[ing]." He noticed it especially during his interactions with other English people, when he felt "glad to have got away from . . . the tradition and history [of English culture]" and the ideology behind comments such as "this is an accepted mode of behavior and this isn't." This, he realized once he had left, had affected the way he lived his life in England; now he felt he had the "maturity and self-confidence" to ignore such ways of thinking. One of the "freedoms" of life in the U.S. was that "I can leave my old identity behind and be who I want," he said. Like the others quoted in this section, Ken was keenly aware of the ways his move had liberated him from the shackles of the English social and class systems. Echoing his words, Tara explained that "as a foreigner in another country, one isn't as constrained. You have very little history, and you can be just about anything you want."

In spite of the class privileges that most of these people had enjoyed in England, they clearly conceptualized their move to a new country as enabling them to get away from the constraints of class that they had experienced there. In particular, interacting with other English people who could "summarize" their class and being forced to do things according to propriety and tradition were aspects of England from which they were glad to be free. Lest we see their complaints about England as disingenuous, I turn now to the ways they did identify the privileges they enjoyed, both in England and in the U.S.

SELF-IDENTIFYING PRIVILEGE

Are We Privileged? Race, Nation, and Class in Self-Definitions

As we have seen, some of the people I talked to believed that their move to the U.S. had freed them from the constraints of the class system in England. However, their sense of privilege also emerged in other ways. Interestingly, when I asked whether they felt privileged to be English, some interpreted the question to be about whether they felt superior because they were English rather than about structural privileges they might experience as a result of their national identity. Although most were loathe to admit direct feelings of national superiority or pride, a sense of superiority came through in a variety of ways.[9] Later in this chapter, I discuss ways that they acted in order to enhance these individual feelings of superiority—notably, in their discussions of their senses of humor and fashion. For now, I focus on the structures of privilege they recognized rather than on any individual sense they might have had that they were "better" than other people. I point to to the ways that race, nation, and class worked together in their structural conceptions of privilege. Their cognizance of their privilege shows an awareness that the constraints they faced were not as severe as those facing other people. Their evaluations of how they are empowered are similar to the work done by Ruth Frankenberg's "race cognizant" interviewees (1993: 159–88).[10]

Defining oneself as a privileged individual takes a certain level of understanding about one's position in the world. Unlike seeing oneself as superior, recognizing privilege involves an awareness of the ways that life has worked in one's favor—that where one is now is not just the result of initiative or judgment but also has to do with structures of inequality that have benefited some at the expense of others. Although some interviewees saw class as a constraint during interactions with other English people, others were prepared to define themselves as privileged on a structural level by referring to their class. They usually did this, however, by noting the benefits that had accrued from their educational opportunities or family background. Although in these cases they did not talk explicitly about their national identity, their Englishness was never far away, as they were talking about English institutions and English opportunities and families. For instance, Hugh answered a question about how being English was important to him by focusing on his family background: "I'm comfortable with the way I am, and I don't want to change it. . . . It's a matter of confidence. . . . I've learned to do [things] from my own family background, and that way seems to work, so that's the way I do things." Although he said he was talking simply about his family, he made this claim in the context of a question about Englishness, which reinforces the idea that his family background and his Englishness are interlinked. Indeed, most of the interviewees felt their families to be the most significant part of England for them—for some, family was the only reason to visit England. But families also provided the starting block for the privilege that they now felt. Craig, for instance, wondering whether he was privileged because he was English, pointed to the opportunities his family had given him: "The travel, the experiences, their attitudes, . . . everything that's been available in my life, [all] comes through my family, financial support from my family." Explaining that his family had paid for his secondary education at a public school, Craig's sense of privilege emerged as a result of his family's class position. He continued by comparing himself with an American friend who "owed thirty thousand dollars" for her social-work education; he noted that his tertiary education had not only been free in England, but "far more comprehensive than the education that they get over here." Clearly, Craig's sense of privilege extended beyond his family to include the educational system in England, and beyond his own class to his national identity.

Living in the U.S. and making comparisons with life here was a primary method for these people to become aware of the privileges they had accrued in their lives. Many felt gratitude for the education system in England; Andy believed that he would not "be where I am now" if he had been educated in the States.[11] Zoe also pointed out that her sense of privilege from being English arose from the fact that "we had the opportunities for a good education, and we didn't have to pay vast sums of money." However, she used the English education system to see her privilege in class terms, aware that not everyone had these opportunities in England: "The university was for the privileged classes only. . . . A lot more people have the chance for more education here than . . . in England. . . . We were lucky because we were in the privileged top 4 percent that got A levels and went to university." Here Zoe combines feelings of national privilege with an awareness that she also had more class privileges than do many people in England. In contrast to studies of middle- and upper-class people suggesting that they believe their position in life to be the result of initiative and ability, these interviewees saw themselves as lucky to have the privileges they enjoyed.[12] Zoe also noted her class privilege in the U.S. in this regard, pointing to her wealthy surroundings as evidence of her luck. She stayed at home to look after her children during the day and said that she felt privileged "being able to live in a lovely house, the fact that [my husband] has such a good job and is well paid. I felt privileged for that in England, and I feel privileged for that here. We . . . have a lot of nice things that [other] people don't have."

Several others recognized their privileged backgrounds but criticized the English education system for instilling in them a sense of superiority rather than an appreciation of that privilege. For example, although she pointed to the "wonderfully rich perspective in English literature" that she had received, Vera also argued that her school had taught her a sense of superiority and snobbishness. "It took me at least ten years . . . to debunk [the] aspect of myself [that thought], well, that [this education] is *the* best thing to have, [and not to be] a snob." Piers concurred, describing himself leaving his public school as "a selfish, arrogant prick. . . . I just wreaked my own particular breed of culture on everyone." Antonia and Harriet both noted how sheltered their all-girls public-school education had been in the context of talking about race relations, suggesting that both were referring to the lack of racial diversity at their schools as well as to their class privilege. These people noted the privileges they obtained from their education, but they were also willing to note the costs associated with these privileges, both for themselves and for others.

Living abroad seemed to help others recognize their privilege. Tara reflected on her social circle in England, which was made up of "my work and my old school friends" from her public school and Cambridge; she determined that she would "volunteer . . . or join an environmental group" if she returned to England to counter the class homogeneity of her friendships. Craig, a doctor, expressed the privileges of his race and class by comparing himself with the "poverty of [his] client group. . . . The people in the worst situations [in the inner-city neighborhood where he worked] are . . . black." As a consequence of this comparison, he felt that he had been given "more opportunities through being white." Gary also defined his privilege by contrasting himself with poor black Americans, although he related this to his status as an English person:

I'm privileged in the sense that I'm [a] white, middle class, . . . reasonably articulate English person. I think that gives me certain advantages over a poor [black] American from [the inner city]. So part of the privilege is just inherent in being white or . . . my class and being well educated, which I think partly goes along with the British part of me, and part of it is that [Americans] take me more seriously.

Gary's comment that "being white, [middle] class . . . and well educated . . . partly goes along with the British part of me" is intriguing. It is not clear in his statements how he sees these different aspects of his privilege working together, but in using the phrase "goes along with" he implies that his national identity is directly related to his race and class status. The Anglophilia he suggests here is also linked to his race, class, and educational background in his mind. I explore these dynamics within Anglophilia later in this chapter.

Having discussed the ways the interviewees became cognizant of their structural privileges by making comparisons with Americans, I will now focus explicitly on their attitudes toward other immigrants. I continue to explore the intersections of race, class, and nationality by investigating whether comparisons with other immigrants affected the ways the interviewees conceptualized their own status in the U.S.

RACE, NATION AND CLASS IN DISCOURSES OF IMMIGRATION

We're Immigrants, Too!

The English people interviewed complained about the constraints of the class system in England but also recognized the privileges that they had obtained from that system. A similar dualism emerges in this section. One group of interviewees recognized their privileged status and criticized the process by which the combination of their race, class, and nationality could work in their favor in comparison with other immigrant groups. These people argued that any privilege they received because they were white, middle-, and upper-middle-class English immigrants was unjustified. Yet another group of interviewees faulted Americans for treating them like other immigrants, because they felt they were different from these immigrants. Members of the second group attempted to distance themselves from other immigrants on the basis of their race, class, or national status.

The first group saw themselves as immigrants and noted the privileges that came with being white, middle-class, English immigrants. They compared themselves with other immigrant groups to make the point that they were well treated in the U.S. In 1995, when the interviews were conducted, anti-immigrant sentiment seemed to be on the rise in the U.S.: Proposition 187, which denied education and medical treatment to undocumented workers, had recently passed in California, and there was talk of denying welfare benefits to all immigrants.[13] Harry reported receiving a particularly Anglophilic comment—"You English seem to see things much more clearly"—from one of his U.S. graduate-school professors. Although Harry admitted to having "a cute writing style [that] lends itself to people feeling affectionate about me being English," he also wondered, "if I'd been Nicaraguan, would [I] have [received] the same comments?" Because his professor marked his national identity, Harry grew suspicious that the professor could not see through it and was therefore not objective about his work. Lucinda also believed that her educational experiences had been biased by her nationality: She said that, compared with other international students, she had enjoyed a "celebrity" status at her high school; she felt that she had been "accepted" in a way that "Japanese or Chinese students [weren't]. They were more fascinated [by me], and they wanted to know as much as they could [about England]." Again, Lucinda points to what she sees as Anglophilia among the Americans with whom she has interacted to contrast her experiences with those of people from other nations.

Diana also said that she had accrued privileges from her nationality, using a different immigrant group to make a point about Americans' Anglophilia. She argued that if she applied for a job in the U.S. and was competing against an Iraqi citizen, "I know I'm going to get the job," which she said she found "horrendous." Gordon and Frank both used the example of Polish immigrants to argue that they believed English people received unfair advantages in the U.S. Gordon believed that Polish people would find inserting themselves into U.S. culture difficult because Polish people have "heavy accent[s]"[14] and come from "a country that doesn't have a strong historical relationship with this country." Gordon's assumption, of course, is that Poland does not have the same "strong historical relationship" with the U.S. as England; thus, he draws on a perceived shared history to explain the privileges that being English garnered.

Frank made a similar point but combined nationality with class status and gender: "As an Englishman, you're supposed to . . . dress, . . . talk . . . and write well, so that's the preconceived idea that the bosses have, so you're liable to get the job easier. Whereas if you're a slob from . . . Poland who worked in a steel mill and you want an executive job, especially if you don't speak good English. . . ." Frank didn't finish his sentence, but his implication is obvious: An Englishman who dressed well and spoke with an English accent would be far more likely to get an executive job than a Polish steelworker. Frank's use of the phrase "slob . . . who worked in a steel mill" suggests that he is thinking of a working-class person from Poland. His comment illustrates the ways that Englishness, middle- and upper-class status, and masculinity can become conflated in stereotypes of English people. Clearly he perceives class, gender, and nation working together to privilege English people. Although he took great pride in his own working-class background, his use of the pejorative word "slob" suggests that he also might be accepting Americans' conflation of Englishness and middle- or upper-class status to distance himself from those from other classes and nationalities.

Frank broadened his comparison to discuss the ways in which he believed his experiences would differ from those of people of other ethnicities and nationalities. If he had been a non-white immigrant, he said,

[I] would have had a lot of strikes against me . . . in the American establishment. . . . Most [Americans] are sympathetic to the middle-class Englishman. [They think,] "He's one of us. He's part of the club. Anybody of a different color is suspect, inferior." . . . Looking back, [my] English nationality and . . . English voice opened doors in [the top echelons of] society that would not have been opened if I were African or Asian.

Here Frank holds white Americans responsible for their racism by asserting that he has been treated differently because of his race, gender, and class. It is also interesting to note the slippage in his remarks between race and class. Although I asked him to talk about his perception of how his life would have been if he had been a non-white immigrant, he first framed his answer by considering his class, gender, and national identities, which implies that he sees the identities of immigrants in these terms. In addition, he seems to equate his whiteness with being a middle-class Englishman. However, his overall point—to recognize the privileges that his white skin and English identity have brought him in America—came through clearly, especially when he compared himself with those with "African or Asian" heritage.

Emily, too, was critical of the racism of Americans who "will talk with an anti-immigrant sentiment in front of you, but they're not including you because you're white. They're basically talking about Mexicans crossing the border. But it's the same!" Her comments show that she is not only outraged that the Americans with whom she interacts are against immigration, but also amazed at their racism and their assumption that she shares their sentiments. She is appalled by their assumption that immigrants are not white and that they "don't even think that people who speak English are immigrants. It's those 'other' people, those 'poor' people who work in hotels." Emily aligns herself with "Mexicans crossing the border" and the "poor people" despised by the Americans about whom she complains to make the point that her white skin and class privilege do not make her any less of an immigrant. In so doing, she criticizes the race and class biases in the discourses surrounding immigration of some Americans. Like other people I talked to, Emily deplored the anti-immigrant sentiment she saw around her during the election campaign of 1996, noting some of the ways that "people with green cards are treated as second-class [citizens]."

The people quoted in this section implied that they were immigrants either by comparing themselves with other immigrant groups or by explicitly claiming that identity for themselves. In addition, they were critical of Americans for failing to recognize their immigrant status and for what they saw as the special treatment they received as a result.

No, We're Not!

However, the attitudes that this group criticized were used by another group to argue that English people were somehow different from, or even superior to, other immigrant groups, implying that they did not see themselves as "true" immigrants. Craig remembered assuming before he came to the U.S. that his race, class, and national status would make obtaining a work permit easier. "Not that I should be treated differently," he said, "but [I thought] I probably would be [because] I was [an] English ... white Anglo-Saxon [professional]. I knew that was wrong, but for selfish reasons [I thought that would be okay]. . . . It was good to know [the immigration process is] even-handed (apart from the Irish)." Craig faulted his assumption that his national, racial, and class status would privilege him in the immigration process by saying that it arose from "selfishness" and claimed to have been relieved to find that it was even-handed (although he also believed that Irish people benefited from positive discrimination).

Diana, Lucinda, and Craig made more racially charged assumptions—for instance, that English people "blend in" in the U.S.[15] Craig said that Americans' comments about his accent reminded him that, "although your face might fit and you don't perhaps look like a foreigner and the clothes are very similar, [you are different]." Craig's assumption that his "face fits" implies that, because of his national, racial, or class identity, he does not look like a foreigner. Indeed, a combination of all three factors seem to enable Craig to make this assumption. Harriet and Imogen also assumed that, as English people, they were insiders. Imogen explained that, in contrast to people of other nationalities, the English did not "club together massively" in the international organization for which she worked. "We're not different enough from the rest," she explained. "We're part of the establishment to some extent." Here she assumes that the English are similar enough to Americans that they do not need to band together to assert their different identity. These interviewees construct an Anglicized notion of the U.S. so that they "blend in" to the mainstream. In constructing this image, they draw on an underlying discourse that they are not immigrants in the ways that people from other countries are: The perceived special relationship between Britain and the U.S. means they see themselves as different from other alien groups.

Others expressed similar ideas. Brad believed that it was easier for English people than for "Spanish [immigrants] to integrate themselves into this society. . . . If I [were] Spanish, I might want to go and live with more Spanish immigrants, [but] there's no English ghetto here." (By "Spanish," Brad was presumably referring to Latinos and Latinas.) In saying that English people are not true immigrants because they do not "go and live" with other English people, he implies that only immigrants congregate together. He continued by explaining that "we don't make an effort to seek out other English people here for reading the *Beano*[16] or something like that! So I think that the English are different than practically every other immigrant group." His choice of "reading the *Beano*" is intended as a humorous example that devalues the notion of people coming together to enjoy aspects of their shared culture. This is ironic in that Brad also told me there were other English people in his town and that a local shop catered to them by importing English chocolate, biscuits, and soft drinks. His animation as he described the shop suggested that, whatever his interpretation of other people's ghettos, he enjoyed the benefits of living in a community with other English people. His comment also implied that he thought English people do not need to congregate in "ghettos" because English culture is mainstream in the Northeastern U.S.

Piers reported that when he first arrived for graduate school in the U.S., he was required to attend an orientation for foreign students. As he told the story, his outrage became clear. He complained about the slow, patronizing speech style of those running the orientation. They asked him how long he had been speaking English. He responded: "'All my life, dammit.' I then proceeded to take the form, correct the grammar and hand it back unfilled." Although his frustration could be interpreted simply as anger at being treated like an ESL[17] student, I read it as anger with Americans for treating him as an "other." Piers seemed to think that he should have received special treatment because he was English—or, at least, that he should not have been subjected to the same orientation that other international students had to sit through. (His actions also imply that he thought he knew English grammar better than the Americans did.)

Hugh made similar assumptions. He was annoyed that his children had been forced by state law to have a series of inoculations before entering school in the U.S.:

> It's like being treated as if you came from a Third World country. [My daughter] Catherine had to have a tuberculosis test, which was, a) daft because tuberculosis isn't very common in England, whereas it's much more common here, and . . . b) [my son] Roger [didn't have to be tested because he] went to nursery school [before starting school].

The implication is that the state law should not have applied to Hugh's children because they were English, not from the Third World. Hugh also pokes fun at the bureaucratic regulations, which seem nonsensical to him, and comments that the U.S. is more disease-prone than England.[18] He thereby asserts his children's right to be accorded special treatment because of their Englishness while devaluing the U.S. on a number of levels. Finally, in these statements he shows his assumption that he and his family are not immigrants in the same way that people from the Third World are, thereby distancing himself from racial and national others.

Dorothy and Andy also expressed annoyance at having been treated like foreigners in bureaucratic matters such as obtaining driver's licenses, credit cards, and Social Security numbers. As Andy heatedly explained,

> I have two points on my car insurance because I am an "inexperienced driver" in New York. I have driven a motor car since I was seventeen. I've driven in a dozen or more countries in the world, but according to New York, I am inexperienced. . . . You feel you are discriminated against, even as an educated, middle-class [professional]. That's not being British. That's being foreign, alien.

Thus, even though Andy claims that does not expect special treatment because he is English, he implies that his "educated, middle-class" status should militate against this sort of "discrimination." New York State, he felt, did not recognize the full range of his driving experience; because his talent as a driver was not taken into account, he believed that he had been discriminated against. Again, Andy assumes that his class status should prevent him from having to abide by state regulations; presumably, he thinks that middle-class professionals are better drivers than those in other classes. He also implicitly criticizes the U.S. for being insular in recognizing only the experiences one has inside the country as valid.

In these sections, I have looked at two sets of responses to being English in America through the lens of immigration. The first group noted the ways in which they thought Americans privileged them *too much*— by giving them benefits because they were English or by treating them as if they were not immigrants. These people noted the privileges that they obtained from their Englishness and felt that this was unfair to others. The second group felt that Americans did not privilege them *enough*. These people believed that they were due special treatment because of their status as white, middle-class English people, and they were often insulted to be treated as immigrants. They drew on a sense of superiority that resulted from their race, class, and national identities to argue that they deserved more privilege than they had received.

Both sets of responses shows the contradictory nature of life in the U.S. for English people. As they grapple with their own identity definitions and those of others, their status as immigrants remains unclear. A factor that further muddies their understanding of their status in the U.S., to which I have already alluded, is Anglophilia.

ANGLOPHILIA IN THE U.S.

Historical and Contemporary Contexts

I turn now to examine the various components of Anglophilia, suggesting some of its causes and manifestations. In particular, I argue that Anglophilia is predicated on race- and class-specific understandings not only of England, but also of the U.S. I show that Anglophilia appears in many different forms before moving on to examine when and where the interviewees encountered Anglophilia and how they responded to it.

Englishness has long enjoyed high status in American culture, despite attempts to define American national culture in a way that excludes the hierarchy and aristocracy associated with England. The fact that many of the country's first immigrants were of British descent may have played a large part in this (although other European groups also settled the new colonies).[19] Of course, the British were despised during the American Revolutionary War period,[20] when the yoke of colonialism was thrown off. At the same time, however, eighteenth-century Americans used English and French etiquette books to define "correct" behavioral standards, and southern "ladies" and "gentlemen" modeled themselves on the manners and mores of the English landed gentry.[21] Europe in general was held in high esteem in the U.S. during the eighteenth and nineteenth centuries.[22] "Dollar princesses"[23] traveled to England to marry aristocrats (a practice made famous in novels such as Edith Wharton's *The Buccaneers* and Henry James's *The Portrait of a Lady*), and the definition of European culture as "high" culture enabled the middle and upper classes to construct a superior self-image to justify their privileges in contrast to new immigrant groups and the working classes.[24]

In the mid-nineteenth century, the idea that the U.S. was part of the Anglo-Saxon "race" began to gain credence in some circles. John Higham has detailed the twists and turns this Anglo-Saxonism took to become racial nativism[25] and cited Henry Cabot Lodge as an example of someone whose Anglophilia allowed him to love things English while despising England.[26] "Boston Brahmins" such as Lodge began to argue for tight immigration controls to prevent immigrants from Southern and Eastern Europe from overwhelming America's Northern and Western Europeans (also known as "Anglo-Teutons"[27]); aided by scientific racism, these upper-class Americans perceived the Southern and Eastern European immigrants—"Alpines" and "Mediterraneans," according to some theories—as inferior to the Northern and Western Europeans, who were also known as "Nordics."[28] Another example of Anglophilia can be found in the institution of quotas to stem the tide of immigrants in the years between World War I and World War II: Britain's quota was set so high that it dwarfed that for the rest of northwestern Europe combined.[29]

Class and race have also been important in modern incarnations of Anglophilia in the U.S. Assumed "blood" ties between the two nations draw on false images of racial and class homogeneity in both countries. When the U.S. Librarian of Congress exclaimed during a 1985 visit by the Prince and Princess of Wales, "I think we are all Anglophiles.... How can we fail to be Anglophiles? Unless we hate ourselves" (quoted in Hitchens 1991: 14), he relied on an old ideology that England and the U.S. share a heritage based on a race- and class-specific notion of Englishness. According to this line of thinking, English people are the archetypal upper-class WASPs,[30] a status to which all Americans are assumed to aspire. The English-only movement and some arguments against multiculturalism follow a similar line of thought.[31] For instance, although Russell Kirk (1993: 9) does note that the U.S. and England are diverse, he claims that if "Americans lose that British patrimony, they must become barbarians, and on their darkling plains ignorant armies of ideologues may clash by night." For authors such as Kirk and Allan Bloom,[32] Anglophilia represents an alternative to "other" forms of culture, and a stereotypical version of English culture as white and male is used to reinforce old distinctions between "high" and "low" culture. Kirk (1993: 90) suggests, for instance, that something called "Anglo-American culture [is] that complex of literature and law and government and mores which still makes civilization possible in both the U.S. and Britain." By contrast, he sees multiculturalism as "anticultural" (1993: 92).[33]

Anglophilia also emerges in popular culture and everyday life. Key the word into a U.S. newspaper database[34] and you will get the sense that Anglophilia is taken for granted as a cultural reference point. The preponderance of British cultural forms is evident in articles about British restaurants and shops; about actors, movies, television programs, newspapers, and magazines; about music, including classical, pop, rap, and house[35]; and about gardening. Even cricket emerges as a category. Apparently, 120 small specialty shops nationwide serve British food and drink—a $3 billion market, according to Tony Matthews, president of the industry group Food from Britain N.A.[36] I found articles describing British restaurants and shops not only in New York City, but also in locations as diverse as Searsport, Maine, and Ridgewood, New Jersey.[37] Some of the comments of the writers bear repeating as examples of Anglophilia. "One visit and you'll chalk the Revolution up to a misunderstanding," Leslie Billera (1999: 37) wrote about a food store in New York City that caters to British palates. And Sheryl Julian (1997) described a Cambridge, Massachusetts, tearoom as "all Anglophile attitude, a cross between a working-class East London café and the dining car on the Orient Express."

Meanwhile, an intrepid *New York Times* reporter demonstrated that there is no shortage of Anglophilia in New York City. Determined to have a weekend solely devoted to Britishness,[38] she watched live soccer games in a bar that received broadcasts by satellite, attended British plays and movies, and ate at all the British restaurants she could find. She drank tea, went clubbing to house and dance music from Britain, took in two British art exhibitions, shopped at British fashion houses, watched British programs on television, and attended a cricket match on Long Island.[39] Similarly, in Boston, a 1996 article proclaimed that "Anglophilia is all the rage," stressing the ubiquity of British accents on local and national radio and of British programs and their derivatives on network, cable, and public television.[40] Meanwhile, films as diverse as *Trainspotting* and period pieces (based on Jane Austen or William Shakespeare or corset-bound Merchant–Ivory productions) have filled the multiplexes.[41] For royal-family watchers, there is a House of Windsor mail-order catalog, membership in "Americans of Royal Descent" (Fussell 1983:119), and a computer database indexing all royal relatives.[42] The Internet has opened an even wider range of possibilities, offering chat groups dedicated to British culture, websites selling British food and goods (at a price), sites with links to favorite British television programs and movies, and even an Anglophiles' singles group.[43] Web surfers can check the news from a British perspective on sites operated by the BBC and ITN;[44] fans of British sports can log on to check their favorite teams' scores[45] or can watch rugby and soccer on Fox Sports World via satellite or cable. Advertising campaigns for BBC America and Sky Sports News draw on the supposed "coolness" of British culture in the U.S. The former has a "Britcom Zone" and "Cool Britannia" evenings; the latter proclaims "The British Are Coming (Again)", combining footage of Queen Elizabeth, World War II, and British rock bands.

Although some commentators have complained about *le vice Americain*, as Geoffrey Wheatcroft (1990) has called Anglophilia, their very disgruntlement points to its ubiquity in American culture.[46] However, it has also been argued, especially in England, that Americans are increasingly seeing English people as the "bad guys" (in movies and in relation to soccer hooliganism).[47] Indeed, one writer commented that wherever Anglophilia is, Anglophobia is not far behind.[48] I would argue that Anglophilia is alive and well today; it simply takes different forms. The orgy of Anglophilic nostalgia that used to make up public television is gradually being replaced by more representative images of Englishness that include, for example, multiracial casts and working-class neighborhoods. Rather than seeing England as a country steeped in history and tradition,[49] people are now as likely to see clothes by trendy fashion designers; music such as trip-hop, ambient-trance, art-rock, bhangra, and Britpop;[50] authors such as Zadie Smith and Meera Syal; and unconventional actors such as Ray Winstone and Kathy Burke as positive representations of Englishness as country gardens, princesses, and corsets used to be.[51]

RESPONDING TO ANGLOPHILIA

Surrounded by evidence of English culture in the U.S., the interviewees, perhaps not surprisingly, perceived Anglophilia all around them. Brad, Harry, and Peter pointed to tearooms and shops serving English delicacies, and many others commented on the number of English shows on television, such as *Are You Being Served?*, *Eastenders*, and *Monty Python's Flying Circus*.[52] Frank remarked on the use of English accents to sell products on television, while Mike and Piers laughed about Anglophilic architectural styles on the East Coast. They found Americans "genuinely nice" about and "appreciative" of English culture, in "awe and wonder" about how lovely England is, and full of admiration for "English institutions and the English language,"[53] to the extent that Americans who "studied in Oxford and Cambridge ... celebrat[e] Britishness ... being more Brit than you are," as Quentin noted with bemusement. As Chapter 4 will show, this admiration often emerged in the context of comments about English people's accents. For instance, Vera mused about how often people say, "Oh, wonderful, I love to hear you talk."

At the time of the interviews, the Prince and Princess of Wales had recently announced their divorce, and there was much eye-rolling among those I talked to about the farcical nature of the media coverage of the breakdown of their marriage. Although many used the royal family and its tradition of pomp and circumstance as their touchstone to sum up Englishness, at the same time they expressed disapproval and sometimes disgust with the monarchy. Emily and Ken, for instance, pointed out that the dysfunctions of the royal family were more representative of England than people liked to think. Most made the point that Americans were far more interested in the monarchy than they were, and they often expressed slight annoyance that Americans assumed them to be experts on royalty, aristocrats themselves, or in favor of the monarchy.

Interactions about the royal family were not the only way that the people I talked to saw American Anglophilia emerging. They had many different theories about why Anglophilia exists: Brad pointed to the fact that the U.S. is a former British colony and that English people were one of the largest original immigrant groups in the U.S.[54] Thus, he said, "there's a lot of identity with the English, particularly in this part of the U.S.... People who ... regard themselves as English hear [about the Revolutionary War period], and so they relate back to that reasonably well." Harriet and Emily noted that "many Americans" have "been on holiday" in England, so there are important connections between the two countries today. Others referred to the political "special relationship" between the two countries, both historically and currently (although some, such as Harry, scathingly suggested that Britain is like "a lapdog" or "the fifty-first state" because it usually backs U.S. foreign policy).[55] Octavia pointed to the supposed lack of history and tradition in the U.S., which, she said, makes Americans envious of those with a long history. Lucinda, meanwhile, remarked that the two countries are similar "probably because of the language, and because they were a part of England for a long time . . . so I think . . . it's easy to be in one if you're from the other."

ANGLOPHILIA AND ACCOUNTABILITY

In their interactions in the U.S., the English people I interviewed felt that Americans saw them through an Anglophilic lens. Indeed, Anglophilia seemed to be a kind of cultural capital, giving them entitlements and privileges that non-English people would not be privy to.[56] As I suggested in Chapter 1, interactions are an important site for the production of meanings; individuals do identity work to create a state of being that appears to come "naturally" to them.[57] The other side of the equation is that those interpreting the actions of an individual also engage in work, holding people accountable for their actions. Thus, they acknowledge, name, blame, excuse, criticize, or analyze the activities of others in light of their own conceptions of appropriate behavior.[58] The respondents argued that Anglophilic Americans interpret them only in light of their national identities. In fact, the people I talked to held Americans accountable for being Anglophiles, often acting in ways that enhance their prestige as English people in the U.S.

Thus, the interviewees often assumed that Americans held them in high esteem because of their Englishness and that Americans were especially warm and friendly toward them because of their national identity. Harriet said she thought her American boyfriend's parents "adore[d]" her partly "because [they think], 'She's English and lovely.' . . . I can't put a foot wrong." By contrast, she thought her own parents were suspicious of her boyfriend when she took him home to England: "'This bloody American! What was I doing? God forbid!' [*in a deep expressive voice*], and it was a joke, but he had a slightly tougher time than I did." Although the difference in treatment that Harriet perceived may have been based on a gender distinction, she framed it in terms of nationalities to make the point that English people are often more hostile toward Americans on principle than vice versa.

The people I spoke with also saw Anglophilia manifested in the "celebrity" or "special" status they seemed to hold in the U.S. Lucinda explained that it was easy for her to fit in because "Americans have this thing about English people. . . . In some ways [I was like] a celebrity when I came over, and so that made it easier." Anne said she felt more respected at work because of her Englishness: "They seem to think that because I have this different accent, it [gives me] a kind of authority." Peter remarked on the "edge" that being English gave him, while Nigel called his accent a "novelty . . . that helps sometimes to break the ice," and Alex said that Americans "regard you as the most amusing thing that's ever appeared on this planet." Here we see these English people believing that Americans respond to them on the basis of their nationality; they hold Americans responsible for the celebrity status they enjoy, arguing that the benefits of being English are a direct result of the way Americans treat them.

In one way or another, these people felt that they stood out in the U.S. because they are English. Hugh and Harriet said that American salespeople recognized them when they returned to stores, and Hugh noted a "slight cachet" that seemed to be associated with knowing him in his new church. Craig told me that his brother found his English accent useful for picking up women, and Emma, Lucinda, and Frances said that English accents had enabled them or their children to make friends in school easily. Mike found people "very interested to know me . . . because I'm English, and to talk about England." Lucinda agreed, arguing that Americans have a special affinity with England:

> Americans . . . really want . . . to have some of the things that England has. So when [they meet] an English person, not that they kowtow to us, but they're more . . . fascinated and they want to know as much as they can. . . . So I don't think [I get] preferential treatment, but . . . definitely more [attention is] paid to me than [is paid to] people from other countries.

It is interesting that the people who made these comments were quick to imagine Americans as attending to their national identity rather than to them as individuals. In other situations, people are loathe to admit that they might receive benefits from an aspect of their identity (for example, in the way that white people and men have difficulty admitting their race or gender privileges). Why are these people so willing to see themselves as benefiting from their national identity?

One reason is that Americans explicitly mark them as English in a positive way. Gordon and Rowena noted that their employers introduced them as "English-educated." Both were aware that they were being used as status symbols; Gordon even pointed out that his boss seemed to see his education as a "badge of honor." But neither seemed particularly disturbed by his or her symbolic role in this Anglophilic self-aggrandizement. Indeed, Gordon claimed that "it actually made me feel proud [of] the meaning that English culture has in this country." Clearly, he experienced the marking behavior on the part of his employer as an affirmation of his national identity.

A second reason lies in the actual privileges some interviewees believed they received as a result of their national identity. Octavia, Diana, and Dorothy, for instance, said they felt their employment prospects had been enhanced by their nationality, quickly associating the ease of their transition to life in the U.S. with Americans' responses to their national identity. Imogen believed that she had been given free subway tokens and access to closed rooms in museums and national monuments because she was English, while Nigel, working as a traveling salesman, found himself invited to people's homes for beer, barbecues, and swimming. In addition, Imogen said she thought that having an English accent made it easier to "strike up conversations with random strangers. . . . They laugh about my silly accent, and it's this neutral thing to talk about." Gary mentioned that it had been easier for him than for "preppie American[s]" to gain access to people to interview on the telephone for his job, and he presumed this was a result of his accent. As these anecdotes show—and as will be demonstrated in more detail in Chapter 4— many of the interviewees played up their English accents when interacting with people in authority in order to ensure that they were taken seriously. Drawing on what they thought they knew about American responses to Englishness, these people worked to gain benefits in various situations.

In their interactions, therefore, these English people believe that Americans hold them accountable for their national identity by drawing on Anglophilic ideas. In return, the interviewees hold Americans accountable for what they believe are Anglophilic attitudes. In many cases, their reactions imply that if Americans want to give them benefits, they are quite happy to take them. As people who find themselves in positions of privilege, they often do not feel the need to justify taking advantage of these privileges. Whether this comes from their own sense of entitlement or superiority is another question, which I will explore in the sections that follow.

RESPONDING TO PERCEPTIONS OF ANGLOPHILIC PRIVILEGE

Placing the Onus on Americans

Most of the English people I spoke with found the phenomenon of Anglophilia attractive and enjoyed the privileges that accrued from it. Alex and Quentin joked about missing the feeling of being special when they returned to England. As Quentin explained:

> I always say that if you say something in America with a British accent, people are 50 percent more likely to believe you than if you say it with an American accent.... I miss that when I go back to England, suddenly not having the funky ... special accent that people appreciate. That's one of the attractions of being in the U.S., because people like English accents and Englishness.

Here Quentin openly holds Americans accountable for the fact that he stands out in the States, placing all the responsibility for his status on the Americans who appreciate him. Likewise, others noted that, while their special status might be unfair to others, they were prepared to use it to their advantage. Thus, although Tara called the privileges she obtained from being English "unfair," she also noted that she was "not going to protest too much." These interviewees' ability to ignore the injustice of their privileges comes from their sense that the privileges are the fault of other people—in this case, Americans. This allows them to deny that they can do anything to change the situation; all they can do is benefit from it. Their attitudes provides some insight into the workings of privilege. In holding Americans accountable for the privileges they believe Americans give them, the interviewees are able effectively to distance themselves from bearing any responsibility for what happens to them. Indeed, they place the blame for their superior status on Americans.

We also see this attitude in their perceptions of Americans as having "a slight inferiority complex" about English people. They claimed that, although Americans might be attracted by Englishness, they sometimes worry that "we are clinging to our Englishness in a way that we wouldn't if we were [living in England]." For Imogen, this meant apologizing to her American friends for preferring English food or tea to ward off their suspicions that she was simply playing up her sense of superiority at their expense. Alex said that she was astonished, after meeting with the lawyer son of a friend, to hear that he had been embarrassed. "[I said], 'Pardon?' [My friend replied,] 'He was so embarrassed because of the way you speak. He said, "I really tried to speak well, but I felt so inferior."' He's an educated man, and yet he felt at this disadvantage. And I wouldn't claim to speak the Queen's English, but that was the reaction!" Others showed less surprise at Americans' sense of inferiority. Diana and Frank, for instance, claimed that they put on an upper-class English accent in difficult situations, admitting that they did so to make Americans "feel small" when they "want[ed] to gain the upper hand." Tara's American boyfriend provided some insight into why Americans might feel small when he told her, "I only tease you because 90 percent of Americans would love to talk that way," implying that her accent was better than those of Americans.

Others had had experiences with Americans who objected to the presumed Anglophilia of other Americans. Imogen said she had once been told, "Don't come here with this foreigner bullshit, because you guys get so many privileges by just opening your mouth"; Stephen also reported being told that his positive experiences in the U.S. were a result of Anglophilia. These comments suggest that some Americans recognize the benefits that come from being English in the U.S. and perhaps feel that positive treatment received by English people is unfair. Harry said he also came into contact with Americans who thought English accents were "really putting on airs and graces." In his estimate, 50 percent of Americans were impressed by his accent, 25 percent didn't care, and another 25 percent actively disliked it.[59] These comments suggest the more negative reactions of some Americans to their Englishness and to Anglophilia.

Gary and William expressed their responses to the presumed American inferiority complex differently. Gary explained that, in his opinion, the English secondary-education system was better than America's:

> A lot of Americans have a chip on their shoulder about . . . the quality of American [high-school] education. . . . I think they are aware that the British education system has a better reputation, and . . . that explains part of the reason I'm taken more seriously in a dinner conversation. . . . They think because I'm British, I'm going to know more about [world events].

Here he attributes his own feelings about the inadequacy of American education to his American friends. Interestingly, Gary spent several years in the American education system—as a child and as an adult attending graduate school. Gary's ideas about the relative merits of the two education systems lead him to play up his accent, making it more English and "much more posh" when he is talking about "academics or anything . . . where I think the British have an edge and it's a serious topic." This is because he believes that Americans will "assume you know a bit more than you might. You sound more authoritative." His reading of Americans' supposed inferiority complex leads him to play up his Englishness and his class status in order to gain prestige and authority in a situation; his behavior is designed to exploit the situation, boosting his own position and enhancing his feelings of superiority.

William had a different way of dealing with the problem. He worried about the fact that Americans thought people with "cultured English accents" were "more clever than you really are or . . . you have a special angle on something, [or] you know more than they do, or you're more self-assured." Because he did not "want to be accused of rubbing it in," he made special efforts to be modest. For instance, he said he tried hard not to criticize the U.S., and when an American criticized England, he tended to agree and "illustrate how they haven't gone far enough in the criticism." He explained, "I try very hard to avoid creating . . . the appearance of being superior in any way and . . . to muck in and get my hands dirty." William's strategy is to recognize the presumed inferiority complex, but to try to overcome it by putting himself on the same level as Americans. In so doing, he assumes that everyone thinks he is superior and tries to show them that they are wrong. Despite his protestations, however, he is operating from a position of presumed superiority during these interactions. Even the phrase he uses—getting his hands dirty—suggests that he is stooping to the level of Americans in his attempt to be equal. However, it is important to recognize that William is attempting to deal with Anglophilia in good faith, trying to find a way to deal with it to enhance the egos of the Americans with whom he interacts. His responses also indicate an implicit critique of the Anglophilia he believes exists among Americans. In the following sections, I address other critiques interviewees made of Anglophilia.

We're Not All Upper Class and from the Southeast

Although these interviewees felt liberated from the constraints of class and tradition and enjoyed their anonymity when they arrived in the U.S., as I discussed earlier, they also expressed concern about the ways that Anglophilia limited Americans' understandings of them. In particular, they criticized the class- and region-specific nature of Anglophilia, which stereotypes English people in Americans' minds and prevents them from seeing individual people with their own identities. Indeed, rather than feeling anonymous, the people I spoke with said they became a particular kind of celebrity in the U.S.: an upper-class person from the southeast of England.

Mike noted that Americans do not understand the "class aspects of one's existence" as an English person. He took great pride in his working-class roots and was annoyed by Americans who "think that you are a member of the aristocracy by nature." Tara, whose background was upper class, became exasperated when people assumed she was an aristocrat. Harry found interactions with Anglophilic Americans difficult because he "would rather they didn't go on about" his being English. People "expect you to behave like . . . this sort of professional English person [who] is not what I want to be," he said. "Who would want to be Terry Thomas? . . . I couldn't bear being that kind of person." His reference to Terry Thomas, a white English actor with an upper-class accent, suggests that he finds that Americans expect him to conform to a class-, race- and region-specific version of Englishness, perhaps to behave in a stilted, "stiff-upper-lip" manner. Other interviewees were more amused than angry about the class-based assumptions that Americans made about England. Alex said she sometimes put on a cockney accent to tease Americans who made class-based assumptions about English people, and Frank noted that "Americans don't get cockney. . . . They don't find that particularly impressive. Lady Diana they find impressive."

Others were exasperated by the way Americans' versions of England were concentrated in the country's southeast. Lucinda pinpointed the problems inherent in answering questions about where she is from: "'I'm from England.' 'I know that, but whereabouts?' 'Oh, I'm from Shropshire.' 'Never heard of it. Been to London, though.' And I just think, 'Well, if you've never been anywhere except London, don't bother asking me where I'm from!'" Harry was somewhat more forgiving, applauding the "honest effort" Americans made to "forge a link," even if they had never heard of his hometown. Diana explained the reliance on class and regional stereotypes: "[As] with any country, people think of the capital city, and therefore they think of London, and they think of the stereotypical . . . English snob only. . . . They don't think of the English working class; they think of aristocrats, which is totally non-representative." Because their regional identities were often extremely important to them, they found having Americans say that they had never heard of Yorkshire or Shropshire or Cornwall frustrating. However, most took it in stride as one of the drawbacks of moving to another country.

It's Hard to Be a Celebrity

Several interviewees found the constant attention they received from Americans wearing. Vera and Alex noted that English people in the U.S. have to become skilled at accepting compliments graciously (or "shuffl[ing] inside," as Alex put it), while Tara found the "inverse snobbery" of a former American boyfriend who relished the Anglicization of his accent "disgusting." Harry was self-reflective about his special status in the U.S. Although he admitted to feeling "attracted" to the Anglophilia he perceived and thought he would "miss the certain status that it gives you," he also felt irritated and constrained by it, saying that he wished he could play his Englishness down. As he explained, describing an interaction with a man in a fast-food restaurant who commented on his accent,

> I just wanted to get a burrito. . . . [Although being English] gives you an automatic celebrity status, celebrities [do] like to hide in the dark and put sunglasses on. I just sometimes wish I could merge. I don't like standing out when I'm just being myself. I don't mind standing out through choice, [but] I don't like the way America distinguishes you.

In contrast to the interviewees who claimed that English people could "blend in" with Americans, Harry notes here the way his accent has made him stand out in the U.S. He wants to become indistinguishable from Americans and likens the experience of being English in the U.S. to being famous (for the negative rather than positive effects of fame). He shies away from this attention because he feels that the Americans are responding to him as a stereotype and that they expect him to live up to their expectations. "They assume that I'm pro–the Queen . . . or that I'm a cockney. . . . I like to think I'm a lot more complex [and sophisticated] than that." Harry's assertion of his independence from these stereotypes is not meant to devalue Americans' efforts to connect; he sees that Americans are "being warm, but the connection they're making is one I don't want."

He continued, "I've learned to play the part, ... because that's what people like. ... They'll repeat things back to me. ... I think it's understandable because ... I'm *so* English—there's no getting away from it. [I'm] not like one of those ... English people who can move between different cultures. I'm English, and there's no hiding it." Harry's recognition of being English as a "part" he plays suggests that he sees Englishness as something he must work at. Yet in saying that "there's no getting away from" being English, he is implying that his nationality is something natural that comes from within. Clearly, he has a contradictory relationship to his national identity: On the one hand, he recognizes the ways he "does" Englishness, but on the other, he cannot hide his nationality. This paradox will recur throughout the book as interviewees express the need to work at something they also believe to be natural—their national identity.

The inconsistencies in Harry's view emerged clearly later in the interview. Although he initially asserted that his Englishness was something from which he could not hide in order to excuse Americans for placing such an emphasis on nationality, he later blamed Americans for the way he expresses his Englishness:

> Identity isn't just something from within; it's from without. And if people keep imposing their views on me, sooner or later I'm going to start playing up to it or performing to it or trying to reject it in some way. But if people are going to define you, it's hard to resist the temptation ... to play to the court.

Here Harry suggests that his English demeanor is the responsibility of Americans, not a result of his own desire "to play to the court." In focusing attention on the Americans' behavior, Harry points to their Anglophilia to account for his actions. Thus, he defines himself according to other people's definitions, despite his earlier protests that he dislikes the class and regional stereotypes associated with being English in the U.S.

The tensions in Harry's assumptions about his Englishness show how the people I spoke to focused on determinants of their identity that they felt were out of their control. Harry believes that he acts in an English way because "people ... impos[e] their views on me," blaming Americans for his behavior in a way that obscures his own role in "doing" his identity. At other moments, he implies that his national identity is natural—"there's no hiding it." Again, his assumption of naturalness functions to diminish his agency in constructing himself as English.

The critiques that English people make of American Anglophilia show the ways in which they hold Americans accountable for their behavior toward English people. As with those who reported enjoying the privileges brought by American Anglophilia, these people seem to believe that the situation ultimately is out of their hands; Americans are responsible for their privileges and, in some cases, for their English-ness—as Harry expresses when he says that his English behavior results from Americans' expectations. In the next section, I point to the other side of the equation: Although English people hold Americans responsible for the Anglophilia they perceive, they also act in ways that enhance their own sense of superiority and that may increase the privileges they receive for being English. I show how they use cultural practices to assert their English identities, sometimes playfully, but sometimes very seriously. I also examine how these assertions enable them to distance themselves from Americans and boost their self-esteem.

NEGOTIATING THE ENGLISH SUPERIORITY COMPLEX

As we talked, it became clear that the interviewees were painfully aware of a superiority complex among the English. Chapters 2, 5, and 6 explore how they critiqued the xenophobia and sense of superiority they saw in other English people. Some said they had moved away from England expressly to get away from its insularity and smugness. Quentin, for instance, reported wanting to "expand [my] horizons beyond what I thought was a rather parochial view that England has of the world. . . . People [there] are rather self-centered in their view that anything that's good in the world has to be English, and if it's not English, it's not good." Others recognized a strand of anti-Americanism present in England, and some found responding to this difficult when they returned to England. The decision to move to the U.S. could be seen as a rejection of this kind of attitude; indeed, some interviewees were explicit about working against this superiority complex. We have already seen William trying to be modest and "muck in" with Americans. Harry noted that when he first came to the U.S., he followed a pattern set up by his English friends. They would "just stay with their English friends," he said, "and not have anything to do with the world they're living in, [but would] pronounce judgments on it." But he soon decided that this type of exclusionary behavior was not healthy (although he still found it hard to make friends with white American men). Zoe also recognized that she would have to work to be accepting of American ways. She said she struggled not to criticize what her children learned at school. When she found that her son had been taught that *W* is a vowel, she confronted the teacher, but then bought an American dictionary and grammar. "I felt that they're teaching my son something different, and I'm going to have to learn to keep my mouth shut because he's got to learn it," she said. "I don't want to criticize the system, because that's not fair."

However, the interviewees also behaved in ways that showed their attempts to maintain or enhance their sense of superiority because of their Englishness. Gary's actions provide a useful introduction to this aspect of identity, because he tried to define himself as English in a way that did justice to his own feelings of pride but also did not belittle anyone else. He explained that he felt

> lucky to have grown up in England at a time when there was such good music, lucky to be able to understand irony in a way that Americans can't. [I think] the English are the coolest people on earth. . . . That doesn't mean that I think . . . I'm better than other people just because they're from California or something.

He is careful to point out that his feelings of good fortune about being English do not mean that he sees himself as better than Americans. His use of Californians as the example refers to his wife, who originally came from that state. Despite his protests to the contrary, however, he does assert English superiority by claiming that English people "are the coolest people on earth" and that Americans cannot understand irony. Gary is a dual-national who spent part of his childhood in the U.S., which makes his wish to devalue the U.S. all the more intriguing. Gary also explained that he assigns American and English traits to himself using his parents as role models: "The old British saying 'Mustn't grumble' holds true. . . . Maybe [I think that] because I saw . . . my British mother who doesn't argue back in restaurants, [but] my father, who is American, does. So I naturally assign those parts of me to those particular stereotypes." Gary was sufficiently self-aware to recognize that he was drawing on stereotypes, explaining that the process of assignation he used was "arbitrary [and] may not hold any validity at all." In addition, he said, "part of the process is simply what I value about Britain and what I value about myself. I sort of cobble [them] together and say, 'OK, this is because I'm English or this is my English side.'" Here Gary tells us that his national self-identification involves combining what he values about himself and what he values about England; in other words, there is little room to feel good about his Americanness. I wondered whether this had some basis in his feelings about his American father, but he was obviously very proud of his father, displaying his father's artwork on the walls and showing me gifts from him. Yet Gary seemed determined to devalue Americans and their national identity; the process that he uses to construct himself as English and better than Americans involves considerable effort, as it means defining himself in opposition not only to his father and wife but also to a part of himself.

Gary's effort to construct himself as superior goes further than this, however. When I asked him to tell me about a time that he felt particularly English, he began to describe his experiences dancing in an American nightclub. First, Gary felt that he was dancing in an English way, explaining that he thought "English men dance better than American men." Then he noted that he was in "a racially mixed nightclub," which he associated with being English because "there is an element . . . of British race relations which is healthier amongst young people than in the States." So Gary identified himself as both white and English, signaling his comfort with racial diversity and black music by drawing on his Englishness. He continued:

> *Gary:* So I'm there, I'm hip, . . . I'm enjoying drinking my English beer. . . . I'm holding [my pint glass] the English way. . . . So generally my stance is English.
>
> *KJ:* How do you hold it differently?
>
> *Gary:* I think English people will hold their pint to their chest and curl their hand around it. This is a bit absurd, but . . . (*shows me how he holds his glass*). Anyway, people have commented on that and said they've seen that happen in England, but not here.

Gary then laughed at himself and seemed a little embarrassed by his assumption that there was an "English way" to hold one's beer glass. He pointed out that this was what other people had told him in order to distance himself from the assumption, but he also seemed to accept that English people hold their glasses differently. I asked him how Americans hold their glasses, and he explained:

Gary: I think Americans just hold their beer out more, . . . whereas a lot of English will hold it close, . . . almost like they are cuddling it. That's something I probably self-consciously do. Also . . . the way I hold my cigarette would be more English than American.

KJ: In what way?

Gary: I've seen more English people hold their cigarette inside their hand *(curls his hand around an imaginary cigarette).* . . . But again . . . I may associate these things with being English when there are plenty of Americans who hold their cigarettes in that way. . . . So all of this could be spurious. . . . But my feeling is that I'm looking English—that's my theory.

Gary again recognizes that his assumptions about English behavior may be completely "spurious." However, his narrative shows the work that he puts into acting in an English way. His words conjure up the dramaturgical perspective identified by Erving Goffman,[60] as Gary is exquisitely self-conscious of the effect his actions have on the way other people view him. He obviously thinks carefully about how to present an English persona to the outside world, and he believes that holding his beer glass and cigarette in particular ways will help people recognize that he is English.

More is involved here than simply looking English, however. When I asked Gary how he felt in the nightclub, he responded by laughing and saying,

Well, I feel better than everybody else. Isn't that obvious? I mean, that's implicit in being English, right? I'm half-joking, but I'm half-serious. I think there is a British sense of superiority, especially when it comes to Americans, [whom we see] as less cultured. That, I would guess, is what I am feeling.

Gary is explicit here about the superiority he feels. What he achieves is the assertion of an English identity through his use of cultural practices, but it is an English identity that sees itself as "better than everybody else." As Gary presents himself as an Englishman in the nightclub, he uses the cultural aspects of Englishness that are important to him to buttress his own self-esteem.

CLOTHES DEFINE THE PERSON

Just as Gary self-consciously presented himself as English in the nightclub by holding his beer and cigarette in a certain way, other interview-

ees used their clothes to construct themselves as English and as superior to Americans. They found many different ways to say that they
found fashion and clothing better in England than in the U.S. Ken was
explicit about his

> instinctive belief that there are some things England does best, like mak-
> ing shirts with the stitching five-sixteenths of an inch from the edge of the
> collar, for example! . . . If I could . . . afford handmade shoes, that's where
> I would get them done, [and] traditional-looking silk ties. . . . Basically [I
> buy] stuff that [I think is] done best there, [although] whether it actually
> is or not is a different question.

The exclamation point in this quote marks an upturn in Ken's voice
where he was possibly laughing at himself for caring so much about
handmade shirts. He obviously recognized that his preference for handmade shirts, shoes, and ties from England might be misplaced, drawing as he did a distinction between his subjective opinion about this and
objective reality. Frank agreed with Ken that English clothes are preferable, although, ironically, he used the American designer Ralph Lauren
as his example of English fashion.

> I like close-fitting suits. I like stylish clothes, the eternal style. I don't like
> Italian [or] American styles. I don't like mod styles. I like traditional. I like
> Ralph Lauren clothes, for instance. He's the nearest American designer to
> English. He makes beautiful suits. If I could afford them, I would buy his
> suits. I like [suits that are] waisted, the old-fashioned double-breasted
> with a higher button. I like plain shirts and clubby-looking [restrained]
> ties. I like English clothing.

Both men showed a preference for the "traditional" style of English
clothing, which obviously came with a high price tag. Ken, recalling a
time that he felt "very English," talked of "working in The City [of Lon-
don] . . . wearing a suit. I looked bloody smart, and I had a silk tie and
the shirt was bought in the right place, and . . . I had a handmade suit
that . . . had four buttons down the cuff and all that kind of stuff." Class
was obviously implicit in his conceptualization of his English style, as
he wore handmade suits and shirts "bought in the right place." Clearly,
his image of Englishness is an upper-class one. At the same time, however, Ken was one of the interviewees who said he found the tradition
surrounding him in England constraining. To explain the contradiction,
he said that clothes are the "things I like about the tradition and history
of Britain, particularly if I can wrap them up and take them back in a

carrier bag to America [and] not have to carry them on my back for the rest of my life." His metaphor eloquently expresses the ways that wearing English clothes enabled him to enjoy and value English tradition without being constrained by it.

Others expressed their assumption that English clothes are superior by comparing them with American fashions. Harriet told me in a melodramatic whisper that Washington, D.C., was "absolutely dreadful for fashion. The stuff the women wear to work is appalling! It's so square! . . . It's so hot here during the summer, and they'll wear these ridiculous pantyhose all summer [and dress] dreadfully, really dreadfully." Meanwhile. Lucinda explained that her father was a very English dresser: "He wouldn't be caught dead wearing loud Hawaiian shirts [like] American men." Here she drew on the stereotypes English people have of American men, as did Stephen, who jokingly responded to my question about whether he had changed his fashion sense since moving to the States this way: "I haven't gone in for the Western look—dark blue Wrangler [jeans] and boots or anything, [and] I avoid . . . Bob Hope checked shorts and long trousers." Likewise, many of the men I interviewed expressed their dislike of sneakers; they voted with their feet, so to speak, by buying their shoes in England (most of them buying Doc Martens).

A surprising number of interviewees still did much of their clothes shopping in England. Some, such as Rowena and Diana, had quickly adapted to American shops and American fashions, but others insisted that they preferred to shop in England. Harriet explained that even grocery shopping had been traumatic for her when she first arrived:

> There's all these different brightly colored packets with different names on them, which your mother never used. You have absolutely no concept which [brand] to pick. . . . Should you go for the one with the green packet [or for] the cheapest? . . . I would stand there almost in tears because I had no basis to make any choice.

"Deeply depress[ed]" by her experiences in supermarkets, she never bothered to find out about clothing stores in America. She conceptualized this decision in terms of the time she had already invested in England

> learning about the quality of the clothes and where you ought to spend your money and what you choose to spend your money on. You know when you go into Marks and Spencer[61] what you're going to get for your

money. . . . You know how to value things. When you come here, you have absolutely no idea as to whether a certain brand is good. . . . I had no way of judging anything . . . , so I don't bother.

Harriet pointed to the assumptions she could make about culture in England: There she had learned where to buy clothes or could use her mother's consumption habits as a model. Clearly, she experienced considerable alienation when she arrived in the States. This is doubly surprising because Harriet had lived in other foreign countries before coming to the U.S. As she commented a few times during the interview, however, she had not expected the U.S. to be as foreign as the other places she had visited, thinking that it would be very similar to England. She noted that buying things in one country to take to another was an expensive habit and was clearly speaking from the privileged position of someone who could afford to do this. Luckily for Harriet, her job took her to England frequently, so she could stock up on clothes, food, and toiletries while she was there.

Although Harriet's alienation may have been more extreme than that of other interviewees, even those who did not visit England frequently often saved up to buy underwear or toiletries when they were there. Imogen jokingly laid down a challenge to me during our interview to illustrate this point: "I defy you to have interviewed a British woman who doesn't buy her knickers in Marks and Spencer!" Indeed, most of the women I interviewed mentioned the shop at some point, although they did not always volunteer whether they bought their "knickers" there! Octavia's American husband said he was shocked at the amount of money she spent at Marks and Spencer, and she admitted that she still bought all her make-up and toiletries in England. As she explained, "I'm not going to waste my money on something here when I know what it is that I like." Imogen was self-reflective about the reasons she would not shop in the States: "I still know where to go shopping in Britain, and I don't really know where to go shopping here, apart from malls, which I can't stand. So of course [I] maintain the illusion that things are better over there. I'm sure they're not, but [I] think they are because [I] know where to buy them." She notes that shopping in England reproduces the notion that products are better there and that this is probably an "illusion" constructed by the fact that she does not know where to shop in the U.S. Shopping in England, then, is another way that people can reproduce the idea that English clothes and products are superior to American goods.

Some of the women were less critical of American fashions, noting that what Imogen called the "revolting shorts and sweatshirts and sneakers" look was certainly more comfortable than English fashions, even if it was aesthetically distasteful. Although Imogen's language indicated her disgust with American clothes, she admitted to feeling "split" as to whether she approved of the "liberation" that came with being able to dress like a "slob" in the States compared with the "trendy people with their strange clothes and their pierced this, that, and the others" in England. Although she found the latter "exciting," she complained that some of her friends in England were "slaves to the wardrobe, [which] seem[ed] like a bloody waste of money and effort." On the whole, both the women and the men agreed that Americans dressed more informally and that they preferred the ways English people dressed—either because they thought it was more traditional or more "far out," as Emily said. However, some people—Stephen and Andy among them—argued that generalizing about fashion was pointless because the world was so "homogenized."

Armed with these (qualified) assumptions about the superiority of English fashion, some of the interviewees set out to do identity work by using clothes to distinguish themselves from Americans. Hugh said he wore a tie to work, despite his colleagues' teasing, "probably as a deliberate thing to say I am different, and I'm damned if I'm not going to wear a tie." Harriet said that her clothing style had remained very English: "If I ever have to start dressing in what I consider to be a dressed-down American way, I'd be very upset." (The "have to" in this sentence comes from the influence of her American boyfriend, to whom she was grateful for never pressuring her not to wear her "outlandish" English clothes). Harriet still buys most of her clothes in England and defined American clothes as frumpy:

> I make an effort not to become American in terms of my dress. . . . When I go back to England, I look at what people are wearing, and I will come back with outlandish things, . . . ridiculous shoes and weird tops, and occasionally I'll wear them out. I don't wear them all the time, but I feel it's very important.

Harriet checks the fashions in England so she can keep up with them when she returns to the U.S. She considers having English clothes so important because it helps her to assert her difference from Americans.

Indeed, because she defines American fashions as dreadful, dressing in what she considers to be an English way boosts her self-esteem. Imogen, too, was aware of the link between her clothes and national identity:

> [Sometimes I] assert my Englishness [by not] wear[ing] stockings in the heat, . . . and people find it a little bit revealing somehow. I mean, even trouser suits, [although] they do wear them, . . . some people have complained. I have had to say, "Well in England, we [wear them]!" [in a defensive tone], which is not actually true, but claiming some kind of cultural difference . . .

Here, Imogen trailed off. It is unclear why she did so, although she might have become self-conscious about asserting a cultural difference that she has just admitted is not true. Whatever the reason for her pause, her words show that she sees wearing (or refusing to wear) certain clothes as an assertion of her English identity. Her story also illustrates how she plays up or plays down her Englishness to suit the moment and to "claim some kind of cultural difference." Hence, we see her using her Englishness to differentiate herself from Americans and to get what she wants out of the interaction.

The interviewees assert their Englishness through dress for a variety of reasons. As I noted earlier, some do it because they see English fashions as superior to American clothes. Others combine this feeling of superiority with claims of distinctiveness from Americans (as Harriet and Imogen explain). And still others were more explicit about wanting to be noticed because of their English clothes. Dorothy, who bought her clothes at Marks and Spencer, said she was thrilled when people in the States commented, "It's beautiful, you must have got [it] from England. I was like, 'Yeah!' (with emphasis). I thoroughly enjoy wearing everything."

The women were not the only ones to recognize the importance of clothes to a self-definition as English. Gary brought up the issue without any prompting, explaining that

> I have a couple of English T-shirts, and I wear them with pride, but I also have a lot of other T-shirts that are not [English]. . . . My "Living Marxism" T-shirt is obviously English because it refers to the Criminal Justice Act,[62] which only English people would know about, so I can go out and English people will know what this is, but Americans won't, which I think is kind of nice.

To express his attitude toward his clothes, Gary first points out that they are not all English. Next, however, he explains how his English clothes function to enable him to assert his Englishness in routine interactions. By wearing his "Living Marxism" T-shirt, he feels he is excluding Americans from his cultural sphere because they will not understand the reference. Thus, through his clothes he can choose to be English if he wants to be, wearing clothes that only English people (or those who know what the Criminal Justice Act is) will understand. So he has the option of using his clothes to exclude Americans and mark himself as different from them. This is similar to the attitude he expressed about holding his beer glass and cigarette in the nightclub.

WE'RE SO FUNNY

Although Gary laughed when he told me he felt superior in the nightclub, he admitted that he was half-serious. His playfulness with the idea of superiority exemplifies the idea that humor often masks a deeper, less lighthearted message. I will now examine some of the ways in which humor functioned to boost the self-esteem of these English people. I am particularly interested in how they used their ideas about their humor to do identity work, constructing themselves as superior to Americans.

The people I talked to were strongly invested in arguing that the English sense of humor is completely different from Americans' sense of humor and that it "sets us apart." They classified this English sense of humor as "ironic," "sarcastic," "witty," "clever," "savvy," "cruel," "cynical," "subtle," "cutting," "self-depreciating," "satirical," and "bawdy."[63] Americans, they said, are too serious, and American humor is too "slapstick and obvious," "in your face" or often simply "not funny."[64] The words they chose to describe English humor make it obvious that they believe English humor to be superior to the "humorless American stereotype," as Tara called it, with which they drew their contrast. Tara's definition shows how believing in a uniquely English sense of humor enhances their self-esteem: "It's a sense of humor which isn't completely obvious, but can be very deft satire. Very clever, . . . sometimes cruel, because if you don't get it you can be part of the joke. . . . People don't take things literally . . . or [people in authority] seriously." Believing that their sense of humor is "deft" and "clever" and that it pokes fun at sacred cows such as authority figures is a sure way to make themselves feel superior to Americans and their supposed "slapstick" humor.

In making these generalizations, the interviewees claimed that irony, sarcasm, and so on were naturally English. Thus, Diana said, "That's where I'm really English, I guess—my sense of humor.... My natural sense of humor offends people, 'cause we're so sarcastic..., and it's comfortable [with other English people] knowing that you will be so totally understood." Here she argues that English people have a "natural" bond because of their humor. Imogen agreed, arguing that "you can't learn [to be English]—the way you know not to like [the TV program *Are You Being Served?*] without being told [is part of a] whole pile of slightly intangible things." Imogen's words effectively distance her from anyone who likes *Are You Being Served?* an English comedy that is now being re-run on U.S. television (but was not being rebroadcast in England when the interviews were conducted). By conceptualizing humor as natural and not subject to change, they could happily define Americans as the non-funny other. Thus, claiming a "natural" sense of humor becomes an easy way to do identity work and assert essential differences from Americans. The interviewees repeatedly cited Americans' enjoyment of Benny Hill's comedy as proof of their lack of a sense of humor (even though the late comedian himself was British); others decided that Americans did not really understand the British comedies on television or couldn't "get out of [*Monty Python*] what we do." At some moments, the interviewees were more charitable. Andy, for instance, made the point that Americans "laugh at things I don't find funny," which implies that English people might be missing something, too. On the whole, however, the message was that things that are "so funny for a British person" are met with a "lack of reaction by American audiences."[65] Emma's idea that "you have to be English" to like certain comedies "or to really think it is as funny as it is" (in this case, she is talking about *The Young Ones*) reinforced the idea that Americans are naturally incapable of "getting" English humor. As Alex said, "It never occurred to me [before] how much of a national characteristic is a sense of humor."

Americans' supposed lack of sarcasm and irony also provided the interviewees with a way to boost their feelings of superiority and put distance between themselves and Americans. Sometimes, Alex said, she got "subconscious pleasure from knowing I'm going to say something that they won't understand," and Peter complained that Americans "don't understand the sarcasm that you and I would have." Harry felt that "I do feel like sometimes my humor's wasted on them" (although he admitted that Americans' sense of humor might also be wasted on him). In believing that Americans are not ironic enough to understand their humor, these people bolstered their own self-esteem at the expense of those they teased. Alex drew a comparison between interacting with Americans and English people: Eight weeks after she and her husband had moved to the States, she said, they attended a dinner party with new English friends, where they had "tears running down our faces, we were laughing so much, and I thought . . . this is what we haven't done. We haven't had [anybody] to laugh with." Most of the others I talked to agreed that other English people, unlike Americans, were on the "same wavelength" in terms of humor. In pointing so aggressively to their unique sense of humor, they show the importance of interactions for the way they understand and experience their national identity. Humor becomes something that they can do to be English. In addition, believing that they have a better sense of humor than Americans enhances their feelings of superiority while enabling them to believe that this superiority is natural. Although their identity seems to be rooted in natural differences, it is reproduced every time they make a joke or believe that Americans don't understand their sarcasm or irony.

Although the interviewees often defined their sense of humor as natural, interactions were important sites for the production of their humor. In their daily lives they used humor to set themselves apart from Americans, sometimes by making fun of Americans, but also by laughing at their own feelings of superiority. As Gary did when he made his laughing comment about feeling superior in the bar, other interviewees playfully asserted their own feelings of superiority. Harriet teased her American boyfriend about English people being "innately superior," but then admitted that she did feel superior to be English. Imogen talked about joking around after seeing a production of *Henry V* about "great England and England's greatest finest blah blah blah, and thrashing the French. . . . But I didn't really mean it. I was just doing it because I knew it would make everybody laugh." Here she uses humor to assert her Englishness and her difference from other nationalities. Although she downplays the meanings behind the joke, she is playing with the idea of superiority—making fun of it but reminding her listeners of it all the same. Even if she "didn't really mean it," reading her story in the context of hers and others' complaints that Americans do not have a sense of humor, one wonders whether she expected them to get the joke.

In these playful moments, the interviewees parodied an attitude of superiority by bracketing it within the frame of humor.[66] As a form of communication, humor is open to multiple levels of interpretation. One can assume that a serious message is embedded in the humor, that the joke itself is the point, that the humor is an attempt to defuse a difficult topic, or some combination of these. In these cases, it is interesting that the interviewees seemed conscious of their choice to invoke a position of superiority at all. The fact that Harriet and Imogen both express sentiments similar to Gary's "I'm half joking, but I'm half serious" comment suggests that these attempts to parody an English superiority complex may be designed both to negate and assert that complex, using the multiple meanings of humor to cover their assumptions that English culture is ultimately superior to that of America.

One can also see the interviewees "doing" humor by examining the counter-examples, the moments in which they had to downplay their sense of humor. Some interviewees noted that they have to change their style of interaction depending on whether they are engaged with an American or an English person. For instance, Quentin claimed that he was much more abrasive with his English friends, especially men. "I have to really tone down my language [and behavior] in America 'cause it shocks," he said. "Jokey aggressiveness that is normal ... in England is taken the wrong way in America." Other interviewees also said they had changed their mode of humor in America. Imogen, one of those who prided herself on her sense of humor, said that she had become more "sensitive," and was even accused of a having a "certain failure of sense of humor" by a friend back in England. Mike told me that he had given up telling jokes because "you just get into trouble telling them [because] they are demeaning to some less fortunate element of the population." Others intimated changes using other means. Harry said that he once could take "relentless teasing" from his friends in England, but now he had "softened up" and could no longer take it. Tara found that people in England "engage in being jokey and humorous and [outwit] each other. They're picking up on other people's jokes.... It makes you have to respond quickly in ways that I don't here. So when I go back, I feel like I've been out of exercise. [I] just can't keep up." Although these stories of change read like evidence of differences between Americans' style of humor and that of English people, they also point to the ways that these English people learn and unlearn certain kinds of humorous interactions. In other words, the "natural" sense of humor posited by Diana at the beginning of this section is not natural at all; rather, it is something that, if it exists at all, is learned, practiced, worked at, and perfected. Not all English people are "naturally" sarcastic. They may (perhaps) be surrounded by more sarcastic shows on television than Americans are as a result of programming decisions or cultural trends, but humor is still something that they must "do" rather than something that they "have."

Another form of evidence showing the work these English people put into maintaining their sense of humor emerges from their consumption of popular culture, especially television. Indeed, the ideas that these interviewees have about an "English sense of humor" seem to come mainly from television. Harry cited *Have I Got News for You* as an example of the cruelty in English humor, while Diana used *Blackadder* as evidence of clever satire. They believed that these television shows expressed something essentially English. Harry, for instance, claimed that Basil Fawlty, John Cleese's character in *Fawlty Towers*, epitomized the "embarrass[ing]" nature of English humor. He found the character "incredibly funny and . . . upsetting . . . This horrible ogre of a man touches a raw nerve in English people [as] he expresses suppressed attitudes that English people would never say." Unsurprisingly, in light of the shows he mentioned, Harry defined his own humor as "a little bit nasty and put-downy" and felt that embarrassment was a vital part of English culture. The TV comedies allowed Harry and other interviewees to define Englishness in ways that made sense to them. Like most of the other people I spoke with, Harry watched English TV shows whenever he could. This functions, I suggest, as a way that these English people can remind themselves about English humor, brushing up on it, if necessary. Watching television and thinking about popular culture are ways to maintain their "natural" English humor by seeing new examples of it, giving them ideas to work with, and giving them clues as to how to define it.

The interviewees noted that it was "refreshing" to be around other English people, "somebody who understands my sense of humor," and that being sarcastic or ironic with them was easier because they could "make references to parts of the culture that you have to be British to know about."[67] However, a few noted that Americans do sometimes "get" English humor. "A few people in this country ... can actually understand ... *Fawlty Towers* and *Blackadder*," Peter said. Piers also conceded that "there's a small select group [of Americans] who train themselves to understand *Ab[solutely] Fab[ulous]* or *Python*." Just as they use English popular culture to help them construct their senses of humor, they point to the fact that Americans can do this, too. If Americans can "train themselves to understand" English humor, perhaps English people are not naturally superior to Americans after all. Indeed, several noted in passing that they had American friends with good senses of humor—"as close to an English sense of humor [as you] can get," said Catriona. The beliefs they expressed about their senses of humor, then, do not hold up under close scrutiny. However, their ideas about the natural superiority of humor provide another way to construct themselves as English in opposition to Americans.

Examining these people's beliefs about their senses of humor provides rich data for understanding the ways that they construct their identities and enhance their own feelings of superiority at the expense of Americans. A discourse of naturalness runs through their understandings of humor—that is, if their humor is naturally distinct from Americans', then it provides a comfortable way to assert their difference from Americans. However, the work that they put into creating and maintaining their senses of humor, using television to brush up on their humor or to help them define an "English" sense of humor, is also evident. In addition, as they use humor in their daily interactions, the interviewees do identity work, acting out their own presumptions about their superior brand of humor. Their playfulness about the issue of superiority is further evidence of this. As they tease Americans about their feelings of superiority, they buttress their own feelings of self-esteem, even though they are "kind of joking."

CONCLUSION: FEELING PRIVILEGED, ACTING PRIVILEGED

This chapter lays out some of the issues that arise from the feelings of privilege and superiority experienced by these English people in the U.S. They feel privileged on many different levels. Having escaped the constraints of the English class system, even those of middle- and upper-class origins experience the U.S. as refreshing and invigorating because of their anonymity. When asked to discuss any sense of privilege they had because they were English, they drew on discourses of race, nation, and class to note the ways their status as white, middle- and upper-middle-class English people was a benefit. They sometimes found it hard to talk about class directly, preferring to recognize their education or family background as something that had helped them along, especially as they compared themselves with Americans. They were more willing to talk about the ways their race and nationality functioned together to enhance their opportunities compared with those of other immigrant groups, criticizing Americans for giving them too many privileges because they were white and English. Another group, those who felt more constrained by their migration, faulted Americans for not giving them enough privileges, arguing that their status as white, middle-class English people should give them a higher status than other immigrant groups.

In discussing their status as white, middle-class English people, the interviewees often drew on the idea of Anglophilia—the love of or respect for English culture that they perceived among Americans. I explored how they thought Anglophilia privileged them and their reactions to these privileges. In particular, I noted the ways they held Americans responsible for their Anglophilia. Unlike other groups who benefit from their identity, most of the interviewees felt no shame or responsibility for the ways that being English seemed to privilege them in the U.S. Indeed, some even attempted to capitalize on what they saw as an American "inferiority complex" to enhance their privileges. Others were more critical of Anglophilia, pointing to its class and regional biases; or they said they just wanted to blend into American society. In these cases, the interviewees also held Americans responsible, implying that Americans foisted an English identity on them and obscuring the work they did to assert their Englishness during interactions.

In the last section of the chapter, I turned from the idea of privilege to examine the ways in which these English people believed they were superior to Americans. I did this to provide some balance to the idea held by my interviewees that Americans are responsible for their treatment of English people. Although some criticized what they saw as a superiority complex among English people, I soon uncovered evidence of the ways they constructed themselves as superior. I pointed to their use of cultural practices to enact their identity as a way to distance themselves from Americans. They used these practices to enhance their own superiority at the expense of Americans and to reproduce their identities as English. In particular, I focused on two aspects of culture associated with Anglophilic notions of Englishness in the U.S.—fashion and humor. In both areas, the interviewees conceptualized themselves as superior to Americans and reproduced their understandings of this superiority through their interactions.

Several themes run through my analysis. In discussing the ways in which privilege is understood by these people, we have seen how they compare themselves with Americans in order to recognize the structures of privilege that enable their lives. I have also shown the ways in which comparisons with others affect their recognition of their contradictory status as immigrants in the U.S. Although one group of interviewees were appalled by the racism, classism, and Anglophilia they perceived among Americans, the other group believed that Americans did not privilege them enough. In both cases, the interviewees held Americans responsible for their status; indeed, throughout my discussion of Anglophilia, we saw the ways they hold Americans accountable for what they perceive as their excessive love of Englishness and English culture. Blaming Americans for their privilege is one way to disavow any sense of agency, for it shifts the focus of attention on to what Americans do, rather than what English people do, to maintain their privileges.

However, by attending to the discourses of superiority that permeate the interviews, I also showed how these English people are active participants in the construction of themselves as better than Americans. Although they cloak this in the rhetoric of naturalness, I analyzed how their conceptions of fashion and humor allow them to do identity work to enhance their self-esteem at the expense of Americans. We also saw playfulness with the idea of their superiority as another technique they used to assert their distinctiveness in a safe way. In all, then, we have seen these people using various methods to construct privileged identities: comparing themselves with others; blaming others for the identities they receive; claiming that their identities are natural and hence unavoidable and immutable; and, finally, acting in ways that enhance and preserve their privileged identities.

4 "Gee, I Love Your Accent"

English People and Americans Interact

Imogen: I do use a lot of English words, and I still naturally spell the English way. I do use a . . . very, very broad slang vocabulary. I don't think I do it intentionally, but certainly a day doesn't go by without someone saying, "What does that mean?" I have to explain, and I obviously do it on purpose 'cause if I didn't like it, I would stop. . . . So I think that's the most prominent aspect of my Englishness.

KJ: You mentioned playing up your accent at work. Why do you do that?

Hugh: I'm determined not to lose it.

KJ: Really? Why?

Hugh [brief pause]: Why? Because I suppose the way I speak is the way I am. That's me, and I don't want to lose the way I speak.

IMOGEN'S AND HUGH'S comments epitomize the strong relationship that many of the people I talked to perceived between the way they speak and their English identities. For both of them, their speech style symbolized a part of themselves; it helped them stand out in the U.S. and provided a way to reaffirm their difference from Americans every time they opened their mouths. Furthermore, both conceived of their language use as natural in some way. This came through in Imogen's propensity to use English spelling and slang and in Hugh's assertion that his speech style is who he is. The implication is that changing his accent would involve changing himself, and that he will not do.

In this chapter, I explore why accents are so important to English immigrants in the U.S. and why the majority of the people I spoke to felt strongly about not losing their English accents. I further develop the idea that identities are constructed through practices and argue that the work the interviewees do to maintain their accents is indicative of deeper identity work. These English people use their accents to negotiate their national identities, playing the accents up or down as they emphasize or deemphasize their Englishness.

I use the data to explore this accent manipulation. First, I focus on the importance of accents in English society to provide some context for the English obsession with accents and to discuss how this might manifest itself among these English immigrants. Second, I analyze the various linguistic practices the interviewees used, showing their considerable skill and flexibility as they negotiate their way between "English English"[1] and "American English." I argue that, as they vary their accents to suit the situation, they are asserting or downplaying their identities as English. In examining these practices, I consider why accents may increase in importance when English people arrive in the U.S. In particular, I point to the ways Anglophilic Americans may value English accents and bestow high status on English people. Although some of the people I spoke to react negatively to this marking behavior, it also increases their self-esteem—and the likelihood that they will continue to use English accents whenever possible. Finally, I discuss the importance of accents to some of the interviewees, such as Imogen and Hugh, as an indicator of national identity. In other words, one of the reasons they see themselves as English is that they speak with an English accent.[2]

IDENTITY, LANGUAGE, AND PRACTICES

As I argued in Chapter 1, identities are "emergent feature[s]" (West and Zimmerman 1987: 126) of social life that are continuously constituted and reconstituted by individuals as they act and interact on a daily basis.[3] These identities wax and wane as they are emphasized or downplayed in situationally specific ways.[4] Because individuals themselves are actively constructing them, their identities may be incoherent or contradictory.[5]

As individuals interact with one another, they use language to account for and give meaning to everyday life.[6] Thus, identities are constructed not only through self-presentation, as Erving Goffman[7] suggests, but also through practice that is named or remarked upon through language. Because language is the communication symbol *par excellence,* it is an important way for humans to constitute themselves as social beings. Focusing on language enables us to attend to the diverse meanings given to identities. It can show us how individuals use language to tease out the variations in identities as they move from one situation to another, draw on one set of meanings or another, or react to one set of interlocutors or another. The use of language ensures that identities themselves are not seen as "essence[s], but [as] *positioning[s]*" (Hall 1990: 226; emphasis in original). Attending to respondents' use of language to defend, describe, define, or decry particular identities provides a dynamic view of identity as "an active, practical and situated accomplishment" (Widdicombe and Wooffitt 1995: 218), one that is mutable, contested, and multifaceted.

In the sections that follow, I explore a variety of linguistic practices used by the English people I interviewed, examining the extent to which they are identity-constructing devices. My data on accents show at least three different ways of thinking about practice. On the one hand, the idea of practice implies a degree of choice, perhaps even an intentional or volitional quality, together with the idea that repeating practices will increase proficiency. In some instances I find these English people willingly negotiating their accents, making choices about when to play them up and down, moving among different situations using different voices to assert or downplay their Englishness.[8] In these cases, the interviewees appear highly skilled and flexible in their ability to do identity work through their accents.

In the same vein, practices may be intentional because individuals know that particular actions will accrue material or psychological benefits. Some interviewees did maintain their accents in situations in which they knew English accents would be beneficial. In Chapter 3, I explored the ideas of Anglophilia and privilege; in this chapter, I develop the idea that practice can have an element of forethought to it. People may act in certain ways because of the structures surrounding them or because they know that they will derive benefits from acting in particular ways. In relation to this, I explore the issue of these people's sense of superiority over Americans. Speaking with an English accent in an Anglophilic context provides a way to build their self-esteem and feel good about being English. Seeing accents as open to manipulation thus enables us to examine the links between language and identity in more detail.

On the other hand, there are also times that these individuals seem not to be conscious of their linguistic practices, claiming one thing at one moment in an interview and either contradicting themselves at another moment or proving something different through their actions. For example, an interviewee might claim that she or he does not vary her or his accent but will then vary it during the interview.[9] This illustrates the incoherent and rather contradictory nature of practices (and, by implication, identities). However, this level of unconsciousness and unintentionality about actions also points to another facet of practices: their habitual nature. Individuals may become so used to acting in certain ways that they are not conscious of repeating practices over and over again. In this case, practices become second nature to them, and they do not even notice the effort that they put into them.[10] These practices might become so practiced that they seem "natural," obscuring the socially constructed nature of identity.

A third level at which practice emerges in my data is performance. Performance theorists have argued that exaggeration and parody are one way that gender identity in particular is produced and then called into question.[11] Similar to the drag queens and pastiche-artists analyzed by Judith Butler who "pump . . . up" gender (Weston 1993; Butler 1990: 5), some of my interviewees engaged in parodying English accents or playing them up for amusement's sake. This provides an alternative way to see practice: It may construct identity, but at the same time it can mock the relationship between linguistic practices and identity.

ENGLISH ACCENTS IN ENGLAND

Accents occupy a rather special place in British life.[12] The diversity of accents is overwhelming in such a small nation,[13] and it seems unbelievable to foreigners that accents can change so quickly over such small distances.[14] Accents are linked to class and region in Britain in ways that are widely believed to be unique;[15] they have been conceptualized as a pyramid, with "RP," or Received Pronunciation, at the top.[16] Described as the ostensibly regionless accent, RP is characteristic of members of the upper and upper-middle classes who have been educated at public (i.e., private) schools. The remainder of the pyramid consists of mild regional accents, with broad local accents at the bottom.[17] The idea behind the pyramid is that non-RP accents—that is, regional and local accents—are more widespread and less prestigious than RP accents. Indeed, according to some estimates, only 3 to 5 percent of English people speak with an RP accent.[18]

The relationship among accent, class, and region ensures that region often serves as a proxy for class in England. Hence, "any regional accent is by definition not an upper-class accent, and hardly an upper-middle-class accent: because in those social classes such accent differences as do exist are not regional" (Wells 1982: 14). The dominant paradigm of accents in the United Kingdom, therefore, is that RP is the only "non-regional" accent (even though it predominates in the southeastern part of the country), and any other kind of accent is seen as "regional" or "local" and therefore tainted with class or "provincial" biases.[19] Obviously, RP also has class biases; however, because it is the dominant accent, these biases generally have been subsumed under the label of neutrality.

According to the interviewees, accent functions in England as a way to ascertain personal biography because English people "can identify anyone in one second by their accent, . . . down to . . . averaging what their parents' income is," as Diana explained. Accents act as clues or markers about the kind of person with whom one is dealing and how one should relate to her or him. That this functions on the level of class is suggested by Diana's comment and by a painful story that Gary related about an encounter he had with an American friend of his wife who had been educated in England at the "right" places (at Eton, a public school, and at an elite Oxford college). He had "extremely refined manners and a very, very English upper-class accent," Gary said. "For all practical purposes, this person was English." Gary had moved around England and the U.S. as a child, attending an English comprehensive school[20] and a relatively unprestigious Cambridge college. His accent was somewhat Americanized but contained traces of the various regions in which he had lived in England. He defined himself as lower-middle class. He takes up the story:

> I found myself almost unable to deal with this person, as the person that I am, coming from Chipping Sodbury, having gone to a comprehensive [school], speaking in various different shades of English accents, but none of them particularly upper class. And I felt tremendously inadequate, despite the fact that I had gone to [Cambridge] and I was entirely intimidated by this person's accent and wasn't able to adjust in that situation . . . and ended up apologizing. He asked me where I had gone to high school, and I said, "Oh, just some comprehensive," which, given my political outlook and the fact that I'm quite pleased [with] where I went to high school, is an appalling situation. And [it] really just fucked me up for a

couple of days. . . . I think the class and the accent and the education issues there really can screw you up. . . . I didn't feel that I could [talk to him as an equal].

Gary's experience illustrates how easily English people can categorize one another on the basis of accents and the class-related emotions that can accompany these categorizations. The wife's friend's upper-class, public-school-educated accent raised the issue of Gary's own accent and educational background and aroused deep feelings of insecurity in him, even though his socialist political outlook decried deferential behavior toward elites. The realization that he was unable to change "the fact that I went to [his comprehensive school] and not Eton" precipitated a kind of identity crisis as he realized that he was, in some way, ashamed of his class background and his accent. His reaction illustrates an important point shown in studies of accents in Britain: RP, the top accent in the pyramid, is routinely associated with status, intelligence, competence, and high culture.[21] Gary's reaction was based on the idea that the Eton-educated, upper-class-accented acquaintance would look down on him for not speaking with an RP accent or for lacking the elite educational credentials an RP accent implied. Interestingly, however, Gary's acquaintance was actually American; the fact that Gary "read" him as English shows the strong, almost causal, relationship between accent and national identity for him.

Gary's crisis also points to a deeper issue about the relationship between accents and identity in England. Despite the prestige of RP, other researchers have found that RP speakers are not ranked highly by non-RP speakers in terms of empathy, kindness, solidarity, honesty, social attractiveness, comradeship, or intimacy within a group.[22] Indeed, the more familiar an accent is to a listener (that is, the closer it is to the listener's accent), the more favorable will be the listener's judgements about that person.[23] Gary found his disgust with himself for devaluing his own accent, background, and education painful because both his regional pride and his political stance told him that he should not conform to the hegemonic RP accent and all that it stands for. His inability to talk to the Etonian-educated American as an equal represents for him an inability to take pride in his accent and background.[24] However, in contrast to Gary's experiences, sociolinguistic studies show that although speakers of "regional" accents may pay lip service to RP, they generally value their own accents.[25] Non-RP speakers may report their eagerness to adopt so-called higher social norms of speech, and even acquiesce to unfavorable judgments made about their speech styles by others, but there is great stability of speech style among these so-called lower varieties of speech.[26] The reason for this paradox is, of course, that accents are a crucial part of identity in England. However downgraded one's accent may be, it is a source of pride and of regional and class consciousness.[27] Thus, Gary's words express his awareness that he should value his accent, education, and background and that he has failed himself in some way by being intimidated by an RP accent.

Most English people arrive in the U.S. highly conscious of their accents because of the importance of accents in English life. They may be additionally conscious of their accents for slightly different reasons. English accents are in a state of flux at the moment, as so-called regional accents can be heard more frequently on television and radio and among those in positions of power. Evidence also exists that RP is changing,[28] and a new variety of English—"Estuary English"—is sweeping the southeastern part of the country. David Rosewarne, the critic who coined the term, argues that this "classless" accent is the result of the convergence of RP and local speakers at school and in the workplace, and he finds evidence of it in arenas as diverse as the House of Commons, regional radio, and The City, and among the younger members of the royal family.[29] In addition, the "conservative RP" accent of older members of the royalty and aristocracy is increasingly subject to ridicule[30] and hostility; even advanced RP (the old accent of the younger royalty) and general RP are no longer seen as unmarked and neutral.[31]

Consider, for instance, the experiences of Tara and Antonia, who both speak a fairly conservative form of RP. They provided a glimpse of Gary's crisis from a different position on the class spectrum as they compared England to the U.S. Whereas Tara says she felt embarrassed about her "upper-class accent" at her left-wing Cambridge college, in the U.S. "I was a complete blank slate." Antonia agreed, pointing to the relative "anonymity" that her Englishness gave her in the U.S. Both find very liberating the fact that most Americans are unable to categorize their class background by their accents. Although Tara's and Antonia's RP accents probably brought them more privileges than constraints in England, both women imply that they were subject to a certain amount of hostility because of the way they spoke[32] and felt "pressure to actually adopt a more working-class accent" in England, as Tara said.

These developments in English accents tell us two things: first, that accents are an endless source of pride, obsession, or simply interest to many English people; and second, that a majority of my interviewees left England at a time that the conventional wisdom about the relationship between accent and class, and the predominance of the RP accent, was under scrutiny. Thus, one would expect to find the interviewees fairly self-reflective about accents and their meanings.

ACCENTS DURING INTERVIEWS

During the interviews, these English people were not only self-reflective about their accents; they also varied their vocabulary and pronunciation, moving between shades of American English and English English and sometimes introducing different English accents or accents from other parts of the world (for example, from Ireland or Australia) into the interviews. Their narratives, too, show that they varied the way they spoke in their everyday lives, perhaps using an American accent when at work or when ordering a cup of coffee and an English accent at other times. This illustrates their skill and flexibility with their accents, as they varied them to suit the situation. Their ability to negotiate accents also shows how knowledgeable they are about accents and how much of their accent variation is intentional.[33]

Harry provided an excellent example of fluidity of movement between English English and American English vocabulary when he described eating "candy" (sweets) and "crisps" (potato chips). The interviewees and I sometimes used English and American words together—for instance, "soccer/football," "vacation/holiday," "mates/ buddies"—because we were unsure as to whether we should be speaking English or American. As Vera explained, "My usages are all mixed up. I no longer know whether [it's] the boot [or the] trunk.... Sometimes I come to a complete halt. I can't say something because I can't remember which language I'm speaking in." Interviewees also consulted me on the English pronunciation of words such as "schedule" and joked with me about the American pronunciation of words such as "niche," showing that they were relating to me as a fellow English person in the U.S.

In addition, they often used different accents to tell anecdotes or jokes or to make a humorous point. Some people were obviously better mimics than others: Imogen, Peter, Frank, Ian, and Alex, in particular, moved in and out of accents to suit their purposes during their interviews. Some of the storytelling involved putting on American accents to emphasize an American's question or comment, and other examples involved using different English accents for comic effect. Imogen, for example, put on what I presume was an RP "wanna-be" accent to make fun of the English propensity to drink tea and a Birmingham accent whenever she talked about soccer. Alex told me stories from British newspapers, enlivening them by putting on various regional accents. And Peter, after saying that he did not play his accent up or down, proceeded to give me a run-through of various accents he used on the phone with English colleagues:

> You tend to . . . probably sound "more of a Londoner" [*in a cockney accent*]. It depends who you are with. I think "if you're talkin' to some kid who's from like Essex [*brief pause*] an' 'e's drivin' 'is XR3-I[34] and all that . . . then you probably star' talkin' abou' like, ''Ow's the Spurs[35] doin' this weeken', Pau'?' 'Oh, pre''y good mate, thanks'" [*in an Essex accent*]. So you tend to bring yourself down or up to somebody's level. "And then again, if you're speaking to" [*in a deep, RP, upper-class accent*] one of the more upper-crusty kind of guys, maybe you'll slow your speech down a bit, you pronounce words a little better.

Although I was laughing heartily by the end of this performance, I had the feeling that Peter grew embarrassed about mimicking an RP accent in front of me, especially since he gave up his imitation of this accent halfway through a sentence. I sensed that most of the interviewees noticed my accent as English (although at least one wondered whether I was American when we first talked, and another thought I might be Australian), and that most seemed to interpret it, correctly, as being an RP accent—or, at least, they identified that I was from southeastern England and had probably been educated at a public school. A couple of interviewees commented on how English I sounded. Frank said, "Well, you're very English. You're not American at all:" Catriona asked me how long I had lived in England, "because your accent is so English." Lucinda told me that my accent was "still very very strong," and Peter said that his accent would probably become more English during the interview because of my accent.[36]

INTENTIONAL PRACTICES: WHY SHOULD I CHANGE THE WAY I SPEAK?

Although many people believe that English English and American English are essentially the same language, a surprisingly large number of linguistic pitfalls await the English-speaking, English-accented immigrant in the U.S., some of them quite subtle. "Jumper," "vest," "biscuit," "suspenders," and "chips" are all examples of words that mean different things in American and English.[37] Much English slang is unknown to most Americans. The interviewees mentioned words such as "loo" and "knackered" as needing constant translation (the former is the bathroom; the latter means exhausted).

Several interviewees described the hilarity that their word choice or pronunciation could induce in Americans. Craig, who worked in a hospital, said: "[If I say,] 'The patient is due in theater at nine o'clock,' they just roll around in laughter, like, 'What play are they going to see?'" (The operating room, or OR, is the American term.) Harry maintained that once every two or three days, "I say something casual and somebody repeats it back to me and tries to repeat my accent," which drives him "insane," although he acknowledged that the mimics mean well.

A general empirical finding in the social-psychology literature is that people are more likely to converge toward a more powerful speaker in any given situation.[38] Thus, people usually change their speech to be like another's out of a desire for social approval.[39] They may also converge to increase their perceived status, competence, or persuasiveness; to gain other economic and social rewards; to conform to their stereotypes of how others speak; or because they believe their interlocutor has converged toward them; or even, perhaps, because they are more empathic.[40] However, none of the interviewees mentioned using an American accent to gain rewards or approval from Americans. Indeed, the opposite was more likely—that they would benefit from using an English accent, as I show later in this chapter.

The literature also suggests that individuals, particularly high-status speakers, may change their speech style to increase their intelligibility, especially in interethnic or inter-national situations.[41] Indeed, one of the main reasons that these English people gave to account for linguistic changes they had made was that they needed to make themselves understood. Miscommunication was especially likely when they first arrived or when they came into contact with a particular American for the first time. Thus, Lucinda spent ten minutes at a meat counter in a grocery store trying to buy mincemeat (hamburger meat), and Dorothy described people at work making "snide comments" about her accent. One might predict that the changes in these cases would be in the direction of convergence toward the more powerful American speakers—the obvious numerical majority in the U.S. who communicate with an expectation of being understood. However, the description given by Piers of the trials and tribulations of ordering a cup of coffee (which in his English accent is pronounced with a relatively long *o*) suggests a slightly different interpretation:

> I'd always walk in and get a bagel and a cup of coffee. "Coke?" "No, that's coffee." "I'm sorry, Diet Coke?" I'm thinking, "OK . . . how do they do it? Coffee, coff, kwafy?" I'm going through every possible thing. I finally come down with something [that sounds like] Brooklyn on the bleeding Mississippi, like k-w-o-r-f-e-e [*spelling out the word*]. . . . A friend of mine finally explained, it's k-w-a-f-y [*spelling out the word*]. Just ask for kwafy. . . . Now they get it. It sounds like somebody has cold feet really quickly, but give me a cup of kwafy.

Although Piers had one of the more "Americanized" accents in the sample, here he is rather sarcastic about American pronunciations. He does mock his own attempts to mimic an American accent, but he also undermines the American pronunciation of "coffee" by saying that it sounds like "cold feet" said very quickly. His humorous attitude reveals a position of superiority, with a kind of amused tolerance for American accents, far from any sense of powerlessness at not being understood.

Piers's story suggests the considerable work he put into making himself understood, but it also suggests the level of detail he noticed in his own accent. That attention to detail was manifested in other interviews and accounts for how conscious the interviewees were about their accents. The following story, related by Imogen, suggests how attuned English people are to accents. The story is about her English friend Jim, who had been in the States for about three months when she invited him to a small dinner party:

> There were . . . six of us British people, and we'd all been in America for slightly different lengths of time and [*laughs*] just halfway through the dinner, [Jim] just went, "You lot are amazing! You're talking at me like I'm a complete idiot! And the ones that have been here the longest are doing it

more!" [*in a high-pitched, excited tone*]. He said he could guess the order in which we all came here, and he got it completely right. . . . It was the going up at the end of the sentence, the questions, . . . the intonation, that was the main thing, talking slowly and not using so much slang. . . . It was very funny. [He said] that we didn't use complicated words [and] we did- n't have glottal stops.

In this vignette Jim, the neophyte English expatriate, accurately guesses the length of the dinner-party guests' stays in the States based on what he perceives as different degrees of Americanization in their speech.[42] Jim's comments extend Peter Trudgill's findings about how English peo- ple Americanize their speech by suggesting that certain types of intona- tion and vocabulary are far better known in England as "American" and are thus more salient for English people assessing, devaluing, adopting, or imitating American accents. Jim pinpointed the questioning tone of American English and marked this as simplistic by combining it with his friends' new, slower speech and their loss of English slang, complicated words, and glottal stops, the hallmark of the new Estuary English. Although on the surface it looks as though Jim is accusing his compan- ions of treating him like a "complete idiot," a closer reading reveals that he is perhaps telling them that they sound like idiots. Imogen explained what Jim meant by "going up at the end of the sentence": "It sounds like, 'Do you know what I mean? Have you got it? Have you understood what I am talking about?' 'Yes, I know what you mean, you bloody idiot!'" The fact that she turned the idiot statement around so that it now described the speaker suggests that she agrees with Jim's assessment that Ameri- canized speech styles are idiotic. Although Imogen laughed a lot while telling the story, the anecdote is a serious comment on the reactions Eng- lish people have to American accents and how they stigmatize them. Indeed, many of the interviewees expressed concern about other English people's reactions to their Americanized speech. This concern can trans- late into a determination to maintain one's accent, perhaps to maintain solidarity with a familiar English network or in-group.[43]

ANGLOPHILIC RESPONSES TO ENGLISH ACCENTS

American Anglophilia also accounts for the preponderance of English accents among the interviewees. English people living in the U.S. gen- erally find that their accents are seen as positive and are often highly valued by Americans. Even when Americans cannot understand what they are saying, the miscommunication is good-humored. Stephen, for instance, told a story about trying to order a hamburger about a month after his arrival. The woman behind the counter responded to his order with, "Gee, honey, I love your accent, but I can't understand a word you said!" Although the fast-food worker could not understand him, she praised his accent all the same—an experience that few other immigrant groups in the U.S. would have, judging by the number of American books and tapes dedicated to losing one's foreign accent.

It is important to recognize the racial and class dimensions of this Anglophilia on the part of Americans. While English accents are valued, immigrants from non-English-speaking countries are not subject to the same praise (although anecdotal evidence suggests that French people may find their accents valued as exotic on the East Coast). Indeed, those whose first language is not English are often subjected to derision; the English-only movement in the U.S. is one example of this mind-set.[44] One of the interviewees, Nigel, tapped into the contradiction embedded in valuing English speech styles but devaluing Latin American ones when he argued that those who wanted to speak Spanish in the U.S. or Urdu in England "should fuck off back to their own country." Although he later included non-Spanish-speaking English people living in Spain in this pronouncement, he also asserted his right to use English words, phrases, and accent: "It's not fucking soccer; it's football!" and "I've called them tom-ah-toes all my life, and I'm not going to change! They know what I mean."

Clearly, the fact that English people spoke with English rather than, say, Chinese or Spanish accents had an effect on how they were perceived. That the interviewees were white and middle or upper-middle class is also an important variable in the equation. Research on the experiences of black immigrants to the U.S. from the West Indies does suggest that they are seen as "better" than African Americans, perhaps because their accents are more Anglicized than Americans',[45] and several of the interviewees noted that black English friends of theirs in the U.S. were not subject to the same degree of racism as African Americans once people heard their English accents. The race and class implications of the Anglophilia experienced by my interviewees are therefore complicated.

The interviewees mused about how "charmed" Americans were by their accents.[46] As noted in Chapter 2, Anne said that "people [at work] treat me with more respect than they do other Americans. . . . They seem to think that because I have this different accent, it [gives me] a kind of authority." Andy explained the benefits of the Anglophilia he perceived, pointing to the effortless ways it allowed him to be different: "You can make your presence felt without patting yourself on the back.... You are a little bit different from the rest of the people in the room, and that can have its advantages. I think you're recognized before you say anything of significance." Imogen felt that she "got to win a lot of arguments," because people assume "I [have] this great level of culture [and speak] and read fluent Latin" (which, she admitted, she does not).

The interviewees pointed to other, more concrete privileges they believed they received as a result of their national identity. Torn-up parking tickets, free subway rides, increased job opportunities, and better luck in singles bars were just some of the "perks" they believed their English accents garnered. Diana, for instance, was certain that her English accent had helped her get job interviews and an apartment: "I knew [the potential landlady] would consider me more respectable if I had a British accent, and I was right. She'd picked my message off the answering machine and didn't bother to answer any others." Mike, meanwhile, mused about whether he could "get away with ... things" because he was English.

The interviewees, then, were aware of the cultural capital their accents produced for them in the U.S.[47] Most found the phenomenon of Anglophilia to be attractive, recognizing and enjoying the privileges that accrued from it. Because they often embraced the benefits of an English accent, their annoyance at Americans' "sense of cultural wonder" is rather surprising:

> I will say ... a Britishism, ... , words that you think are used over here but they're not, like "jumper," for example ... and people will react to that like, "Wow!" They will find it really quaint and interesting in an almost patronizing way, that you can speak in a different way, that for you this word means something else.

Instead of feeling that he is the outsider because he uses the word "jumper" (which means sweater), Mike faults Americans for failing to take cultural differences in their stride. In England, he suggests, people "will not react to an Americanism in a wild manner.... We will say, 'Oh, that's an Americanism; he's an American,'" and that will be that.[48]

As Mike continues his explanation, he provides a clue to the nature of these interactions. He explains that English people "might not have a particularly high opinion of the Americanism being used." Although this may be true of English reactions to American accents, the opposite accounts for some of the reactions English accents receive in the States: The marking of English speech is usually the result of Anglophilia. Thus, English people are at an advantage in these interactions because their accents are valued over American ones (and they usually value their own accents over American ones, as I show later). American Anglophilia may be expressed in diminutive or patronizing tones—that an accent is "cute" or a particular word is "quaint"—but Americans' underlying motive is usually positive. However, in spite of this and the humor with which the interviewees told these stories, they also find it annoying to be faced with constant reminders of their cultural difference. Harriet says she was quite put out by a salesman's response when she expressed surprise that the shop did not sell telephone batteries:

> I said, "Well, what is the point of the phone if you don't have any bloody batteries?" . . . The salesman wandered around the shop from there on after saying, "Please say 'bloody batteries' again. I love the way you say 'bloody battery.'" It was ridiculous! He loved the combination of my English accent saying "bloody battery"! . . . I have never been back since. I was like, "The man's a weirdo! What is he talking about?"

Although the salesman's Anglophilia shines through, the fact that he was enamored of Harriet's accent obviously embarrassed her tremendously. She laughed as she told the story but was uncomfortable enough with the interaction to stop going to the shop. Although she may have been flattered, she also felt stigmatized (albeit positively).[49] Americans' positive reactions to these English people's accents can detract from whatever they are trying to get out of the interaction. In Harriet's case, her frustration (exemplified by her use of the word "bloody") is ignored by the salesman,[50] who instead focuses on how charming he finds her accent. What is interesting in these interactions is that most of the interviewees do not change their accents even though they may dislike the Americans' comments. Indeed, they may even play the accents up to suit the situation and accrue more benefits.

Playing Up Accents

The interviewees were apt to take advantage of Anglophilic responses to their accents. For instance, Craig said that if I'm . . . wanting to get my point of view across [or] wanting to make an impression with somebody . . . , I probably do have a more clipped term, and emphasize the English accent . . . to a greater degree simply because they . . . take more notice of you . . . and you suddenly become more eloquent. . . . It manipulates the situation. You can have people thinking that you are saying something more important than you actually are!

Indeed, despite their recognition of the potential unfairness to others, the interviewees were often quite prepared to use their accents and special status to their advantage. Diana saw links between her gender and her national identity in this regard:

If people are going to be so dumb as to run a system . . . totally on appearances or how you sound, then . . . I'm going to play them at their own game. I use the bit about the accent . . . in the same way as I use [being] small and blonde and female. . . . You get looked at differently and . . . if you've got a British accent, I've been told that you sound a bit more intelligent, so I use that to my advantage.

Although she characterized this as "playing a game which I totally disapprove of," she was prepared to play the game to win, using her petite size, femininity, and Englishness to get whatever benefits she could from the "dumb" people who "run" the kind of "system" where these things matter. The "dumb" people she is referring to are clearly Americans.

Imogen also modified her speech style to fit the situation, distinguishing between Americans who would know what she was talking about and those who wouldn't: "I know perfectly well to say 'bathroom,' and when I'm out in some public place, I'll say 'bathroom' without thinking. . . . But when I'm in a crowd of Americans who I know have been exposed to European [culture], I'll say 'loo' without thinking." Although Imogen claims not to think about this, she is obviously conscious of her audience on some level and adjusts her vocabulary accordingly. Gary also noticed his accent changing depending on the subject of conversation: His accent sounded more English, he said, when he was "talking about Britain or Europe . . . or something which I think Britain is well known for." These situation-specific changes point to the ways that accents become the object of practice; these English people actively work to make themselves understood by different groups of people in different situations. They put effort into varying their accents and vocabulary, showing a high degree of knowledge about the minutiae of American English and English English, and considerable skill in being able to do this translation work on the spot. That this involves effort is exemplified by Harry's comments about how refreshing it felt to talk to other English people: "It was like being bathed in clear waters for a few seconds when I heard the accents and people speaking. It was like, 'Ah, I don't have to concentrate.'"

The variations in these people's accents do more than ensure their intelligibility, however: Imogen and Gary's examples in particular show that they are working to assert themselves as English in particular situations. By speaking with an English accent when the conversation moves to Europe, Gary can remind his interlocutors that he has an insider's knowledge of this topic, and that they should therefore see him as an Englishman. Likewise, Imogen's ability to size up her audience to determine whether they will understand "loo" shows that she is able to continue to use English slang as a "prominent aspect of [her] Englishness." Accent forms a link between the individual and her or his identity, a way to turn identity on or off. These English people feel English when they think they sound English. Thus, when asked to read in church, Emma "felt very English, because when I talk publicly, my accent is very strong ... because my mother always taught me ..., if you read in church ... you project and you talk clearly, and so I do." Others made sure to use English accents to make a good impression or when they first met people. For instance, Lucinda noticed that her mother's accent "comes on very heavy, gets very snotty ... and becomes very English in a matter of five seconds [when] something's not going her way, like if a policeman pulls her over." In addition, perhaps, to hoping to gain some kind of special treatment from a police officer, Lucinda's mother may rely on her English accent to enhance her self-esteem in a difficult situation.

Emma also admits that she sometimes speaks with an English accent to show people that she is English. If she is playing with her children in a public place or hears another English accent in a restaurant, "I start to talk very very English [*putting on a very upper-class accent*]. It's very funny, and it's not deliberate sometimes. Well, sometimes it is, I think. Sometimes it's like, 'Well, I'll let them know I'm English, too,' so I'll speak in an English accent." Emma clearly states her awareness that she needs to feel English in situations where other English people are present. For Emma and for Gary, it is important to prove that they are English in an interaction. When confronted with another English person or with a topic of conversation related to England, their motivation is to use their accents as ways to mark themselves as English. They assert their national identity via their speech style, either to show their right to be in the conversation (in Gary's case) or to show that they are just as English as other English-accented people (in Emma's case).[51]

In contrast to these interactions, Harry explained the accent work he does when speaking to Americans:

> I'm so used to explaining myself in every second sentence, so used to interrupting myself mid-sentence to explain the word I just used or the phrase I just used, then diving back into what I was saying, by which time the whole point of the thing is just dead. . . . I've developed a very different style of speaking, and now I'm talking to [you], it's like I don't have to translate.

Indeed, I noticed how many English slang terms came up during the interview, such as "divot," "tosspot," and "thickie" (all of which mean "idiot"). Harry's strategy seems to be to retain his English accent and vocabulary (although his intonations were slightly American at times), but constantly to translate it for Americans. He is essentially bilingual but refuses to speak the language of the host country in a straightforward manner. Instead, he uses language to mark himself as different from Americans while still ensuring that he is intelligible. This strategy is similar to the one used by Nigel, who said, "as they say over here, shit happens," to mark Americanisms in his speech as foreign to him so that he will not be mistaken for an American himself. Harry and Nigel illustrate the aspect of choice in the linguistic work these interviewees do: They show that they know how to speak like Americans but choose to accentuate their difference from Americans through their speech. Indeed, Nigel's and Harry's communication styles point to a strategy that was common when interviewees interacted with Americans: Most of them either maintained their English accents or exaggerated them as a form of linguistic divergence. These English immigrants play up their English speech styles to assert and affirm their national identity, both for themselves and for others. By speaking with an English accent, they maintain their credibility as English people and want to be held accountable as English, not American.

"I'M So BORED WITH THE U.S.A."[52]

Although the British punk band The Clash[53] was bored with the U.S.A. for reasons that differ somewhat from those of these English people (in

"I'm So Bored . . ." The Clash was singing about American cultural impe-rialism), the title of the song sums up an attitude that many interview-ees expressed. Although they acknowledged the material benefits of American Anglophilia, they also responded with boredom and annoy-ance to the marking of their accents. As Diana said, Americans seemed "dumb" to care so much about their accents. Their frustration often went hand in hand with a sense of entitlement and superiority that interactions with Americans engendered. Peter, for instance, described asking for the bathroom in a bar:

> I was like, "Excuse me. Where's the bathroom?" And the guy goes, "Par-don me?" [in an American accent] "Where's the bathroom?" [louder] "I'm sorry, sir" [in an American accent] "Where's the bathroom?" [louder still] "I'm sorry, sir; I have no idea what you are talking about" [in an Ameri-can accent] "Where's the fucking ba-athroom?" [in a very loud American accent, emphasizing the long a] "Oh, it's down the end of the bar on your right. Why didn't you ask?" [in an American accent].

The story is interesting for the rote repetitions of Peter's question, per-haps to emphasize what he sees as his own patience and to contrast it with the bartender's inability to answer what Peter thinks is a simple question. His anger shows through as his voice gets louder, until he uses the adjec-tive "fucking" to mark his frustration with the situation. The fact that he prefaced this story with the comment, "Americans are not great thinkers. . . . I mean I love the American people, but if you don't say things the way they're used to hearing them, they don't understand," shows that he holds the American bartender responsible for the miscommunication as "not [being a] great thinker." According to Peter, it is a failing on the part of Americans if they are unable to understand an English accent. A different reading of this story is that the bartender is deliberately pro-voking Peter in order to get him to speak with an American accent. Of course, Peter, stuck in his mind-set that Americans are rather simple, would not understand that the bartender was getting the better of him; he could only see that he was the one speaking English properly. As an Englishman in England once said to me about Americans, "Ask them what language it is that they are bastardizing." The implication is that Americans are in the wrong for speaking American English.

Peter and Diana were not the only interviewees who enhanced their self-esteem by speaking with English accents; many of the comments in the previous sections can be read as instances in which the interviewees felt superior when they sounded English. In addition to providing material benefits, then, Anglophilia and its attendant accent manipulation provided psychological benefits to these interviewees. Speaking with an English accent provided a way to feel good about themselves.

Additional evidence for the assumption that English accents were superior emerged as those interviewees who had children worried that their children were picking up American accents. Frances proudly displayed her daughter saying, "How now brown cow?" (with round *o*s) to me to show off her English accent; when Emma asked her daughter what was in a bucket, she laughingly said, "Ha! That's English water, if you ask me!" (She pronounced "water" with a southern English accent—wah-tah—as opposed to the American wadder.) Gary, whose wife was pregnant, responded to my question about how he felt about bringing up a child in the U.S. this way: "Well, I don't feel very good about it, frankly, which is not a nice thing to say since I'm married to an American. . . . But I'd much rather bring the child up somewhere else." When I asked why, he replied, "Well, accent has something to do with it, [although] it's a very superficial reason." Earlier in the interview he had expressed a desire to retain his own English accent and said that he did not like to see Shakespeare's plays performed by American actors, all of which suggests that he valued English over American accents (although he does attempt to downplay it in this quotation). Dorothy, whose daughter was enrolled in American day care, noted that her daughter's accent and behavioral patterns were developing in what she defined as an American way:

> *Dorothy:* She's got this drawl on these words . . . , and in a way I can't understand what she is saying. I think, "Oh, no; she's going to be so American!" . . . When you first have a baby, . . . you think, "Oh, my gosh; she's going to be American no matter what you do!" Then you forget. . . . Then when I went back to England . . . , I listened to all these children with this English accent, and I [thought] "Katie's not like that at all. She's loud!"
>
> *KJ:* Do you think she is louder than English children?
>
> *Dorothy:* I think that English children, just like we, are . . . naturally more reserved.

As Dorothy explained how loud her Katie was, her voice took on a rather plaintive tone, suggesting to me that she was not happy about the "American" way her daughter was growing up. Her definition of what an American is comes from Katie's accent—the drawl that Dorothy cannot understand sometimes and her loud voice mark her as different from the English children who are "naturally ... reserved." Thus, for Dorothy in this example, her daughter's accent signifies personality traits that she defines as not English; accent has become a marker of what she dislikes about America and Americans. This raises another issue: that many of the interviewees with children were married to, or were living with, American partners. Even though they had made life-long commitments to Americans, most still felt comfortable deploring American accents as embodied in their children's voices.

The strong dislike of American accents among the people I talked to is also evident in the vehement language they used to discuss changes in their English accents. Rowena said she was "disgusted with herself" when she heard an "American twang" in her voice. Catriona said she was "horrified" when people told her she was losing her English accent. And when people comment on the Englishness of her accent, Dorothy said, "Thank God I've still got it!" Tara admitted that she used to get "terribly embarrassed [or] really defensive" when people told her that her accent had changed, although she claimed to have grown less so by the time the interview was conducted. As Rowena continued (putting on an upper-class English accent) when I asked her why she felt disgusted: "I don't think the Americans speak as well as we do. They don't pronounce their *ts*."

Clearly, many of the interviewees' friends and family in England had the same negative feelings about American accents: Quentin thought he was seen as a "traitor" when he returned home because "my voice, my vocabulary is a bit different, my accent is a bit different."[54] Piers laughingly said that people would think he was an "ignorant ... fool" because of his American spelling. Most of my interviewees had some experience of English people negatively evaluating Americanized parts of their speech.

In addition to devaluing American accents, those I spoke with also expressed admiration or sometimes longing for English accents. They valued English accents as a way to differentiate themselves from the American out-group and to enhance their own self-esteem as English people.[55] I interpret these feelings not only as expressing superiority to Americans, but also as agreeing with American versions of Anglophilia. They learn, when they are in the U.S., to see England as "cute" and "quaint," through American eyes. Not only do they prefer English to

American accents, but their words imply that they sometimes hear English accents as outsiders would or revel in them as something that is different, unique, and interesting. Catriona "love[s] to hear the English accents" on the BBC World Service news, and when Harriet hears a "particularly nice English accent," she thinks, "Oh, maybe I should make more of mine," suggesting that both women value English accents as they perceive Americans to be valuing them. Harry watches the television show *Eastenders* religiously because

> I . . . enjoy watching people talk in English about things that matter in England, and it's the nearest I get to it. . . . It's more than just watching a soap; it's like a cultural thing now for me. . . . I really enjoy the way they talk to each other and the accents they have and the fact that I understand what they're getting at.

Harry's viewing pleasure arises partly from his status as a former insider in English culture, in that he can understand *Eastenders* on a level at which most Americans would not (he later says he would have to "translate" for an American viewer). However, there is also a sense in his words about relishing the accents per se—he enjoys listening to the accents as a "cultural thing" and as a way to get in touch with "things that matter in England." Likewise Gordon derives pleasure from the sound of English voices, linking his amusement with "cliché[s]" and "stock movie[s]." He explained that

> I find the people are very funny . . . in the way they interact . . . , and the way that people speak is very musical and very expressive. . . . And my family['s] . . . obsession with tea, which is a cliché, but it's true. I mean, you go back and within ten minutes there's . . . a whole cacophony of, "Do you want tea love?" "Oh, I'll make a cup of tea." "Put the kettle on for a cup of tea." I mean, it's like something out of a stock movie . . . , but it's real.

This implies that English immigrants' images of England are mediated through popular culture, perhaps even the same popular culture from which Americans learn their Anglophilia.

Others spoke of finding humor in English accents: Emily said she laughs when she hears herself saying "lorry instead of truck"; Catriona was recently reminded of the English habit of calling French toast "eggy bread," which caused much hilarity; and Diana admitted that she found the "British accent very amusing." These interviewees were listening to English voices through an Anglophilic lens, able to see what Americans find so quaint and amusing in English speech. In addition to the humor, however, one often finds a belief that the English way is better. So, for instance, Tara reveals that she is "glad I'm an English English speaker. And I think that sometimes . . . , not all the time, a lot of British professionals I know . . . write better than Americans." These people obviously value English linguistic abilities over Americans', and in some cases this is mediated through the lens of popular culture. They see England in terms of clichés (like the tea story) or admire the way English people are portrayed on television or radio. They also adapt to the American idea that English accents are amusing (although this is not such a stretch because accents are used as a form of humor in England). When I asked them what they defined as important about England, many of them pointed to the tradition of literature, the "high cultural standard of language," or said that they saw England as a "repository of the spoken word, spoken well."[56] Thus, the determination to hold on to their English accents is clearly a way for many of them to maintain positive self-esteem.

CONSCIOUSNESS AND INTENT

Is this accent manipulation always intentional? Social-psychological research shows that speakers who modify their linguistic practices often are not aware of the "objective" reality of theirs or others' speech patterns.[57] Although positing a relationship between identity and accent may seem to presuppose a degree of consciousness and intent about what one's accent sounds like, identity-constructing practices can also be unconscious and unintentional. For instance, Erving Goffman's[58] dramaturgical approach to the self does not presuppose that we all feel like actors all the time. Indeed, the beauty of symbolic interactionism and ethnomethodology are that they make explicit aspects of social life that are otherwise taken for granted or so habitual that they seem like second nature.[59] Peter moved among cockney, Essex, and RP accents in one of the earlier excerpts; yet he told me that he did not play his accent up or down. Other interviewees also contradicted themselves, claiming not to have changed their accents or vocabularies, but using American phrases or words during the interview. Still others were self-reflective about their accents or vocabularies, such as Tara, who reacted in mock horror when she heard herself use the word "neat" during the interview. Imogen mused about whether she used English slang on purpose. "I don't think

I do it intentionally," she said, "but certainly a day doesn't go by without somebody saying, 'What does that mean?' I have to explain, and I obviously do it on purpose, 'cause [if] I didn't like it, I would stop." She rightly points out that although it may be unconscious, she must derive some benefit from it or she would stop doing it.

These people also varied in the degree of intent they had about their linguistic changes. Some, such as Piers, were determined to Americanize their accents from the moment they arrived, whereas others, such as Alex and Hugh, were determined to maintain their English accents. Some were prepared to change certain aspects of their speech—for example, pronouncing tomato as tom-ay-to—while others refused to adapt to American pronunciations of French imports such as "niche" and "clique." William said he had not intended to change his accent, arguing that he was "too old to change it anyway." However, he had made some changes, saying "bath" with a long American *a* rather than with the shorter southern English *a* (or baaath versus bah-th). Despite his willingness to Americanize some of his speech and spelling, in the next breath he told me that "Americans can't write," positioning himself as linguistically different from Americans. Decisions about changing or maintaining one's language, then, are not a one-time or all-or-nothing event. Individuals may be conscious of their language in different ways at different moments and may intend to change some aspects of their speech but not others.

Some of the interviewees grappled with the contradictions raised by William's comments: How could they value some aspects of their Englishness while not wanting to emphasize the fact that they are English? Mike took pains to point out that he was not a "disgruntled Brit abroad," while others said they did not want to mix with other English people while in the U.S. As Harry explained, "You get a lot of Brits who spend their time abroad and say how great Britain is, and you think, 'Well, why don't you go back there if it is so great?'" Thus, some looked down on the English abroad who still defined themselves as English or who played up their accents. Stephen expressed his dismay at

people who've been here fifteen or twenty years [who] must know how an American says 'yogurt' [*says it American-style, with a long* o] and "tomato" [*with a long* a], and yet they still insist on saying it the English way. . . . I guess I don't understand that. . . . Maybe it's a statement by them . . . that they are British.

Although Stephen told me that he had adopted many Americanisms, his overall accent was among the more English in my sample. His exasperation with the "more British than British"[60] expatriates was echoed by Antonia, who denied playing her accent up, saying, "No. If anything, the reverse, because I think . . . there are quite a lot of arrogant English people who do do that a bit, . . . are very affected, and I find that so irritating. . . . I'd be so upset if anybody ever thought I was doing that." Yet Antonia also admitted that she enjoyed her expatriate status. Her accent did not sound at all Americanized to my ear; she was also one of those who felt liberated from the baggage that came with her upper-class RP accent in England. Indeed the disjunction between Stephen's and Antonia's words and the voices that I heard echoes other contradictions among the interviewees. I found that the need to distance oneself from other English people or to point out those people who remained *too* English often coincided with the desire to keep an English accent oneself. For instance, Nigel told me about some Union Jack T-shirt–wearing English immigrants whose English accents and behavior had disgusted him, yet he also said that he would not play his accent up or down, that people would just have to accept him the way he was. Again, his accent was very English to my ear.

In contrast to those whose English accents were so habitual that they were not conscious of them, others with whom I talked were self-conscious about their accents. Some characterized an English accent as affected, arrogant, or fake. Harry said he understood why Americans might think that the "rounding off of vowels" might sound "fake like you're putting it on." Imogen admitted that she sometimes felt "stupid" when speaking with an English accent, and Anne said she had stopped listening to the BBC World Service because it sounded "pompous and strange." Again, however, despite their self-consciousness, these people did not have noticeably Americanized accents. Although they were able to hear English accents from what they thought was an American perspective, their perception did not necessarily influence the way they spoke.

ACCENT AS PERFORMANCE

We have already encountered interviewees displaying their skill with accents (Peter's ability to move among cockney, Essex, and RP accents is a good example) and using their accents to exaggerate their Englishness to Americans (Harry's bilingual backtracking springs to mind).

Now I turn to situations in which individuals self-consciously exaggerated their accents to parody their Englishness.

When these interviewees talked about playing up their accents in certain situations, they seemed to define "up" in two different ways. Some took "up" to mean simply putting on a stronger version of whatever their original English accent was, whereas others interpreted my question by defining "up" as moving up the English class scale or making their accent more like an RP accent. Some seemed to use both conceptualizations of the question, implying that they thought that having an English accent meant having an upper-class English accent. Frank, for instance, moved his accent up the social scale because he was ashamed of his accent, although he tried to fight his shame:

> I don't like my voice. It sounds like a jumped-up cockney kid from South London. . . . I'm proud of being a cockney because my parents were cockneys . . . but, at the same time, inculcated in[to] my brain by the system is the thought that that's low class. "Well-bred people don't speak that way" [*in an upper-class accent*].

Frank's difficulty in coming to terms with the prescriptions of the English class system illustrates how accent is equated with class in England. Even though Frank had lived in North America for forty years and had built a successful career as a corporate executive, his voice still had the capacity to make him feel "low class." This shows the hegemony of RP as the accent to which everyone is supposed to aspire.

However, Frank had other reasons for changing his accent to "a modified version of high British." He changed it, he said, if "somebody gives me a hard time and I want them to feel that I'm superior, 'cause that's the way [Americans] think of the British. Anybody with a superior accent is a Lord." He further explained that Americans "don't get cockney. . . . They don't find it particularly impressive." This behavior conforms to the finding that individuals may accommodate to the stereotypes that they think others have of their accents.[61] Others complained about English people who played up the upper-class version of Englishness held by Americans. For instance, Stephen said he disliked English people who conformed to "a certain view that a lot of Americans have about England, which is a quintessentially middle- or upper-middle-class English lifestyle and way of doing things and . . . language." Alex agreed, telling a story about some American friends who had complained about the regional English accents in a *Masterpiece Theatre* production on public television:

> I think their idea of how British people speak is . . . the programs they see on TV, which tend to be well-spoken English. [They said,] "Well we weren't happy with their accent" because the other main players had spoken with a very upper-class accent, and these were more normal accents. And I pointed out [that] a lot of programs you'd see on British TV they'd never import over here because they'd never be able to understand them.

These quotations suggest that some Americans have a class-specific notion of how English people speak, and that English people may draw on this notion as they interact with Americans. Indeed, playing up their accents with Americans may mean conforming to this particular version of Englishness, perhaps further institutionalizing it.[62]

However, performance theory suggests that exaggerated parodies of identity-specific practices somehow call into question the link between the identity and the practice.[63] Some interviewees exaggerated their accents precisely for this reason—to mock the assumption that a particular accent made them English. Specifically, they often made fun of the RP accent in order to undermine the link in their listeners' minds between RP and Englishness. Catriona said that she sometimes reacted in jest, for instance when told, "I think you're losing your accent." She replied, "Oh really? That's terrible. I can't have that happen! [*in an upper-class English accent*]." Tara "act[ed] out . . . a royal family voice" as a joke while Harry played "the English jester because that's what people like." Alex, reacting to Americans who were dissatisfied with a non-RP accent, explained, "Sometimes I deliberately don't speak the Queen's English because it amuses me. . . . I'll say, 'Well, like, darlin', you wouldn't like it, now would you; I could easily talk like that' [*in an East London accent*]." Here we see these English people performing their accents as if they were actors, using their skill with accents as a way to parody the version of Englishness uppermost in most Americans' minds. It must be said, however, that the majority of those I spoke to were more likely to exaggerate their accents in situations in which they would gain benefits than to be humorous.

NEVER MIND THE ACCENT. WHAT ABOUT ME?

Although I have provided evidence that these English people often defined themselves in terms of their accents, I return now to their frustration with others who defined them solely in linguistic terms. Regardless of whether the outcome was increased prestige, they often found the process of being defined by others upsetting. Emily sums up the embarrassment of having one's accent monitored and commented upon (while pointing to the integral place of her accent in her personal identity):

> *Emily* [*in a high-pitched, sycophantic voice*]: "Oh, I could listen to you talking forever!" It seems sort of corny or odd. This is how I talk. It's almost on the borderline of being intrusive. It's like saying to someone, "How did you get to be so fat or so thin?"
>
> *KJ:* It's part of you?
>
> *Emily:* Yeah, it's like, "Are you entitled to comment?"

Peter, too, objected to Anglophilic comments about accents: "If I had a dollar for every time I heard, 'Oh, gee, I love your accent' [*in an American accent*], I'd be the richest guy on the block! . . . Give me a break!" Yet if someone he liked was impressed, he admitted, he would play his accent up. This suggests the contradictory nature of my respondents' feelings toward their interactions with Americans. Having one's accent marked may be annoying, but they understand that it comes from a positive desire for connection on the part of the American (and are prepared to benefit from it, if need be). Lucinda explained the mixture of annoyance and understanding that such comments engender: "I know no one means it offensively, and it really is a compliment, but . . . after a while, I get so annoyed. . . . It's comments like, 'Where did you get that [accent] from?' and a couple of times I'd say . . . 'K-mart. It was on offer.' I mean, what kind of stupid question is that?" Their irritation arises not from feeling threatened or discriminated against, or even from disagreement about the attractiveness of their accent. Rather, their responses suggest a need to regain control over the interaction by trying to deny the salience of their accent, perhaps to remind people that they "come with the accent" (in Tara's words). Lucinda's sarcastic reply downgrades the stress her interlocutor has placed on her accent. Likewise, Peter said he responded with, "I haven't got an accent. You've got an accent," and Harry and William both said they pointed out that they liked Americans' accents. Although they used different methods, all three were pointing out that Americans have accents too, and that they are really not as special as the American is making them out to be. They are trying to de-emphasize their English accent and lessen its import in the interaction (although Peter's comment implies that his speech style is normative in comparison to that of Americans).

One of the reasons that these interviewees objected to this marking behavior was that they believed it reduced them to an accent. Although the marking is generally complimentary, they feel that Americans are not paying attention to them in their entirety because of Americans' Anglophilia. The implication is that it is their English accents, not something unique to each individual, that attracts the praise. Stereotyping occurs in that they are being seen as group members rather than as individuals. The stereotyping, however, is of group members who are prestigious rather than devalued.[64] So Tara said, "It's so stupid. It's as if people are listening to the way I say things instead of what I say. It's not *that* funny." Other interviewees used almost the same words to express their frustration with American reactions to their accents. In addition, Alex noted the "glazed look" that comes over Americans when they listen to her voice rather than the content of her message. These interviewees, then, wonder whether they are being taken seriously on the basis of their merits or their accents. Stephen reacted with annoyance to comments by Americans that his accent made him sound well educated: "You really want people to think you're educated because of what you're saying, not the way you're saying it." Craig wondered whether people were more interested in him when they first met him because he is English, and Harry summed up the concern: "You lose purity in terms of your perspective of people. Like, there's a guy at work that I really like, but apparently he has only heard me speak a few words, and he said I'm really cool just 'cause I'm English. And was that because I'm English or was that because of who I am?"

These interviewees suggest that Americans may be glossing over something unique to each individual by focusing on accents. However, we have seen other evidence that accents provide an important way to maintain their English identities; they may be more than their accents, but their accents are extremely meaningful to them, too. Ironically, the intrusive comments about their accents generally garner them prestige or power in a situation, because they are defined as speaking well or as being well educated or intelligent. In addition, the humor that Americans find in English accents is usually good-natured and used as a point of connection rather than differentiation. American Anglophilia, then, provides English people with opportunities. Although they may feel irritated by constant comments about their accents or find making themselves understood difficult, their own feelings of superiority are reinforced by Americans.

The marking process that Americans engage in during these interactions reminds these people of their Englishness. Identity is being forced onto them in situations in which they may not want it. Other scholars have noted situations in which people wish to refuse the group membership being foisted on them by others,[65] although this usually occurs with identities that are stigmatized. The generally positive connotations of English identities on the East Coast makes this situation slightly different. These interviewees are held accountable for their national identity,[66] yet they will not change their accents to prevent this from happening, presumably because they know their accents are valued in the U.S.

CONCLUSION: DOING ACCENT, DOING IDENTITY

In this chapter, I have stressed the work involved in "doing" identity through linguistic practices. I have shown that the interviewees' accent negotiations illustrate three different conceptions of practice. First, I pointed to their ability to change their accent depending on the situation. They emphasize it when they hear other English people speaking or downplay it when they need to be understood by Americans. I argued that this shows the flexibility of practice as they "pass" in one situation or another. Situating English accents within the context of U.S. Anglophilia, I argued that some of the interviewees' linguistic practices show reactions to the delight many Americans take in English accents, and that these people receive material benefits from speaking with English accents. I also examined the ways in which the interviewees themselves valued their speech styles, showing how this Anglophilic context may shape their morale and self-esteem. Next, I examined their unconscious and unintentional uses of accents, arguing that this shows the habitual nature of practice. Even though they may not approve of other English people using English accents in the U.S., their own linguistic practices are so ingrained that they seem like "second nature" to them. Third, I argued that in some situations, these English immigrants exaggerate their accents as a performance to parody the upper-class accents they believe Americans expect from them. Their accent negotiations are one aspect of the identity work they do to manage their national identities as they decide how English or American they want to be. Their ability to use their accents to their advantage shows the agency they have in producing their national identities.

Throughout the chapter, I have explored the ways that these individuals construct their national identities using linguistic practices. Many of my interviewees would agree that they have to work at their accents. Emma and Gary, for instance, self-consciously used their accents to assert their Englishness in various situations. However, others suggested that their accents were ingrained so deeply that they seemed natural. The fact that they found it hard to "do" an American accent reinforced their idea that their English accents were a natural part of them. Although one could say that they were simply poor actors, they drew a distinction between mimicry and habitual, everyday speech patterns, which suggests the depth at which accents operate for them. Imogen, who seemed skilled at moving among different accents during the interview, explained that while visiting a friend, she was introduced to a person who was "from the IRA. . . . He was . . . a major Irish person and the person I was staying with said, 'Just don't open your mouth. But if you have to, speak in an American accent.' I couldn't. I couldn't do it [*laughs*]. It wouldn't come out. But if I'm imitating someone, it comes out perfectly American." Apart from the Irish question here,[67] it is noteworthy that Imogen finds herself unable to change her accent in one situation but perfectly able to do so in another. The implication is that speaking in an American accent would mean putting on an act, which she is prepared to do within the frame of a joke[68] or as an exaggerated performance, but not within the frame of everyday life. Vera had a similar experience when a teacher in a speech-therapy class asked her to "speak American":

> I don't think I can do it, really, [but] I said, "Well, I can do it for you if you like." . . . I thought it was terribly put on, but apparently it worked out as being [OK]. . . . I suppose I speak French with a very good accent, [but] I would find it very difficult to speak with an American accent all the time.

Vera and Imogen each claim that they cannot "do" American accents, although they are both able to in other circumstances. This is similar to the fear that others, such as Lucinda, had of sounding "phony" if they used an American accent. Vera claimed that her attempts at an American accent sounded "put on," and Imogen said she could only "imitate" Americans. Compare this with Mike's assessment of friends from Central England who had moved south and "changed [their accents] like that [*snaps his fingers*]. . . . I always tend to mistrust their personalities as if there's something sort of weak within them." These quotations suggest that changed accents are somehow "false," as Nigel said, and that to modify one's speech would involve not being true to oneself. The implication is that if English people were to speak with American accents, they would lose part of their identity.

Thus, the heart of the matter is that accents symbolize much more to these English immigrants than just the way they speak. Tara and Rowena both spelled this out forcefully, Tara explained to Americans who teased her about her accent that "it's just the way I am. . . . I come with the accent." Her words, like Imogen's quoted earlier, imply that she is powerless to change her accent, but also that her accent is "the way [she is]." She sees her accent as immutable and natural, an aspect of herself that is deeply embedded. Rowena also conceptualized her accent as a part of herself. She said she did not want to change it, because "I don't want to try to be something that I'm not." Again, having an American accent would involve changing who she really is.

In using the idea that their accents are a core, almost natural, part of their selves, these speakers imply that the identities arising from their accents are biological essences. Indeed, Alex also explained her determination to keep her English accent by drawing on this idea: "Because, blow it,[69] that's me! And, no, I'm not going to lose it. . . . I was telling you . . . about that lady who's been here forty-six years, [and] it's as if she stepped off the plane today. . . . She said, 'I refuse [to adopt an American accent] because I'm British.' And that's me!" Not only does Alex consider her accent "me"; it is also what makes her British. However, Alex also suggests the agency she has regarding her accent. Her friend refused to adopt an American accent; Alex is also determined not to lose her accent, but clearly she plans to work toward this goal. Likewise, although Hugh believed that "the way I speak is who I am," he also talked about his determination to keep his accent in terms of what he did: "I like who I am and the way I do things." Both ultimately define their accents in terms of how they act and what they must do to keep them. Thus, the process of identity construction involves working, acting, practicing, and doing in order to define themselves as English. In defining identity in this way, we see its contradictory nature. These people feel that they must work to maintain something that they believe is already core to their being. Through their linguistic negotiations identity seems to be already constructed, yet it is also always in need of reconstruction.

The question also arises of what being a person with an English accent means to these people—what they think an English identity is. Their words suggest that their accent maintenance is due to more than aesthetics, to more than the privileges they garner, and to more than maintenance of group cohesion and self-esteem. They suggest that accent is a powerful indicator of the kind of person that they are.

5   White Mischief?

Doing Conceptual Work with
Empire, Race, and Gender

England's not the mythical land of madam george and roses
it's the home of police who kill black boys on mopeds
and I love my boy and that's why I'm leaving
I don't want him to be aware that there's
any such thing as grieving

> Sinéad O'Connor, *Black Boys on Mopeds*

IMAGINING IDENTITY

BENEDICT ANDERSON begins his book *Imagined Communities* with an excerpt from a Daniel Defoe poem, *The True-Born Englishman: A Satyr:*

> Thus from a Mixture of all kinds began,
> That Het'rogeneous Thing, *An Englishman:*
> In eager Rapes, and furious Lust begot,
> Betwixt a Painted *Britton* and a *Scot:*
> Whose gend'ring Offspring quickly learnt to bow,
> And yoke their Heifers to the *Roman* Plough:
> From whence a Mongrel half-bred Race there came,
> With neither Name nor Nation, Speech or Fame.
> In whose hot Veins now Mixtures quickly ran,
> Infus'd betwixt a *Saxon* and a *Dane.*
> While their Rank Daughters, to their Parents just,
> Receiv'd all Nations with Promiscuous Lust.
> This Nauseous Brood directly did contain
> The well-extracted Blood of *Englishmen.*[1]

The satire is well chosen, reflecting as it does some of the peoples who make up what we now think of as "the English." Although there are many more groups of people who should be added to this list of the ancestors of English people, the myth predominates that the English are a race unto themselves, and that the "nation" of England is a

141

homogeneous grouping, with all English people descended from the same (white) stock. Anderson argues that nations are like individuals in that when we come to write their biographies, we seek to situate what they are like *now* in the context of what they were like *then*.[2]

The narration of the "life story" of nations usually emphasizes continuity with the past by the use of selective memories, motivated forgettings, invented "traditions," and the treatment of myths as reality.[3] Weaving a symbolic thread from the past to the present is an attempt to create a coherent narrative that makes political and cultural sense. As Defoe's poem shows, the numerous groups of people who conquered and colonized parts of England—such as the Vikings, the Romans, and the Normans—are often conveniently "forgotten."[4] By also ignoring the English descendants of immigrants from Africa, the Caribbean, and the Indian Subcontinent, the collective memory of a purely white "English England" can become a reality in people's minds. The construction of myths such as these is politically motivated: Cultural and political elites have a vested interest in conceptualizing modern versions of English identity as if they have always been that way. The selective use of the past to inform the present creates hegemonic images of what England is (and apparently has always been) like.

Anderson (1983: 22) uses the term "imagined communities" to describe nations as groupings of people who have never met, but who imagine a common history and a comradeship with everyone else in their community. With the help of invented traditions and politically motivated images, individuals imagine a basic similarity among group members, believing that their community is homogeneous and that they all imagine it in the same way.[5] Despite the heterogeneity of most communities, collective identities are often represented and defined as if each individual who holds that identity is absolutely the same, or believes in the same ideals as her or his fellow identity holder. The definition of the identity becomes hegemonic because it requires the exercise of power (and sometimes force) to make it stick, and also because it must have people's "active consent" (Hall 1986: 19). Although consent is rarely complete under hegemony,[6] it can be hard to challenge a hegemonic outlook when one's imagination has been constrained. Indeed, hegemony works to legitimate the ideas of dominant groups in the public discourse.[7]

In the case of Englishness or other national identities, hegemonic conceptions can come from many sources: from the government and the

laws it puts into practice (for instance, immigration and nationality legislation that makes it harder for Africans, Asians, and West Indians to
become citizens[8]), from the media (especially advertisements, newspapers, films and television programs, political satirists and cartoonists),
and from groups as diverse as novelists, the clergy, business people, and
sports personalities. All have the potential to create new images or to
draw upon historical images of Englishness, perhaps updating them in
some novel way—as did the cartoonist who depicted Margaret Thatcher
dressed as Britannia[9] during the Falklands/Malvinas[10] conflict—but
using their power to define or redefine Englishness for the rest of us.
The images and definitions, however, are usually white: John Bull
dressed in his Union Jack hat; Britannia with her shield and helmet; the
businessman in a bowler hat with his "brolly"; Diana, Princess of Wales,
adorning magazine covers; a football hooligan shouting racist and xenophobic abuse at other fans.[11] People come to accept these images as representations of England and Englishness, or even as "stor[ies] they tell
themselves about themselves" (Geertz 1973: 448).

But do people really believe those stories? My analyses in this and the
next chapter show that the people I interviewed understand and respond
to these hegemonic ideas of Englishness in different ways. Sometimes
they accept them, and sometimes they do not; sometimes they will act
on them, and sometimes they will not. They may struggle to modify or
challenge dominant conceptualizations or unthinkingly acquiesce in
them. As they define Englishness, their imaginings "are structured in
ways that admit certain possibilities and not others" (Connell 1995: 65).
Their active engagement with hegemonic understandings of the social
world "convert[s] initial situations into new situations [and] makes the
reality we live in" (Connell 1995: 65). This is the conceptual work that
they do to (re)produce particular versions of Englishness.

One of the benefits of examining peoples' reactions to hegemonic
versions of Englishness is that we see the potential for structures and
ideologies to be challenged and changed along with the moments in
which there is active consent. Even though these imaginings may be
unconscious or unintentional, they are a form of conceptual identity
work, a way that national identity emerges from the activity of individuals on an everyday basis.[12] In focusing on the ways they create
meaning using images of England, I show what they imagine English
identity to be.

RESPONDING TO THE IMPERIAL LEGACY

In 1997, Britain finally handed Hong Kong back to China. For some, this transition represented the end of an era, the end of the British Empire. However, scholars have noted for some time the declining significance of Britain in the world political economy. Britain watched the erosion of its status as a world power as its former colonies threw off the yoke of imperialism. It has been beset by internal crises, such as skyrocketing unemployment in the 1980s, the 1984 miners' strike, and the widening economic divisions between the North and the South. Welsh, Scottish, and Irish nationalisms have continued to grow, and Britain has alarmed its European partners by dithering about the extent of its involvement in the European Union. Despite Thatcher's assertion that "the lesson of the Falklands is that Britain has not changed" (quoted in Chambers 1993: 45), Britain clearly has changed—as shown not least in the election of "New Labour" in 1997. The end of imperialism, however, does not necessarily mean the end of an imperial mind set, as Thatcher's words illustrate.[13]

Thatcher was probably not thinking about race relations when she claimed that Britain had not changed. However, the Falklands/Malvinas conflict did raise important issues about the relationship among race, nation, and imperialism. As Conservative commentators used race to decide who belonged in the nation, they implied that white Falklanders did but that "West Indian or Asian immigrants [to Britain] living next door" did not (Worsthorne, quoted in Gilroy 1992 [1987]: 52). Paul Gilroy's[14] analysis of this and similar modes of thought, suggests how whiteness and imperialism go hand in hand to construct a homogeneous white national "we." As I suggested in Chapter 1, European imperialism encouraged the formation of white identities based on the idea of the "other," so that white European colonizers could define themselves as different from, and superior to, colonized others.[15] White middle- and upper-class men constructed themselves as the standard by comparing themselves to who they were not—black people, women, and the poor or working class.[16] Imperialism was also predicated on the power of men over women: While white women served as wives, missionaries, and workers, white men "made and enforced laws and policies in their own interests" (McClintock 1995: 6). White women did, however, have some power over colonized women and men. They were also seen as responsible for protecting traditions and producing future imperialists, making them "ambiguously complicit" in the colonizing process (McClintock 1995: 6; Ware 1992). The guiding forces justifying the treatment of the colonized, however, were paternalism and racism, combined with the demands of capitalism.[17]

The imperial mind-set, with its racialized and gendered underpinnings, is still evident today. Immigration and nationality legislation, for instance, has functioned to exclude from British citizenship black people from former colonies and to define married women as dependent on their husbands.[18] Thus, the 1971 Immigration Act excluded nonpatrials, who were mainly from the West Indies, Africa, and the Indian Subcontinent, but included patrials, mainly whites from Canada and Australia.[19] The 1981 British Nationality Act consolidated this by abolishing most of the remaining categories under which colonized or formerly colonized people could become British citizens, although white Falkland Islanders were classified as British citizens.[20] In addition, the 1971 act allowed male patrials to pass citizenship to their wives but not vice versa.[21] Although women were finally given the right in 1981 to transmit British citizenship to their children—even those born abroad— much of the legislation still does not treat men and women, especially black women, equally.[22] Although nations are often imagined as female,[23] the paradigmatic citizen often has been assumed to be a man,[24] a situation exacerbated by the assumption that women's primary sphere of influence should be as wives and mothers rather than as full citizens.[25] Thus, nationalism, racism, and sexism have all been vital in defining some categories of people as less than true citizens.

CRITICIZING ENGLISH ARROGANCE

In light of these interconnections among race, gender, and imperialism, it is noteworthy that the people I talked to did not usually conceptualize the "imperial hangover" (as Gary quipped) in terms of their racial identities. As white English people, they found their racial identities fairly unproblematic. Only occasionally did they make implicit connections among race, nation, and imperialism. Sometimes, however, they did define imperialism in gendered terms in their choices of metaphors and examples. The imperial legacy usually emerged when I asked what it meant to them to be English; how they defined English culture or summed up England; when they were aware of being English; what they disliked about being English; or, in some cases, whether they felt proud to be English. In other words, imperialism and the post-imperial condition were important components of their imaginings of England. I suggest some of the ways these people responded to the ideas, ideologies, and narratives about imperialism that surround them, doing conceptual work to imagine their national identities. This is similar to Frankenberg's notion of "discursive repertoires." As Frankenberg (1993: 16) explains, " 'repertoire' captures . . . something of the way in which strategies for thinking through race [are] learned, drawn upon, and enacted, repetitively but not automatically or by rote, chosen but by no means freely so". Thus, in analyzing their responses to the imperial legacy, we can examine how they defined their national identities, drawing on or rejecting hegemonic discourses.

Quentin summed up the attitude many of the interviewees had about the imperial legacy by saying that England has "an arrogance that stems from some previous glory days which are long gone. [It is an] ex-colonial power . . . sitting on its laurels that have long faded, gradually waking up to the fact that . . . to get ahead, to compete in the world, there needs to be . . . a loss of arrogance." This focus among many of the interviewees on England's arrogance, which is incompatible with its current position in the world, may stem from their move to another country. Once they leave England, their contempt for England's size and what they see as its inflated self-importance may grow. After all, they now live in a country much larger than England that sees itself as the primary global power. Some even ridiculed the "special relationship" between Britain and America that British politicians have held so dear. (Ian argued that the U.S. saw the smaller country simply as an "air base" for military maneuvers in the Middle East.) Others echoed the disdainful attitude toward a declining England, stressing its size and its ranking in the gross-domestic-product ratings, which showed it lagging behind Italy as a "fiftieth-rate power."[26] Ian said, "England is not nearly as significant as it thinks it is. . . . It's a stupid little country that doesn't realize its position in the world, which is somewhere between Greece and Italy." Emily, too, argued that England "thinks a great deal of itself. . . . It's hard for people to give up on that power." These people distanced themselves from the post-imperial legacy by criticizing England for failing to recognize or come to terms with its declining power. England has shrunk in importance in their minds, and they see its superiority complex on the world stage as rather ridiculous. The contrast between their admiration for English culture, expressed in this and other chapters, and their disgust at England's inflated self-image is stark. Their disdain suggests an "imperially cognizant"[27] discursive repertoire, one that recognizes and decries the self-important "imperial hangover" from bygone days.

The people I spoke to drew a distinction between English institutions and government and English culture, showing what they felt comfortable criticizing about England and what they did not. Some had been disdainful of English post-imperial arrogance even before they left, especially as it was embodied by the Conservative Party.[28] Quentin explicitly noted his need to turn his back on the superiority complex he associated with England, and Piers said he decided to go abroad after finishing public (private) school in order to knock off his xenophobic "Rule Britannia and fuck the rest of the world" edges. Harry and Gary both said they had left the country because of the Conservative government's policies, and Ian blamed Thatcher directly for the "real fucking poverty" that accompanied the decline of northern England's industrial base in the 1980s amid the "mindless vitriol that came out of the Tory Party." He also lambasted the Conservatives in the 1990s for speaking "as if it were the Edwardian days when the empire was still there." Brad, who described himself as a "European," was also incensed by the antics of the Little Englanders within the Conservative Party. Gary, in discussing what he saw as the English inability to "accept that foreigners may be better at something than they are or may even be in a position to tell them what to do," criticized English institutions rather than English people per se:

> The English don't have [the] capacity [to learn from other countries]. But I'm speaking generally, you know, in terms of nationality, not in terms of English people, 'cause I know so many English people who aren't like that at all. British *institutions* are reluctant to learn from other countries—that's what I'm getting at.

As they criticized England, then, they usually imagined some grouping of the power elite rather than ordinary English people or English culture. This separation enabled interviewees to reconcile the pride in English culture that they expressed at other moments and maintain a positive form of national identity.[29] Thus, the men quoted here could wax lyrical about English beer but maintain their distance from the xenophobic mind-sets of English elites.

CONSCIOUSNESS, GUILT, AND SHAME

This first set of people constructed discursive repertoires that criticized hegemonic versions of Englishness. A second set went beyond this critique and spontaneously asserted feelings of shame or guilt about Britain's imperialist past (and present). As Frankenberg (1993: 174–82) suggests in the case of her interviewees who drew on "race cognizant" discourses, shame and guilt can be limiting, but they can also be constructive.[30] In Frankenberg's study, the women who moved beyond feeling guilty about their complicity in racial structures were able to do meaningful anti-racist work. Following the work of scholars who have examined racism among white feminists, I suggest that it is important for white people to locate themselves as beneficiaries of structures of oppression in order to understand the experiences of those who do not benefit.[31] Although Richard Rorty suggests that guilt is useless for white liberals because it can become immobilizing,[32] it does have its functions. For instance, it may indicate to an individual that something is wrong with the narratives she or he has been taught.[33] The interviewees expressed feelings of guilt and shame in different ways. Some internalized the guilt, embracing it as their own, while others used it to distance themselves from England and Englishness.

Mike, who belonged to the former group, argued that because "we fucked the world up in the nineteenth century, [it is] difficult to gain any sort of moral high ground being English." This points to his own sense of responsibility and shame about England's past. Imogen and Frances also described their feelings of shame when confronted with the results of colonialism in the Caribbean and Africa. Both women characterized these as moments in which they experienced their English identities very strongly. Frances spoke of a specific experience imbued with the imperial legacy that occurred when she lived on a Caribbean island. She described the island as "like a little colony" and said that she first became aware of her Englishness when she moved there. She had rented a small apartment beneath a house owned by a black couple and was astounded to learn from them that, in the 1960s, "they couldn't go to the cinema or be out on [the] street after a certain hour because they were black. . . . You think, well, what undercurrents of resentment there still must be amongst people who had actually suffered that." It is noteworthy that Frances had to leave England to gain some understanding of the history of racial discrimination. Although she noted this as a time when she felt very English, it may also have been easier for her to understand institutionalized racism because she could see it as "foreign" in a way that she would not have been able to in England. Imogen said she had had a similar experience while traveling in Africa: She was embarrassed "by our colonial past. . . . I felt this urge to say 'I'm sorry' when they [told] us about the terrible things that had happened in the past." Both women were confronted with the legacies of the empire in such a way that they felt both responsible and apologetic. In some ways, as Frankenberg points out, this can be quite a limiting response to the history of imperialism and racism. Taking responsibility for something that you yourself did not do "generates backlash, because people don't know why they have to hate themselves, they don't remember doing anything horrendous in their lives" (as Cathy Thomas, one of Frankenberg's interviewees, explained [1993: 174]). The danger is that internalizing this shame and embarrassment can lead to individual guilt, which can become immobilizing and self-defeating.[34] However, at the same time, it is noteworthy that both women recognized their nation's role in the horrors of colonialism.

Members of the second group were more likely than members of the first group to externalize guilt and shame. A representative of the second group, Diana, expressed shame about England's past and present actions in the world arena when I asked her whether she was proud of being English:

> I don't know what there is to be proud of in a country that went out and conquered the world and introduced slavery to a lot of places [and] still has its troops in Northern Ireland, [that] won't take America's advice on Northern Ireland, but gives its advice on everybody else's problems. . . . I think Britain is absolutely appalling to keep a facade of good manners concealing that total oppression and everything in the past.

In Diana's forthright condemnation of Britain's role in slavery and of its policies in Ireland, we see her unswerving desire to distance herself from Britain's past. She was also critical that this past had been masked by a veneer of good manners, denouncing these manners as two-faced.

Her outrage became more specific in the next sentence, as she pointed to the class and gender discrimination inherent in "men's clubs," which were "signs of one person getting it over another person," and in the monarchy, "which was incredibly corrupt and horrible, and symbolized somebody making themselves exclusive." Diana was happy to point her finger at specific groups of people for being exclusionary, but she kept herself distant from those she accused, who at one point were explicitly men (and implicitly upper-class and white; presumably other men would not have been invited to join "men's clubs"). She also criticized the tendency to gloss over the effects of imperialism, implying that it would be better for people to take responsibility for the oppression, corruption, and exclusivity.

Harry also wanted to distance him from England because of its imperial legacy:

> [I don't] think of England as a cool country to belong to, personally. . . . I think of its imperial past and . . . its treatment of Ireland, and if I was going to take pride in a nation, that wouldn't be the one I would pick. It's not really one I would . . . stand up and shout, "Hey, I'm English!" because it's a sort of embarrassment sometimes.

Throughout the interview, Harry returned to this theme—that he wished he could avoid being English. Indeed, as I show in Chapter 6, he expressed a desire to be Irish.[35] In this excerpt, he wanted to deny feelings of national pride that arose from being English because of its problematic history. Like Diana, he used historical abuses to justify his sense of shame about being English. Unlike those who felt the need to say "sorry," Harry tried to split himself off from England, externalizing his sense of shame and guilt. Interviewees such as Diana and Harry seem to want to expose the "total oppression" in English history by refusing to be proud and by discussing Ireland, where the negative results of imperialism are still obvious. In so doing they imply that English people need to be open and critical about the past.

Others addressed this theme by pointing to the ways in which adverse consequences of imperialism were glossed over. Gordon noted that England had faced few consequences of "the negative effects on other cultures of imperialism," expressing disbelief at how "former colonial countries overthrew British rule, but then . . . happily subscribe[d] to the Commonwealth." And although he said he was proud of the way the empire had been "wound down" ("with obvious and horrible exceptions, like Cyprus and Malaya and Kenya"), Ken also admitted that he was embarrassed by the Commonwealth, "a club that doesn't have any point." Frank criticized a television program he had seen in which Dr. Livingston's grandson retraced his forebear's journey in Africa, "behaving like the colonial gent." Ken also mentioned the "upset and chaos [caused by] the ludicrous European race to grab all of Africa" and the bloody wars precipitated by calls for independence.

As these people reflect on the impact of imperialism on their national identities, the shame, guilt, and critical knowledge that they express show that they are not forgetting the imperial legacy. Bearing in mind that successful nationalism requires motivated forgettings and selected rememberings,[36] this is an important counterweight to hegemonic imaginings of England. Indeed, these people might even be able to use their feelings of guilt to imagine a new version of Englishness, a version that does not erase the experiences of people colonized by the English. Frances and Imogen, for instance, may be more able to see themselves as beneficiaries of institutionalized racism. By expressing feelings of shame, guilt, and even anger about being English, these people work to critique Englishness as they experience it. Their attempts to make Englishness live up to their ideals are forms of conceptual work as they try to create new ways to be English. It is noteworthy, however, that few of the people I talked to mentioned race in the context of imperialism.

"ALWAYS LOOK ON THE BRIGHT SIDE . . ."[37]

Others were more muted in their critiques of the British Empire and its legacy, using definitions of Englishness that were more in keeping with hegemonic discourses in their paternalism toward former colonies. Their strategy can be seen as similar to the "color-evasive or power-evasive discursive repertoire" upon which Frankenberg's (1993: 139) white interviewees drew to talk about race. In her study, the users of this discourse thought in assimilationist ways that tended to ignore racial differences, arguing that everyone has the same opportunities, and thus blaming individuals if they failed to achieve their goals.[38] Translating this to my own interviews and to questions of imperialism, a power-evasive discourse became evident when my respondents avoided addressing the dynamics of power and the oppressive and discriminatory practices that are part of imperialism. Instead, they looked on the bright side. Not all of those I quote in this section drew wholeheartedly on this discourse. As with Frankenberg's respondents, they tended to move in and out of different discourses during each interview. Thus, although Craig said he felt positive about the imperial spirit in England during the Falklands/Malvinas conflict, he also saw problems with it. He reminisced about this time as a moment in which he felt that the left and right had come together, and "there was a national patriotism [or] national identity ... harking back to the [days of the] empire. I guess. ... 'No one's gonna mess with us.' Maybe that's a good thing about it ending, though." His final comment, said laughingly, shows the ambivalence he felt about the imperial mind-set, however. On the one hand, he felt good about the national unity in what he perceived as a time of crisis, but on the other, saying, "No one's gonna mess with us," reminds him that harking back to the empire can stir up chauvinism and xenophobia (especially as his next sentence contained a critique of extremist politics). Although Craig was somewhat nostalgic for the days of the empire, as he imagined England he quickly noted that costs were associated with an attitude that put patriotism before everything else, suggesting that he was at least somewhat cognizant of the negative aspects of imperialism.

Others used the power-evasive strategy more comprehensively as a way to deny completely the realities of the empire and its legacy, combining it with a paternalism that drew on the idea that the colonizers knew what was best for the colonies.[39] Quentin, for instance, worked with many Indians and found himself defending the empire to them:

> They tend to be the ones, at my age at least, [who] go on about how India's still suffering from British colonization. So we just get launched into, "Yeah, look at what Britain gave you in terms of the civil service, roads, education, blah, blah." It sounds like a Monty Python sketch from *Life of Brian*, but that's when I'm most defending Britain.

Quentin, who traveled extensively for his job with an international organization, refuses to accept that India's current situation may have something to do with the effects of British imperialism. Not only will he not admit any responsibility on behalf of Britain for the post-colonial situation, but he also actively defends colonization in a paternalistic move. Indeed, he attempts to inject humor into his account of these interactions by referring to the scene in the movie *Life of Brian* in which a Roman soldier details all the benefits to Judea of the Roman Empire. This reference is obviously an attempt to lighten the mood, but it also implies that Quentin is not taking the complaint seriously. It is a power-evasive move. Like the Roman soldier, Quentin can see only the positive outcomes of the process of colonization, arguing that India would not have modernized without Britain's influence. His unwillingness to give credence to his colleagues' complaints bolsters his own sense of pride in the imperial legacy, pride that may translate to his feelings about his identity as English.

Some interviewees showed a rather skewed understanding of events. Gordon, for example, argued that

> the wars [of independence] weren't particularly bloody. It was basically an administrative change in power. . . . It was very peaceful. In India, the only violence was after Britain left. . . . The logic of empire must have played itself out completely in that there was nothing else to do but to withdraw and return sovereignty to its rightful hands.

In this comment, Gordon denies that Britain played any role in precipitating the violence engendered by imperialism. He seems to be claiming that the British withdrew willingly once "the logic of empire [had] played itself out," rather than recognizing the tenacity with which Britain held on to its colonies. Although none of the interviewees had any claim to expertise on the legacy of imperialism, the narratives that they used to justify Britain's role in colonization are interesting because they point to the ways that people may have been taught to evade power differences. For Gordon to argue that the violence in India occurred only after Britain had left probably means that, like Quentin, he had heard only positive things about the empire. Nigel also drew on what he had learned about the empire as a boy, when "half the world was pink" (that is, marked on the map in pink to show colonization by Britain). When he was a child, he argued, "in a lot of countries they were still living in mud huts . . . and they still are, so what's gone wrong?" Here Nigel describes former colonies in terms that suggest he thinks they were and are uncivilized and primitive. The term "mud huts" conjures up the racist imagery used to justify colonialism,[40] and Nigel paternalistically implies that Britain should have done a better job of civilizing the inhabitants of these huts. His power-evasive discourse treats former colonies as essentially different from Britain, and implicit in this is the idea that they were (or are) inferior.

Those who drew on the discursive repertoire of power-evasion saw the empire as essentially benign, "civilizing" the colonies to bring them peace and prosperity. The men I have quoted in this section also assessed the imperial legacy using extremely paternalistic discourses. In so doing, they drew on the hegemonic narrative of Britain's role in conquest and colonization. They ignored the ways in which colonial exploitation contributed to Britain's prosperity, the decimation of colonized peoples, the introduction of slavery, and the political and economic repercussions of divide-and-conquer policies that still exist today, as former colonies depend on the so-called First World for economic survival. In other words, when the interviewees drew on the power-evasive discourse, they constructed their national identities as essentially benign and innocent,[41] advocating that former colonies "look on the bright side" of imperialism.

CULTURAL RESPONSES TO IMPERIALISM

Another set of respondents extended these feelings of pride in the imperial legacy by pointing to the ways in which imperialism had disseminated English culture across the globe. While they drew on a cultural-discursive repertoire to take pride in English culture, they often used a power-evasive discourse, as well. Several mentioned how easily they interacted with people from the Caribbean or India who had been educated in the "British system of education." Indeed, when I asked William what made someone English, he cited an Indian colleague who had been educated in India to illustrate his reply: "You've got to be educated there. You have to have spent some part of your formative years there. There are some mannerisms, ways of pronouncing words, aspirations, background, the way people project themselves which is characteristic of being English." By "there," he seems to mean England, and yet in so saying, he extends Englishness to his Indian colleague, implying that India is still part of the British Empire. He believes he and his colleague have a "common heritage [as a result of] our education in Britain [and] in India, which was implemented from a similar point of view." However, he is also using his cultural pride in the imperial legacy to expand his definition of Englishness. Likewise, Mike cited the Marxist social critic and sports writer C.L.R. James to help him define Englishness: "Here is a Trinidadian. He's coming to England and really becoming—

or, at least, some part of him [is]—getting involved with class struggle and with English cricket, and becoming an Englishman in a sense in that way." For Mike, being English means "being able to appreciate and enjoy a whole network of social and cultural forms," which include cricket and the class system. This involves expanding his definition (as William did) to include anyone who appreciates English culture. In contrast to those designing immigration and nationality laws, William and Mike imply that anyone who appreciates the "joys" of Englishness— whatever his or her race or national background—should be defined as English. The cultural repertoire thus had radically revisionist potential for hegemonic discourses.

Some interviewees found focusing on culture in their discussions of empire very enjoyable, because it let them reminisce about the English cultural forms they loved while feeling positive about the legacy of colonialism. For the men quoted in this section, sports emerged as an important by-product of imperialism. Mike argued that "the one good thing that came out of the British Empire was the fact that we . . . invented and exported a certain type of team sport, which has now become very interesting and exciting to me—soccer, . . . rugby and cricket." Yet turning cultural imperialism into a positive aspect of English culture evades the consideration of issues of power and inequality in imperialism. Instead, Mike compared the international nature of the sports he enjoyed with the insularity of American sports. In the U.S., as English people like to point out, the "world" often seems to mean only North America.[42] Mike was incensed by some of his American friends' response to seeing a rugby scrum on television, because he felt it showed American culture at its most insular.[43] In this part of the interview, he stood up and waved his arms around, shouting in disbelief, to mimic the Americans, "*'Look at them! Look at that! Look at that! Oh!'* They will be absolutely flabbergasted, and they will say, . . . 'What is this? What is going on here? There must be more efficient ways of moving the ball around!'"

Mike uses Americans' cultural insularity to provide a contrast with the internationalism of English sports and culture. Ironically, in doing this he points to American cultural imperialism: "We, the rest of the world, know a lot more about America than they know about us." This could also be said for the English, whose export of cultural forms ensured that they did not have to take indigenous cultural forms seriously. In fact, the one thing that made Harry proud to be English was that England, or Britain particularly, gave the rest of the word soccer, . . . cricket and rugby. . . . Wherever they went, they set up their little boys' clubs and played their little games. I think [it] has done great things for England. That's why . . . there's still some warmth retained for English imperialism. . . . Wherever you read about soccer clubs, whether it's Buenos Aires [or Athletico Madrid], they'll say this club [was] founded in 1912 by a Welshman and a Scotsman . . . or something.

Both men locate the internationalization of sports as the most positive part of the British imperial legacy. Although this may be true, focusing on culture enables them to feel good about the aftermath of imperialism. Harry even points to the "warmth retained for English imperialism" (despite the fact that he uses "a Welshman and a Scotsman" as his examples).

However, I also saw some self-consciousness about this strategy. Both Harry and Mike pointed to the gendered nature of their responses in focusing on sports. Mike said, "I'm sounding like a man here, maybe," and Harry laughed at how "male" his answer sounded. It is perhaps not surprising that men spent more time extolling the joys of these sports than did women (although women were as likely as men to mention football hooliganism[44] as a negative trait associated with Englishness). However, it does point to the ways discourses about the legacy of imperialism can still be male-defined. That Harry thought of the colonialists setting up "boys' [sports] clubs" is no accident. Interest in football, rugby, and cricket in England focuses almost exclusively on the men's game. Spectators are usually men, although more women are becoming fans of football in particular, and the ethos of the games tends to draw on the qualities associated with hegemonic definitions of masculinity: competitiveness, aggression, physical strength, and skill (not to mention high salaries). Indeed, Michael Billig[45] argues that sports function as a peacetime form of war with which men can identify. These men, then, view the cultural benefits of imperialism through a lens of masculinity, thereby implicitly pointing to the dominant role of men in the colonizing process.[46]

Harry, however, also showed awareness of the traumas that underlie sports. In explaining his belief that the spirit of sports can heal wounds, he pointed to the Christmas Day soccer match during World War I[47] and to the World Cup, arguing that the camaraderie of sports "has the potential to soothe sores and to make everybody feel that they're equal because they're at the World Cup. . . . And it also provides an acceptable funnel for nationalist xenophobia, the way it allows you to feel proud . . . without having to . . . fight anyone." Harry's sentiments are noteworthy because they are underpinned with an understanding of tension among different nations, that there may be "sores" that need soothing as a result of British imperialism, and that nations may not feel "equal" at other times. Also, he is aware of xenophobia among people of different nations, for which soccer provides an outlet, he believes. So he focuses on sports to gloss over the negative aspects of the empire while paying attention to the hurt and ill-feeling that the empire has left behind. The "acceptable" face of xenophobia came through in his interview, too. Despite his avowed hatred of nationalism, he joked about "devious . . . Johnny Foreigner" using footwork and tactics different from those used by English soccer players and admitted that he could be "really racist" when England was playing in the World Cup.[48] Although sports obviously have the "potential to soothe sores," they can also rile up nationalist sentiment (as English newspaper headlines before England–Germany soccer games show[49]). By conceiving of sporting events as a "safe" place to experience racism and xenophobia, Harry evades the results of these emotions. As the relationship among soccer hooliganism, racism, and far–right-wing groups in England shows, the "nationalist xenophobia" that emerges is not safe for everyone.[50] Relishing the cultural aspects of imperialism runs the risk of glossing over the experience of imperialism itself. To quote Frank, "I don't think England gets enough credit. I know they've milked . . . all the countries and their wealth . . . , but they did a lot of good. They spread a lot of civilization, [like] traditions, . . . cricket, [and] literature." Again England emerges as the superior civilizing force—a repetition of the "look on the bright side" attitude.

"You've Got to Have a Sense of Humor About It"

Another power-evasive strategy, which Quentin used earlier, is to make a joke out of the post-imperial moment. Alex used this strategy, too, pointing out that it is impossible to take Englishness seriously because "if you're in a society that ruled the world and then lost empire and the lot, [then] you've got to have a sense of humor [about it]." She contrasted this with Americanness, which she thought must be a "serious business," citing the questions for aliens on U.S. immigration forms:

> "Are you intending to set up a prostitution racket?" Or "Are you intending to smuggle firearms and narcotics?" . . . You have to fill in a form and tick that, and I think any country which seriously exposes themselves [*sic*] to daily ridicule with that form really is beyond belief. That just makes me howl with laughter.

She is amused by the idea that the questioners would seriously expect smugglers and pimps to admit to their intentions.[51] By comparison, Alex imagines the English as a group whose past disappointments and defeats have created a setting for sarcasm and cynicism and a willingness not to take themselves too seriously—certainly not as seriously as Americans, who she believes do not share her irreverent sense of humor. Yet a serious note underlies this humor, which comes through when Alex jokes about interacting with U.S. immigration officials. With her head held high, and using a fake upper-class English accent, she answers their questions rather officiously, laughing to herself and thinking, "This is the voice of the British Empire. We didn't go off to conquer foreign climes [to then] succumb to idiots like you." Here her attempts to mock American officialdom result from a sense of superiority, which is buttressed by her sense that Britain was once a great conquering nation. She seems to imagine herself as a lone representative of the British Empire, refusing to give in to the petty demands of people she considers beneath her (although this is all framed in terms of a joke). Yet she is using her assumption of power to boost her own morale, an assumption that draws on an essentialist discourse that the members of the former British Empire are much better people than lowly American officials. Her playfulness with her national identity enables her to make fairly xenophobic assumptions, all the while laughing at herself for her pretensions.

Alex was also very willing to laugh at England. She and Mike were both amused by the idea that English people (particularly men, they implied) are thin, ineffectual, weedy, and uncomfortable in positions of authority, and both contrasted this with what they saw as the aggressive masculinity of American authority figures. Alex explained:

> I find you arrive at London airport and you think, "Well, I know I'm [in England] because there's this staff milling around [and] they've got this

weasely look about them." You're not really sure what they are doing. Airport officials [in America] are all this sort of "aggression, aggressive uniforms, and crew cuts and walkie-talkies" *(in a deep voice)*. You know you're back in New York, whereas in London there's all these slightly seedy looking individuals. It's so funny, these cartoon impressions of the United States and Britain.

She emphasizes the Americans' masculinity by putting on the deep voice, and she obviously finds the stereotypical images she has drawn of the two countries very amusing.

In contrast to the masculine images of the U.S., several of the men I talked to stressed a more feminized version of Englishness. Gordon highlighted the feminine aspects of English working-class culture, arguing that women held the communities together even though they lacked power at institutional levels. He also said he could identify English tourists in the U.S. by their clothes and the fact that the men were "unmasculine" and "relaxed with their body movements" as they walked. (Here he sloped his shoulders down and around to show me what he meant.) Both Gordon and Craig self-identified as unmasculine men, the latter by talking about weeping when his insecurities got the better of him. And although Gary's American wife found England too sexist, he said he knew a lot of "strong English women" and "a lot of English men who are not strong or . . . fine, who Britain has treated . . . very badly." (His reference was to high rates of male unemployment in England in the 1980s.) These men's responses show that gender is a more complex phenomenon than simple binary differences between women and men. They acknowledge the role of women in English society, but they also suggest that men do not have a monopoly on strength and power. Gordon, in particular, identifies Englishness with femininity, refusing to see national identity only in stereotypical male ways.

Mike continued the point, stressing in a very ironic way the macho nature of the police in the U.S. (exacerbated for him by their carrying guns[52]), saying that they look like white fascists. He said that he is reminded that he is not in England

when[ever] I see policemen with guns, . . . in fact when I see policemen in particular, 'cause they always look like they're members of the Third Reich, [where I live] anyway. They're not these sort of thin, ineffectual-looking British bobbies who are absolutely no use. They're big . . . , blond white people with guns and big muscles.

Mike is more explicit about using white images here and stresses the fascist connotations of the guns, uniforms, and muscles of American policemen. Both Mike and Alex, then, contrast English officials with their larger, seemingly more efficient, and certainly more aggressive American counterparts, in what is perhaps a metaphor for the idea of a small and weak post-imperial England compared with their idea of the U.S. as a huge, violent world power. In examining the playful nature of Alex and Mike's ideas about the ineffectual nature of English authority figures, we have come full circle, returning to the image that the interviewees had of a declining and rather pathetic England.

A MASCULINE STORY?

The people I talked to provided insights into the ways in which gender works with the imperial legacy in their imaginings of England. As they discussed the empire, they used gendered language. Diana, for instance, expressed disgust with "men's clubs," which symbolized "one person getting it over another person." Relating this to imperialism, she implicitly drew links among privileged echelons of masculinity, exclusion, and oppression. In contrast, as Quentin and Nigel talked about the "civilizing" benefits of the empire, they used the very discourse that Diana critiqued—that of a paternalism in which they took pride, or the idea, as Frank said, that imperialism "did a lot of good." Harry and Mike also responded in gendered terms to imperial culture, stressing football, cricket, and rugby—all, until recently, games with predominantly male players and fans—as the legacy that gave the English a "reputation [as] nice . . . gentlemen" with "courtesy and manners," as Harry suggested. Ironically, the narrative becomes more complicated here, as Harry balances his feelings that football is fundamentally positive with the overwhelming negativity of nationalism and hooliganism (again, mostly among men) that football can engender.

The story of imperialism told by these interviewees, then, is a story dominated by masculinity—that is, until we revisit the comparisons of England and the U.S. with which I started and ended the chapter. The criticisms of English arrogance—that it is "pathetic," that it has "crawled into a small shell and said 'don't disturb me,'" or that it is "like the swan, . . . paddl[ing] like shit under water, [but] appear[ing] to be moving gracefully along,"[53]—all suggest a smaller, weaker, emasculated version of Englishness than the paternalistic colonizing force described earlier. Combining these critiques with Mike's and Alex's stories about "seedy" and "ineffectual" officials in England, compared with American police ("big, blond white people with guns and muscles"), we can see how gendered images play a part in the assessment of the post-imperial moment. When these interviews were conducted in the mid-1990s, England seemed weak and feeble to the interviewees.[54] The question arises, however, as to whether painting England in these terms of decline functioned as an excuse. To see England as a tiny nation, pathetic in its demise, is perhaps to see its "imperial hangover" as nothing more than a bad headache—certainly not as a country with a history that has "fucked the rest of the world up," as Mike so eloquently put it.

CONCLUSION: RESPONDING WITH DISGUST OR PRIDE?

I have focused here on how these English people responded to the legacy of imperialism. I started and ended by examining the contempt that some interviewees felt for England in the post-imperial moment, pointing out that the imperial legacy found its way into their national identities via a strong distaste for elite or hegemonic discourses that attempted to resuscitate imperial pretensions. Another group expressed shame about England's past—some internalizing their guilt in a potentially damaging way, while others externalized the shame, arguing for a strategy of critical openness about the past. In criticizing the hegemonic definitions of Englishness, these people all did conceptual work as they attempted to imagine a new kind of Englishness that would not be complicit in the exploitation and oppression of others.

I then moved on to examine the discursive repertoires of those who used power-evasive techniques to think about the empire. These people have learned to think of Englishness in ways that avoid issues of power, domination, and inequality. They constructed the imperial project as benign, using definitions of Englishness that coincided with hegemonic versions. This generally resulted in feelings of pride about being English rather than a desire to distance themselves from England.

Another group focused more explicitly on the cultural legacy of imperialism, and their words helped to highlight the gendered nature of the imperial project, especially as it related to sports. They also expressed pride in this legacy and sometimes used a power-evasive discourse.

However, there were also moments in which the radical potential of the use of culture emerged: As they bonded with people from former colonies, they expanded their definitions of Englishness to include these people, in direct contrast to official immigration and nationality legislation. In addition, those who focused on culture sometimes looked below the surface of their narratives to see how culture could gloss over negative effects of imperialism. In light of the literature I cited, it is striking that many were able to talk about imperialism without mentioning race. However, they did use discourses of gender to understand imperialism. One group (approvingly) pointed to the paternalism of the colonial project and the imposition of male-defined sports on colonized countries. Yet, finally, post-imperial England emerged as small, weak, and powerless, especially when compared with its big, strong, powerful ally across the Atlantic.

6 "The English Are . . . Not Racist, but . . . Just English"

Imagining a White Nation

You could see they were English, though how this was, since they were mostly gleaming brown and both elegantly and scantily dressed, it would be hard to say. A pinker skin-tone under the brown, and then the pristine, non-domestic look this kind of English had—untouched, however untrue that may be.

A. S. Byatt, *Still Life*

IN THIS CHAPTER, I explore the links between Englishness and race in the narratives of the people I talked to. As with the previous chapter, I am interested in whether these English people were able to challenge dominant images of Englishness, images that have usually been white and male. In particular, I ascertain whether their attempts to rethink hegemonic understandings of Englishness constitute a kind of conceptual work, as individuals refuse to think of England in racially stereotypical ways.

White people often take whiteness for granted as a race—that is, when they talk about "race," they think of people who are not white. Whiteness also has often been taken for granted as the dominant version of Englishness.[1] I therefore investigate the places where the people I talked to imagine Englishness as white (and sometimes as male), both unconsciously and consciously. In so doing, I explore how white people understand their own race and their relationship to race more generally, bearing in mind the point that whiteness itself is a social construct.[2] Because their identities as white emerge in both the U.S. and England, the narrative in this chapter moves between the two places.

"RACING" ENGLISHNESS

As I argued in Chapter 5, colonial expansion abroad enabled the English, and other Europeans, to conceptualize their (white, and often male, middle- or upper–class) selves in opposition to the "other." That is, they conceptualized themselves as not black, not "savage," not "childlike."[3] The fact that blackness and Englishness have been seen as "mutually exclusive" (Gilroy 1992 [1987]: 55) is a direct result of this imperial past. Despite, or perhaps because of, the part that ideas of the "other" have played in the construction of English national identity, there is considerable denial about racism in England's past and present.[4] Although black people have lived in England for at least four hundred years,[5] collective amnesia about England's role in colonization, slavery, and racial stereotyping was common until relatively recently.

In the 1950s and 1960s, people from the Caribbean, the Indian Subcontinent, and Africa began to emigrate to England, throwing the results of its imperialism into sharp relief. As the title of one famous book about race in Britain suggested, the empire struck back,[6] as citizen-subjects of the crumbling empire came to the "mother country" and claimed their right to be there. Stuart Hall (1989: 17) characterized black immigration to England as "the return of the repressed," pointing to the ways in which images of the black "other" moved from being a psychoanalytically internal "threat" to a "threat" that was visible inside the national borders.

The existence of large numbers of people who claim both English and black identities[7] has not changed the assumption in some quarters that the two are mutually exclusive, as the title of Paul Gilroy's book *There Ain't No Black in the Union Jack* shows.[8] He argues that the use of phrases such as "the Island Race" and the "Bulldog Breed" to describe the English illustrates the blurring of the terms "race" and "nation" and that the phrases "rely on that very ambiguity for their effect" (Gilroy 1992 [1987]: 45). Pointing to the way Enoch Powell's "Rivers of Blood" speech and his infamous question, "Who are we?" was taken up by Thatcherism, Gilroy shows how "the black presence [was] constructed as a problem or threat against ... a homogeneous, white national 'we'" (Gilroy 1992 [1987]: 48).[9] Again, Englishness becomes synonymous with whiteness in these discourses.[10]

Although racism still constructs the black subject as "other" (Hall 1988: 28), additional factors have contributed to something of a re-evaluation of English (and British) national identity in recent years. During the 1970s, 1980s, and 1990s, it became increasingly clear that some Welsh, Scots, and Northern Irish refused to think of themselves as British. In addition, during the Thatcher years, many in England itself became alienated from the definition of Englishness. This group included people in the north of England, the region hit hardest by supply-side economic policies; trade unionists, who were treated with barely disguised contempt by the British government; blacks, who suffered skyrocketing unemployment and racist treatment from the police and media; and progressives, who were shocked by racism and by the nationalism of the Little Englanders and Eurosceptics within the Conservative Party in its dealings with the European Community. As Hall (1989: 14) wrote:

> You're left with the English as a tight little island somewhere around London with about twenty-five souls and the Thatcher government hovering over it. And they are continually asking the question—not only about the rest of the world but about most of the people in their own society—"are you one of us?"

The answer, it seemed, was invariably "no."

Most of the people I interviewed left England during the 1980s, many because they were disgusted with Thatcherite policies. Moving to the U.S. complicated their racial identities as well as their national identities. As white English people abroad, they had a unique perspective on race relations: They could cast a critical eye over race relations in both their host country and back home. These comparisons could force them to understand the relationship between their whiteness and Englishness in new ways. To explore this possibility, I investigated the comparisons they made between the U.S. and England about race relations.

MAKING COMPARISONS

The U.S. as "Raced"

Sometimes discussions about race relations emerged spontaneously during the interviews. When they did not, I asked people how they thought their experiences as immigrants would have been different if they were not white in order to help them consider their racial identities.[11] They had mixed responses about whether race relations were worse in England than in the U.S. Although some were critical of the racism they perceived in England, others, as I will discuss, felt that race relations were more problematic in the U.S. The comparisons were usually implicit in their discussions of race relations and racial identities because of their own experiences moving between the two countries. In the analysis that follows, however, I am not interested in ascertaining whether race relations are better or worse in the U.S.—that is, whether the interviewees were "right" or "wrong"—as much as in how their thinking about race provides insights into the relationships between national and racial identities.

Race Relations Are Worse in the U.S.

Many of those I talked to found the U.S. "raced" in a way that they had never encountered before. The U.S., they claimed, had forced them to think of themselves as white for the first time. For instance, Ken, Mike, Diana, and Emma all argued that they had become much more conscious of race since they had come to the U.S. "I never really thought of myself as being white until I came to America," Mike said, even though he had grown up in an ethnically heterogeneous town in England. Ken said he noticed how "WASP-M" (white and male) the City of London was only when he returned to England for a vacation, because he saw race relations "with fresh eyes." Imogen, as I shall discuss later, believed that she had learned to fear black people in the U.S.

In conjunction with this heightened awareness of their own whiteness, the majority thought that race relations were worse in the U.S. than in England. They cited a variety of reasons to account for holding this point of view: Ian, for example, noted that the first slaves arrived as the burgesses met in Virginia in 1618; Gordon, Brad, Imogen, and Frances pointed to segregated housing patterns in the U.S.; Tara, Frances, and Gordon thought that interracial relationships might be more common in England than in America; Harry, Mike, and Ian complained about identity politics as a source of tension in the U.S., arguing that this inhibited people of different races from forming friendships; others[12] pointed to the lack of racial and ethnic minorities in positions of power and their over-representation among the poor and in low-wage work; Emily argued that most of the anti-immigrant sentiment she saw in the States was directed against immigrants of color; and Diana, Emma, Tara, Peter, Ian, and Octavia thought that racism was more extreme and virulent in the U.S.

In making these arguments, the interviewees showed that they saw the U.S. as charged with race in a way that England was not. For instance, Ian told a story about watching a European film with an American friend who was stunned by the portrayal of a character in a minor role who was played by a black actress. The race of the character was not relevant to the film, and Ian's friend argued that this would rarely happen in an American film. Ian agreed, commenting that in the U.S., "a black character . . . always means something more than the character." He felt that race was "a pathology" in the U.S. Having originally come to the U.S. to study African American history, he had changed his field because he thought his white skin and his refusal to agree that there was such a thing as "black psychology" made it hard for him to succeed there. Together with other interviewees, he found a reliance on identity politics essentializing and disturbing. In his words,

> It is an axiom of history that we can re-create the lives of people who lived centuries before and understand how they loved and thought and taught. . . . And yet when it's gender or when it's race, that breaks down. [People say,] "You can't understand because you haven't experienced racism," which to me is simplistic beyond belief.

What did the American awareness of race mean to these people? For some, such as Ian and Emily, it meant being critical of the "interest . . . in differences" in the U.S., seeing it as something that stifled open discussion. Others, such as Anne, thought the emphasis was successful. She characterized the U.S. as "more multicultural" than the United Kingdom, saying, "They have this great series of holidays [such as St. Patrick's Day] to remind people of their origins and traditions." She was proud of her workplace, where "we have people from all over the place," as was Brad, who worked with "a fantastic range of racial groups." Tara enjoyed multiculturalism in terms of the number of international cuisines available to her, but she also expressed more serious ideas about the different experiences a black English person might have in the U.S.:

> You might feel that there was a group of people [in America] who are much more ardent about breaking down racism and much more cohesive, and you might feel like you'd found a great world. On the other hand, depending on what part of the country you're in, you might find racism that was really overt and uncomfortable.

Here she expresses the positives and negatives of the attention paid to race in the U.S. (as these people saw them)—that there is much greater awareness of racism as an issue that needs to be dealt with, but that this is so because racism may be more virulent than in England.

Ian stressed class as an axis of difference to make another argument about the differences between the two countries. In England, he argued, race intersected with class in ways that potentially mitigated racism (although he thought this only "in [his] better moments"). To illustrate, he told a story about a white man he had met while working in an unemployment center in the north of England. This man, who had spoken Urdu and Punjabi fluently since childhood, was employed by his Pakistani landlord doing heavy manual labor for a pittance. He had had a heart attack at twenty-four and was told by doctors that he would have to rest. He went to the center, homeless and in rags, because his landlord had evicted him and fired him. According to Ian, this man

> did not have an ounce of racism in him. He never said, "that 'Paki' bastard, blah blah blah." It was, "that landlord bastard, that employer bastard" because he had too many friends that were Indians to blame it on being Indian. Whereas . . . the biggest moaners about getting their dole checks were the people who, six months before, had been the most Tory Thatcherite critics of welfare. [These were the owners of small businesses who had said,] "They're fucking unemployed, lazy bastards never do any work" . . . and then they'd lose their job and they'd be straight down . . . the unemployment center, saying, "'Course there was a fucking 'Paki' standing in front of me; he gets his welfare before I do." They were the racists, locating all of their anger . . . on this poor old Pakistani guy. But the guy who really suffered, he wasn't [racist].[13]

Ian's point was that class and race function in complex ways in England. The young homeless man had grown up in integrated neighborhoods, and his class-consciousness was far more acute than any negative racial consciousness. Ian, himself a Marxist, argued that racism was more effective in the U.S. than in England because American workers have less working-class consciousness than do their counterparts in England. He used his experience working in the unemployment center to argue that English racism in its current guise is a petit bourgeois phenomenon. As a vehement critic of Thatcherite economics, Ian locates racism as a product of Thatcher's Britain, arising as it does from people who have been taught to blame others for social ills. This story shows, among other things, that Ian was highly conscious of race relations before he moved to the U.S. His experiences in America, however, had led him to believe that race operates to divide people more effectively in the U.S. than in England, and his story implied that there was more racial integration in England.

In tending to conceptualize the U.S. as racially charged in ways that England was not, these people were able to separate themselves from American race relations. Some thought about the emphasis on race in positive cultural terms, as something that gave them access to interesting holidays and cuisines. Others found the American reliance on essentialized racial-identity positions problematic and felt that these divided people unnecessarily. In general, they gave the impression that they saw themselves as outside the racial discourses of the U.S., looking in and usually finding fault. We see this attitude in more detail in the following sections.

They Take Race So Seriously

The English people I spoke to developed the idea that America was more "raced" than England by pointing out how seriously race is taken in the U.S. They argued that the discourse about race did not allow for any questioning of the status quo. Imogen noted that people "jump[ed] down my throat" when she asked what she thought were innocent questions about race relations in the U.S., such as "why black people have to be called African Americans." She noted, "There is a tension, and . . . you can't speak your mind about it. You can't even let yourself think about the issues; you can't even investigate the issues here, for fear of offending somebody. That's a shame, because they are complicated." Imogen made the U.S. sound like a police state, but she seemed sad that there was no room to discuss the issues. Mike echoed her complaint, explaining that he felt race was often "shoved under the carpet" in the States in a way that it was not in England. He cited as counter-examples his friendships with people from the Caribbean who agreed with him that

> there is . . . a channel of humor between the white man and the black man in the Caribbean. [It's] a racial channel of humor in which one's identity as being black and white is not something that is disguised, but it's a very narrow channel, and it's a very delicate one. But it can still be used as a form of cultural communion, whereas I've found here that . . . it's just better not to get into the race thing, . . . not to use that as a way to form friendships with people.

Mike linked this with the "failure of the sense of humor"[14] that many interviewees noted about Americans, as discussed in Chapter 3. However, Mike took pains to point out that "I don't want to seem like somebody who is proposing a racist form of humor, because I think that is essentially bad," but that he also said that it is impossible to "make jokes about being white" in the U.S. Again, Mike stressed that he knew that "there's every reason to be tense about [race] in America," and that he did not mean to imply that if Americans just "loosen[ed] up about this race thing," all their problems would disappear.

Mike's comments are interesting because of the discrepancy between how he frames them and what he actually says. He implies that people are more relaxed about race in England, but he talks about his interactions with people from the Caribbean. Mike is one of the people who claimed he had not thought of himself as white until he moved to the U.S. Extrapolating from this, the relaxed interactions he now has with people from the Caribbean about race, where they joke about his being "a horrible white person," are different from the interactions he had at his racially diverse school in England, whose population consisted of English children whose parents or grandparents had immigrated mainly from India or Pakistan. Indeed, elsewhere in the interview he claimed that his interactions at school were racially neutral, which suggests that he did not joke about being white in England (although he might have been more relaxed about it).

Imogen adds to this contradiction a little, explaining that she was much more comfortable about her white skin with her Indian American friends than she had been with English people who had Indian ancestry. Indeed, she laughed about how her Indian American friends in the U.S. teased her about being a "whitey," but then told me a story about going to an Indian restaurant with her family while visiting England. Imogen was very friendly, asking quite detailed questions about the etymology of certain words on the menu, which caused great consternation among the restaurant staff. Her family were very embarrassed and later told her that her behavior had been inappropriate "and made them feel bad. And it shows how my attitudes toward Indians has changed. I do remember when I [first] met Indians here, I was always trying not to be offensive." Thus, she used this anecdote to talk about how her attitude toward people of Indian ethnicity had changed as she applied a consciousness of race she had learned in the U.S. However, her story also suggests the ways that race relations in England differ from those in the U.S., at least regarding interactions between whites and people of Indian ethnicity.

Reading between the lines of these stories, it seems that at least some of these English people had nostalgic ideas about race relations in England. They imagined it as a racial utopia compared with the U.S., a place where everyone got on regardless of the color of their skin (although Imogen's experiences in the Indian restaurant proved otherwise). Yet at times they compared race relations in the U.S. with their interactions with people from former colonies rather than with race relations in England. Although we shall see later that some interviewees admitted that England was a racist country, seeing the U.S. as raced enabled others to avoid the question of race in England or to claim that England had a healthier attitude toward race. Thus, they were able to use issues of race to enhance their own self-esteem as English people.

Responding to Ethnicity

Further evidence of the interviewees' critical attitude toward Americans came when they complained about Americans' tendency to emphasize their ethnicity.[15] Peter joked around with this idea, conducting an archetypal conversation with an imaginary American who felt this way (complete with American accents in all the right places):

> They're always [saying], "I'm half-English, half-Irish, half-Scotch." Well, [that's] three halves. . . . Never say you're Scotch, because that's a kind of whisky. . . . And they're never Americans. They're always something else. I find it very amusing. "I'm Italian," . . . "Oh yeah? Been there often?" "Oh no, I never went there."

His irony coincided with that of others who complained about Americans' tendencies to "hyphenate" their national identities. As Nigel said, "They're not African Americans; they're Americans." These people attempted to belittle the salience of ethnicity for Americans, trying to push them instead simply to claim a national identity, sometimes in a way that mocked the ethnicity claims of Americans.

They also showed an urge to respond to claims of ethnic identities by drawing on their own national identities. This was evident in their outraged responses to interactions with pro-Republican Irish Americans. These kinds of interactions usually encouraged them to feel "more English than normal."[16] In other words, criticism of England's policies in Ireland brought their national identities to the surface. They had three main complaints about these interactions, all of which helped them to see themselves as English. The first complaint was that second-, third, and fourth-generation Irish Americans claimed to be Irish. As Peter mocked, "My mother's grandfather's budgerigar's cat's mother was Irish." The interviewees said that these people had "no right to claim to be Irish" or called them "plastic paddies."[17] Thus, they devalued the ethnicity claims of Irish Americans by making fun of them or arguing that these people were not truly Irish. One wonders why the claim to ethnicity aroused so much ire. Perhaps as first-generation immigrants, the interviewees wanted to retain a monopoly on the authenticity of their ties with another country.

However, these people also took interactions with pro-Republican Irish Americans seriously when they felt threatened. Thus, their second complaint concerned the rudeness with which they said these Irish Americans approached them, a stark contrast with their relationships with Irish people from the Republic of Ireland. Peter quoted an interaction in which someone had walked up to him and said, "You fucking English should get out of Ireland [*in an American accent*]." Other interviewees had similarly conflictual interactions with Irish Americans. In these situations, they clearly felt "more English than normal" because their Englishness was being marked in a negative way. In comparison to these difficult interactions, Peter and Craig both had friends from the Irish Republic, several interviewees had Irish relatives, and Catriona was married to an Irishman—a situation that she said took some Americans by surprise. (Frances had married an Irish American and said that interactions with his family could sometimes become tense.) Their third complaint, and the third way in which their national identities came to the fore, was explicitly concerned with the attitude of some Irish Americans toward the IRA. They argued that American supporters of the IRA did not understand the complexities of the situation in Northern Ireland, were too quick to blame the British government, tended to "glamorize" the IRA, and seemed to find it acceptable that their money would kill "women [and] little children."[18] The interviewees drew on their own experiences of terrorism in England to explain their anger with Irish Americans who supported the IRA, and, in so doing, asserted their English identities. Frances contrasted the ubiquity of bomb scares in London with the gradual awakening of Americans to terrorist threats. Frank mentioned the news of a bombing in England that had occurred on the day of our interview, saying, "The bloody Irish. . . . It could be me, it could be my kids if I was still there." Here he clearly identifies with English people, thinking "it could be me" as way to emphasize his links with England.

Thus, the people quoted in this and the previous section wished that Americans would take race and ethnicity less seriously until they came to an issue in which they themselves had a strong investment. Either they mocked the ethnicity claims of Irish Americans or portrayed themselves as having more authentic understandings of the Irish situation, both of which were attempts to undermine the seriousness of Americans' ethnicity. Ironically, in attempting to refute the ethnicity claims of Irish Americans, these people drew more heavily on their own national identities as English.

The majority of the people I interviewed felt they did not understand the conflict in Northern Ireland completely but tended to defend England when confronted by Irish Americans, thinking that they at least understood the situation better. Having said this, it is important to note that not all of the interviewees shared these views. As they did with colonialism earlier, some interviewees acknowledged and decried Britain's role in Ireland. Gordon noted that "we've fucked the country for five hundred years" and said he felt "thoroughly ashamed" of that. Gary characterized himself as a "republican"—that is, committed to ending the British presence in Northern Ireland—and Ian said he had participated in a demonstration supporting the IRA during his student days in England. Diana thought it was "obvious" that Britain's presence in Northern Ireland was wrong, as did Craig, although he was concerned about what would happen in Northern Ireland if the British withdrew.

DOWNPLAYING ENGLISH RACISM

I will now examine the relationship between national and racial identities in more detail, investigating the ways in which the interviewees tried to downplay the racism of individual English people. They did this using two main strategies: first, they made excuses for it, saying that it was thoughtless or unconscious or was said without malice; and second, they argued that England was smaller, older, and whiter than the U.S. As an example of the first strategy, Ian, who was adamantly critical of racism elsewhere, pointed out that "my dad ... still calls black people 'darkies,' and he doesn't think this is a bad thing. . . . He grew up with P. G. Wodehouse as his model, and he doesn't mean it maliciously. . . . It's him and his mates down the pub. It's the classic kind of unthought-ful racism." Ian whispered the word "racism" at the end of this state-ment, showing how uncomfortable he was labeling his dad a racist, and he used the fact that his father grew up with racist role models as an excuse for his language. Lucinda also excused her grandfather's racism:

> I think the English are very very [*brief pause*] not racist, but I always say, just English. [They are] very concerned about who they are, their history. They're English, not necessarily patriotic, not like here in America. . . . I think of my grandfather, who really is very racist, and he always makes comments about the "nignogs," and I'm like, "Grandpa, you can't say this. I mean, not now, anyway. I know when you were growing up it was OK." But I think that the English . . . haven't had as much experience . . . of being a melting pot for as long as Americans. I think there [are] definitely racist underlyings, really.

She implies that it was "OK" to use racial epithets in her grandfather's day, thus downplaying his racism. So she ends up excusing both her grandfather's and "English" racism by implying that they are inherent in being English. In arguing that the English are not racist but English, she conforms exactly to the relationship between racism and national-ism spelled out by Gilroy.[19] She implies an exclusionary identity of "we" that is related to racism and patriotism, defining who is "English" and who is not (although she denies that Englishness is related to patriot-ism). Clearly, she is thinking only about white English people here, because these are the people she assumes have a history in England. She also agrees with the comments of other people I talked to that history plays a part in England's inability to deal with race relations fairly, because the country has not been "a melting pot" for long.

Others expressed far more discomfort with the racism of white Eng-lish people, and yet they still made excuses for it. Tara talked about "unthoughtful and ignorant [racism] from all classes of people, white people" in England, using "phrases that people would never [use] here, [such as] 'black as the ace of spades,' . . . as if it is relevant [and] an OK thing to say." Although she was critical of irrelevant racial marking, she undermined this critique by claiming that it occurred because people are "unthoughtful and ignorant." Frank was less willing to make excuses for white English people, pointing out that my mother still referred to black people as "darkies" 'til the day she died. . . . They may pay lip service to tolerance, but I think your average Anglo-Saxon Englishman is one of the most racist animals on earth. England was never open to immigration until relatively recently, and . . . all they knew was [how to] subjugate . . . them.

However, his comments suggest another angle that these people used to excuse English racism: They argued that England had less of a race problem because it was older, smaller, and had a larger majority of white people than the U.S.

Stephen responded to (presumably American) critics of race relations in England by pointing out that "people generalize about [race relations on] the East Coast of America and don't consider the heartland and the West, because . . . it's much more like England out there in the sense that the proportion of ethnic minorities is a lot lower." The implication of his defense of England is that the smaller proportion of black people in England than on the East Coast of the U.S. exonerates England from the possibility that it is more racist than the U.S. Imogen also pointed to numbers and relative levels of integration when she critiqued the American system of busing students over long distances in order to integrate schools. "I can't imagine that there are that many homogeneous schools, state schools [in England], . . . and if they were homogeneous, then it would be because there weren't any black people within a hundred miles, [like in] Yorkshire or somewhere." Imogen assumed that most schools in England were already integrated unless other (presumably acceptable) reasons existed for segregation. These reasons might involve region—that is, schools might be all-white because no black people lived nearby. Or they might involve class—that is, state schools might be integrated, but she did not expect public (private) schools to be. Although it is true that racial and ethnic minorities in England tend to be concentrated in the Southeast and Midlands and in the large cities,[20] Imogen's comments belittle Americans' attempts at integration while ignoring the fact that England makes no such attempts to achieve educational equality.

Others used the same argument—that England is smaller, older and whiter than the U.S.—to explain England's greater propensity toward racism. Yet these interviewees' comments still functioned to excuse England. Anne pointed out that "it takes people longer to adjust to new cultures" in England, because the "vast majority of people are white,

Anglo-Saxon Protestant." She noted that England is "a fairly old country and . . . , it's made up of people who've been there a long time [who] tend to be a bit set in their ways." Arguing that England is not open to new cultures because it consists of "people who've been there a long time" whitewashes black people out of history.[21] Gordon was more explicit about this: "When I think of English . . . , I do think [of white people] because predominantly and historically it sort of exclusively . . . has been white people." Ken also explained racism this way: "To set foot in England is to understand why [questions of race and assimilation] are still a problem. . . . It's a very crowded old country. There's too many people there who want it to go on being the way they think it used to be for that to change very quickly." Again, although it may be true that the majority of the English population historically has been white, the effect of their comments is to erase issues of power, inequality, and racism under the benign idea that white "people [are] a bit set in their ways."

A portion of my conversation with Imogen sums up this willingness to excuse English racism and downplay the negative aspects of race relations in England:

> I learned, not racism, but . . . to be frightened of black people in this country . . . , and it's not like I've come from an ethnically homogeneous place. I was never frightened of black people before, and when I got [here] I was. I couldn't understand it at first, . . . couldn't understand why black Americans are not . . . at the same level of disadvantage [as Jamaicans].

First, she returns to a familiar theme—that the U.S. is racially charged in ways that England is not. To express this, she claims that she learned "to be frightened of black people" in the U.S., suggesting that, in her experience, blackness in the U.S. is infused with negative meanings that do not exist in England. She had thought of a few reasons that her attitude toward race could have changed:

> There's a lot less [black people] in Britain—is it 5 percent in comparison to 17 percent [in the U.S.]? . . . It certainly seems to me that . . . there's less racism in Britain. . . . There's fewer of them; they've come more recently; and then . . . their culture and self-esteem and self-valuing systems are much more intact. . . . Obviously, there's no guns, and there's fewer drugs, but . . . those are the means by which their disadvantage shows itself. [long pause] But, then, racism against Indians . . . is as bad or worse than racism against blacks here. I don't know, but I suspect it's very bad. You

hear stories. . . . I don't know whether they're true and how representative they are, but you certainly hear stories.

The reasons for Imogen's different attitude toward American black people include the idea that England is whiter than the U.S. Contrary to the others quoted in this section, she implies that this makes England a less racist place. Although she recognizes that racism against Anglo-Indians may be worse than racism in the U.S., she undermines her claim by saying that this is the result of "stories" she has heard, which may be unrepresentative. The passage shows how she struggles with the meaning of race in both England and the U.S., carefully weighing the evidence of her own experiences against what she has heard. Ultimately, she uses the evidence to justify her experiences of racial consciousness, colluding in a denial of racial discrimination and racism in England compared with the U.S.

In this section, I have shown how these white English people deployed the interrelationships between race and nation to enhance their own self-esteem and distance themselves from Americans. They used the U.S. as a racial "other" to construct their racial identities via comparisons that were generally favorable to England. Hence, they argued that the U.S. is raced in ways that England is not—that Americans take race relations too seriously or that they are more racist than English people. In addition, they made excuses for any racism they did identify among English people. In so doing, they drew on their own racial and national identities to define a version of whiteness that seemed better to them than the ways in which whiteness is constructed in the U.S. In the next section, I delve more deeply into the issue of whiteness, examining how it intersects with Englishness in the narratives of the interviewees.

RACE AND NATION

Whiteness and Englishness

Getting white people to talk about their racial identity is usually quite difficult unless they are members of groups such as the Aryan Nation or Ku Klux Klan.[22] As Frankenberg recounts in her study of white women and race, requests to talk only to white people are often met with hostility, the assumption being that if one is interested in whiteness, then one must be racist.[23] Attempts to discuss white privilege itself are

often met with blank stares or denial. However, more and more scholars are drawing on the insights of empirical and theoretical work in the
study of racial and ethnic minorities to examine whiteness as a raced
category.[24] A new category of social activists, "race traitors," has also
emerged to question the race privilege that white people receive.[25]

Nevertheless, white people who are interviewed about their racial
identities tend to see their race as bland, formless, or cultureless.[26] One
of Frankenberg's interviewees (1993: 191) argued that whiteness "only
takes shape in relation to other people." Although many white people
see whiteness as empty, uninteresting, or amorphous, "white cultural
practices mark out a normative space and set of identities" (Frankenberg 1993: 192) which are often invisible to the bearers of a white identity. For instance, the assumptions white people make about their own
daily lives often entirely ignore the ways that structures of racism privilege them at the expense of those without white privilege.[27]

Several of the interviewees expressed attitudes in keeping with the
ambivalence about whiteness noted by Nick Hornby (1992: 47–8), a
white English writer:

> The white south of England middle-class Englishman and woman is the
> most rootless creature on earth; we would rather belong to any other com-
> munity in the world: Yorkshiremen, Lancastrians, Scots, the Irish, blacks,
> the rich, the poor, even Americans and Australians have something they
> can sit in pubs and bars and weep about . . . but we have nothing . . . we
> want. Hence the phenomenon of mock-belonging, whereby pasts and
> backgrounds are manufactured and massaged in order to provide some
> kind of acceptable cultural identity. Who was it who sang 'I Wanna Be
> Black'?"

Indeed, Hornby (1992: 48) suggests that white, middle-class, suburban
English culture defines itself in relation to other people who seem to
have much more interesting cultures:

> How we all wished we came from the Chicago Projects, or the Kingston
> ghettos, or the mean streets of north London or Glasgow! All those aitch-
> dropping, vowel-mangling punk rockers with a public school education!
> All those Pogues fans from Hertfordshire singing Irish rebel songs![28]

In keeping with these attitudes, Harry explained his teenage "Irish
romantic fantasy," in which he claimed "some kind of genetic Irish
bonding" with his revolutionary Irish grandfather as part of his rebel-
lion against his parents. However, he also noted that his pretense that

he was half-Irish came from his socialist political convictions and from dissatisfaction with his identity. "Being white, middle class, and English is [like being] the enemy, the dominant power," he said. "It's kind of hard to feel—it's not easy being [*brief pause*]. Actually it is easy. . . . I can't complain, but it's the last prejudice that's acceptable in some ways, you know [*brief pause*], to say, 'You white male bastard.'" Here Harry expresses his desire for some culture that is not "the enemy," showing he has a sharp understanding of the negative ways that his identity as a white, middle-class English man can be conceptualized by those who do not share this identity. He feels like "the enemy" because he believes he is seen as complicit in, or even guilty of, the oppression of other people. His hesitations, backtracking, and contradictions show how hard it is for him to express the bitterness he feels about this. He is not sure that hating himself for his identity is the answer. No wonder he wanted to shed part of it and claim an "acceptable cultural identity" (Hornby 1992: 48) as a "disenfranchised oppressed minority." He knows that his life is easier because he is white and that he benefits from the material rewards of having white skin in a racist society. The fact that he does not approve of white privilege makes the contradiction harder: He wants to complain about anti-white sentiment that he suffers but knows that it would be disingenuous of him to do so because he is privileged in so many other ways. Finally, he does complain, drawing on the ideology of a "backlash"[29] to buttress his point by claiming that calling white men "bastards" because of their identity is a form of prejudice. As Frankenberg notes, when guilt and shame about one's identity spiral inward and become individualized, they do little to raise consciousness or create social change.[30]

Responding to Whiteness in the U.S. and England

I will delve deeper into Harry's racial attitudes to examine how race and nation functioned together for some of the people I interviewed. Harry, who expressed ambivalence about his own whiteness, distanced himself from the racial ideologies of white American people in oppositional ways. He described the not-guilty verdict in the O. J. Simpson criminal trial as a "defining moment" for him—a moment when he realized that he did not share the view of the other white people in his office who thought that Simpson was guilty. He said he found their "white rage . . . sickening." Harry defined himself as an outsider by refusing to collude with their understanding of events. He also told me stories about other confrontations he had precipitated at work about issues of race and class and then described an incident in which he had gone out with white friends of a co-worker for the first time and got drunk:

> [I] completely let loose, and instead of being discreet or tactful, . . . I just said everything I thought: . . . "Well, tough shit. You had it coming. It was your turn. . . . I think it's about time. Five years of you putting up with discrimination against you won't make up the centuries of—." I just got into it because I can't stand listening to those privileged white kids whine about losing out to affirmative action.

Here Harry attempts to distance himself from white privilege by confronting the backlash ideology. He does not want to listen to white people complaining about affirmative action and decides to "let loose" and explain his frustration to them. Perhaps his slightly heavy-handed approach is explained by his feeling that "except when they're good friends, I just don't like white men." Here, then, he completely removes himself and his friends from the picture so he can blame other white men for racism and complicity in racial structures of oppression. However, he conceptualizes his experience of whiteness in terms of individual interactions. He did not say that he disliked racist and sexist structures. He said that he did not like "white men" (which he attributed in part to his hatred of his single-sex public-school education).

The role gender plays in this excerpt is particularly intriguing in that Harry expanded on his dislike of white men by expressing his discomfort with stereotypical masculine behavior: "As soon as I'm with a group of people who are acting like lads, I just think, 'I have to get out of here.'" Yet there were contradictions, too, as sometimes his gender-consciousness took a back seat. Thus, he admitted to letting sexist behavior go by "with a nod and a wink, especially if I'm drunk and with a bunch of friends," although "I like to think that I'm sort of a feminist and above it all." Harry moves in and out of different identities as he tells his story—denying his identity as a white man (especially in relation to Americans), but then foregrounding his masculinity when he is "drunk and with a bunch of friends."

There is nothing particularly odd about any of this. Sometimes the people who are hardest to confront are the people we care for most. However, Harry's honesty about the differences between his ideology and his actions suggests another interpretation, as he described a different situation in which his identity as an English white man became relevant. He found himself in a pub in England sitting next to a friend of a friend, a white skinhead man who appeared to be a member of the National Front, an extreme right-wing, racist political party in Britain. "I'm sitting there, and I'm thinking, 'This is the enemy; this is kind of strange,' and I said, 'This is a weird situation. I think I'm going to go.' And he said, 'Well, what do you mean?' and we carried on talking, and he was just a poseur. The things we found in common were football and music." Several aspects of this interaction intrigue me. First, and most obvious, is the fact that Harry managed to talk civilly to a racist English skinhead but earlier could not contain his frustration with the white Americans he also had just met who complained about affirmative action. Second, how did Harry decide this skinhead was a "poseur"? And even if he was, why does the fact that the man posed as a racist skinhead not trouble an avowed anti-racist? It does not seem, from the narrative he recounted, that Harry confronted the man about his racist appearance. Third, Harry used this story to explain that, although he might have things in common with white English men—namely, football and music—he did not have anything in common with white American men (because he assumed that they play different sports and listen to different music).

Again, Harry's gender identity surfaces, although this time more implicitly. It is noteworthy that the points of connection Harry found with the skinhead included sports, something that he claimed had the potential to "soothe sores" (see Chapter 5). Gender, race, and nation work together here, as Harry feels able to form a brief alliance with a man with whom he can converse about the sport he loves. In this case, masculinity and national identity allow Harry to overcome the differences between his definition of whiteness and the skinhead's. Although he begins this story by asserting his dislike of white men, it becomes clear that it is only certain white men that he dislikes.

Put together, these analyses suggest why Harry might be moved to say, "I think there is something much deeper [going on here] that I'd rather not think about." Harry's motivation is that he wants to distance himself from the racist attitudes of white Americans, not those of white people per se. In other words, he can find something about which to connect with a racist English person that he cannot find to connect with American people who express racist attitudes. Thus, his national identity trumps his anti-racist sentiments. In this case, prejudice and racism, defined in other situations as his antithesis, are ignored in favor of English culture. Harry experienced his whiteness, then, in very contradictory ways. On the one hand, he was ashamed of it and felt guilty about it. On the other, he found a way to distance himself from whiteness by identifying white Americans as "the enemy."

Turning for a brief look at Gary's identification of himself as white suggests that this analysis may apply to other interviewees. Gary took pride in his knowledge of black music, positioning himself as a white English man as he discussed dancing in a racially diverse nightclub in the U.S.:

> I think English men dance better than American men, white men, so . . . I'm an English white guy that's . . . in a racially mixed nightclub. . . . There's an element of British race relations, which is healthier amongst young people than in the States, and so I . . . associate that with being British. So I'm there, I'm hip, I'm into this music, which is black music, but I feel entirely comfortable with it, and we know that British people consume more black music than American people, American white people.

Gary identifies strongly with black music not as a way to deny his whiteness, but as a way to assert his Englishness (and his masculinity). Whiteness becomes benign through the lens of his national identity. Not only are English race relations "healthier," but "American white people" are not "hip" enough to enjoy black music. Thus, he uses the combination of his whiteness and Englishness to distance himself from American whiteness.

Both men, then, combine their racial and national identities so that their whiteness takes shape in opposition to American whiteness. White Americans become the focus of their negative feelings about race relations in the U.S., while they assume that race relations in England are unproblematic. Thus, they claim a relationship between race and nation that distances them from Americans, perhaps to erase their own feelings of culpability in the workings of race relations. As Frankenberg's work shows, whiteness is often seen as an identity that is racist, guilt-ridden, bland, or invisible.[31] To carve out a positive feeling about whiteness, these people rely on their national identities so they can see American whiteness and English whiteness as ontologically distinct. In addition, Harry and Gary's masculinity plays an interesting role in this process. For Harry in particular, masculinity allows him to connect with other men, ignoring his feminism and anti-racism when it suits him. I now examine other ways in which the respondents' white identities emerged during the interviews, asking how else they might imagine England as white (and sometimes as male or upper-middle class).

IMAGINING A WHITE ENGLAND

Despite the ambivalence toward the white, suburban, middle-class, person from the south of England that Hornby identified, the people I talked to often acquiesced, albeit unconsciously, in the idea that whiteness is invisible, using it as the unmarked version of Englishness. Indeed, when they identified typical English people, some of them excluded non-whites altogether.[32] Most of the comments in this section further explicate Frankenberg's power-evasive or color-evasive discursive repertoires[33] in that they show interviewees refusing to engage with the issue of racial difference in England. However, they add a new dimension to Frankenberg's ideas. Most of the people I quote here are not consciously trying to avoid thinking about race; race is simply invisible to them as a category when they think about Englishness. As Peggy McIntosh showed in drawing up a list of ways in which her white skin privileged her,[34] white people often do not think about their whiteness and do not understand how their assumptions exclude others. Here we see interviewees agreeing with the hegemonic images of Englishness identified in Chapter 5 in that that they do not attempt to subvert those images.

Because the interviewees themselves were white, it is perhaps unsurprising that white images were the first thing to come to their minds (although we have also seen that they are far more prepared to recognize the racial diversity of the U.S.). Indeed, as Peter Gould and Rodney White argue, the "mental maps" we have of one another and of our environment tend to focus on what we find important: ourselves.[35] These unconscious imaginings teach us about how people perceive those around them and may be related to how they act toward others. These images show how easy it is for exclusionary definitions of Englishness to rise to the surface. They illustrate how, as Gilroy suggests, Englishness and blackness are often perceived to be mutually exclusive.[36]

So far, I have uncovered a fairly contradictory portrait of these English people: They have moved in and out of different discourses about race throughout this and the previous chapter. Hence, although some felt shame and guilt about colonization or questioned the hegemonic ideals of post-imperial England, they were also inclined to deny much of the reality of the post-imperial legacy. In addition, they have tended to downplay or excuse English racism while seeing the U.S. as racially charged. Harry oscillated between complaining about his white male identity and feeling he was not entitled to complain, then confronted some white people about their racism but not others. Although the relationship between personal ideologies and behavior is unclear, we can speculate that the images people use to imagine their nation has an impact on their own practices. If their underlying ideas about Englishness are informed by images that exclude people on the basis of race and gender, then they will be less likely to confront racism and sexism when they see it in their own lives[37] or in larger structural arenas such as government policies. Examining their unconscious images of Englishness, then, points to some of the motivations underlying their actions and, for this reason, can be considered a form of unconscious conceptual work. As they imagine English people, they are constructing some people as "typically" English and some as not.

Some interviewees unconsciously invoked whiteness to describe what English people look like. Harry laughingly said that "on the beach . . . you can spot English people a mile [away]. They're just the ones who . . . are white, and Scottish people are blue virtually. You can just see that. . . . It is to do with the heat." Here Harry uses skin color to describe English people's appearance. Gary, too, focused on the sun when he discussed negative feelings about being English: "I feel terribly constrained by the fact that I sunburn easily, and I associate that with being English." Gary thus unconsciously argues that a facet of being English is having white skin. Both men extrapolate from the United Kingdom's temperate climate, Harry to argue that whites from the British Isles look out of place on beaches, and Gary to make the connection between sunburn and Englishness.

Emily echoed the focus on skin color and its relationship to the weather in descriptions of English people. After she described her feelings of alienation from England, an Australian friend told her, " 'Well, of course you don't look English! You're not gray enough!' That was her feeling, that people there [looked gray], both in the way they were dressed and physically. They don't get much sun, and a lot of people, I guess, don't eat that well. They look pretty pale when you come to think about it." Emily focused on the unhealthy aspects of life in England to account for the different color of the people there, although she also argued that women in England were less likely to color their hair or wear makeup, suggesting that the dull tones she perceived were also the result of cultural practices. The fact remains, however, that she was talking only about white people, as one can see from her use of the adjectives "gray" and "pale."

Apart from explicitly mentioning color, the racial coding of English people as white (and as male) arose in the examples the interviewees chose in order to describe English people. Harry, for example, told the following story about a trip to Europe:

> I was sitting in Prague [and] this guy came out of the train station wearing Union Jack shorts. . . . He had like a skinhead or something . . . like that. He had some T-shirt with a British slogan on it. He was shouting and singing and staggering along the street with his friend, half-drunk, . . . shouting abuse at [everyone]. Here's me and my friend . . . sitting there with a bunch of Swedes and Yugoslavs and Germans . . . and they're all saying, "So there's the British." I'm thinking, here we are sitting here . . . and you'd never guess we were English. But [that] guy—he's English! . . . The only time you ever notice people's national identity is when they parade it.

Here he admits diversity in definitions of Englishness by contrasting himself with the drunken Englishman. Unlike that man, Harry sat quietly in a multinational group, watching a stereotypical parade of national identity. That the man he described was white is suggested by his skinhead-like haircut and by his clothes. Union Jack shorts tend to be associated either with football hooligans traveling abroad or with a certain racist punk or skinhead ethos. Note also that this man was engaged in stereotypically hegemonic masculine behavior—drinking and taking over the street by hurling abuse at passersby, which suggests that Harry conceives of stereotypical displays of national identity in male terms.

Diana also used mainly white and male icons to describe typical English people:

> There's millions of typicals. There's the farmer, . . . the bowler-hat guy, . . . my brother, . . . the punk on Carnaby Street. . . . There are too many images. I think. There's the Sloane. I don't have one typical English person. I could give you a typical American—the sloppy T-shirt and sneakers, just baggy

clothes. Typical white American or typical Hispanic American. I couldn't give you a typical English person.

Although Diana asserts that there is no typical English person, she names a few ideas, and all except one are unequivocally male and probably white. The "Sloane" is the odd one out here, because Sloane Rangers can be upper- and upper-middle-class people of either gender, although the term is usually used to describe women.[38] It is also noteworthy that in this passage Diana marks Americans as raced by refusing to generalize about all Americans and limiting herself instead to white and Hispanic Americans, but that English people do not emerge as racially diverse. A few minutes later, she confirmed that her typical punk is white and male. "I suppose the average white, middle-class American doesn't have to cut his hair strangely and say swear words a lot to prove something, whereas the average English white person often does." The "bowler-hat guy" she mentioned is a city gent who is more than likely white, according to two interviewees who had worked in London's financial district.

Although Diana discussed these images while ostensibly refusing to generalize, her use of white and male versions of Englishness came through. When discussing how other people (probably Americans) view English people, she also used male images: "They think of the stereotypical things, like . . . the English snob . . . like Lord So-and-so and not Mr. Average at all. Yes, I think that's the image they would have of an English person." Here, Diana is aware of the upper-class bias in others' stereotypes of Englishness (and her own "typicals" covered a range of potential classes), but these responses are still gendered and, to some extent, raced. Lord So-and-so and Mr. Average are obviously men, and implicitly white.

Likewise, Andy said:

> The English [come] in so many different groups . . . and you could see characteristics that I would epitomize of Yorkshiremen or the typical Essex boy—that's me! . . . I don't think there's a typical British person unless you went for the . . . bowler hat and brolly brigade [or] John Bull with his flag . . . waistcoat. No, I don't think so. I think over here people generalize too much, [and] I don't think there's a typical American either.

Although Andy pays lip service to diversity, he thinks in terms of male icons to illustrate this idea and arguably in terms of white ones as well, which rather undermines his point. His diversity only covers region and class. Although he claims that there is no general type, his examples use white and male images of English people—thus making unconscious claims that whiteness and maleness are representative of England. Quentin similarly refused to generalize but proceeded to talk in terms of male icons: "I have different images of what a British person is like, that extends to some out-of-work shipbuilder from Newcastle to an ex-Eton, Oxbridge guy working in the foreign office and everything in between."

Only two people used female images as a way to identify with Englishness. They were both women, and in so doing they drew on examples that related to them personally. Vera told me of her amusement at seeing a woman in London with an "English face" wearing an "extravagantly romantic hat." Her face was "round, countrified [and] devoid of makeup." Like Frances (who found American faces too "smooth"), Vera associated Englishness with a lack of makeup. It transpired that the woman with the English face reminded Vera of herself. When I asked her what was English about the face, she continued:

> Well ... you see it in the faces in the [paintings in the] National Gallery. A sort of insouciance, total un-selfconsciousness in the wives and children of country people. Rather fresh-colored, maybe that flaxen part of English people, and fairly red cheeks and that sort of innocent look in their eye which is really, "Here I am. I am an English person. Just take me as I am." There is no guile. It's an English look that they have about them, that ... I find very funny.

For Vera, Englishness is conveyed by a carefree and uncontrived attitude; one can't help but wonder whether she is contrasting this innocence to Americans. Meanwhile, the Englishness she perceives is also "fresh, ... flaxen, [with] red cheeks," a white, but female, version of Englishness. Likewise, Lucinda, identified strongly with a female cousin, drawing on very class-specific images to describe her as "very English":

> She likes to wear this white [lacy] blouse and a ... flowery skirt [from Laura Ashley]. The way she carries herself, she's very upright [and] vivacious ... going to, not wild parties, [but] parties. ... In America, ... if you're going to a party, [it's] down the street. But there, if you go to a party, you go for the weekend. ... And it's your friends from school, because most, [well,] a lot of people, seem to go to boarding school.

Lucinda's version of Englishness is located in the experiences of those close to her. For her, being English involves wearing expensive clothes and going to parties with one's boarding-school friends, activities that are not likely to be open to working-class or most middle-class English people. In her imagination, then, English people are likely to be just like her—upper-class white women. Lucinda and Vera imagine Englishness as female but only by using the images closest to them, as if they cannot think of a range of female images similar to "Lord So-and-so" and "John Bull."

Although the interviewees tended to use white and male icons, they were much more likely to note their racial bias than their gender bias. Thus, Craig pointed out that because we had already discussed race relations in the interview, he was aware of the "Afro-Caribbean [and] Indian populations that are second-, third-generation British." However, "if it is an immediate thought, it's difficult, then it's kind of . . . white Anglo-Saxon British [or] Celt." Gordon claimed that, although he had always been "open-minded about ethnicity," when he thought of English people, "I do think, I suppose, of white people." In addition, when Catriona returned to England after two years in Ireland, she said, she "landed at Heathrow airport, and I was absolutely amazed at the amount of black people that were there because at that time there were very few in Ireland." These anecdotes and comments suggest the effort of will some people had to make to recognize that black people could be English. Again, this suggests the ways that whiteness operates unconsciously as the unmarked and invisible national category.

This section has shown the racial, gender, and, to some extent, class bias that exists in these interviewees' imaginings of England. Just as "people" is so often assumed to mean men, because women have to be marked as women, English is often assumed to mean "white" and "male" unless otherwise noted. Thus, these interviewees' assumptions about Englishness make whiteness (and to a lesser extent, maleness) the neutral and unmarked category, its normativity invisible to most of them. Indeed, most of the work on whiteness shows that comparisons need to be made with other racial groups before whiteness becomes noticeable. One of the defining characteristics of white privilege is that white people assume that everyone shares the same worldview and privileges that they enjoy until they are confronted with people who do not.[39] It is this unconsciousness about the workings of difference that gives whiteness its unmarked status. Because it is unmarked, white people assume that their experiences are neutral and normative; they sometimes cannot see how their racial identities structure their experiences and worldview. As paternalism emerged as part of the imperial legacy in Chapter 5, gender comes into focus here in terms of male images of Englishness. The interviewees were much more likely to see diversity in terms of region and class than they were to recognize gender divisions in English society, especially in relationship to the ways they imagined England.

A RACIAL CONSCIOUSNESS OF ENGLAND

White people are not always unaware of their racial identities, however. More explicit questioning about race usually encouraged the interviewees to recognize their whiteness. Hence, in this section, I examine the words of some of the same people to analyze how they thought about their racial identities. This occurred in two main arenas: in taking anti-racist stances and in thinking of themselves as immigrants.

Those who took explicitly anti-racist stances were often able to engage with the meaning of their white identities. Frank, Gordon, Harriet, and Emma all noted with disapproval the overtly racist remarks they had heard from friends and family in England. Ken and Anne felt that England was not a successful multicultural society because there was "no desire on the part of the larger body to assimilate the smaller ones." Diana, Gary, Quentin, and Frances expressed little doubt that racism was rife in England, while others criticized the racial homogeneity in certain parts of England.[40] Still others noted the racism of certain politicians in England and the exclusionary and xenophobic attitudes they found intolerable in England.[41] By commenting on racism and racist attitudes, these interviewees had to consider, at least implicitly, their own racial identities. In pointing to the ways that racism affected others, they would be aware of their own relative privilege because negative stereotypes about race did not affect them.

Ian was among those who spontaneously brought up the significance of race relations in his life by telling me about his experiences in the U.S. and England.[42] He had a keen sense of his own anti-racist stance, claiming that he had been a "vocal critic of racism and racist ideas through all my twenties." He told me about his formative years at a diverse city college in England, about his Marxist political activities as a student, and about his attendance at the Rock Against Racism concerts in the early 1980s. Ian was very sure about his own position vis-à-vis other racial groups, refusing to accept essentialized racial positions and arguing that he saw himself as a white man only when others placed that identity on him.

Other interviewees had less centered anti-racist histories and were less sure about the ways their racial positions enabled them to think about race. For some, this stemmed from a lack of experience, usually because they had only become interested in race relations since they had moved away from England. Diana and Ken, for example, both felt unqualified to comment on the ways that race functioned in England. Others made different arguments as to why they were unable to speak about race with authority. Emma, for instance, was self-reflective about her own attitudes toward race both in England and in the U.S. She was shocked by the racist language she had heard at an all-white school in Yorkshire and wanted to claim that she was not prejudiced. However, she also said:

> Obviously I can't categorically say [that] because I don't have the experience. . . . But I don't feel any animosity or anything toward any race, even in England, how they've moved in. . . . I mean, my brothers have made "Paki" jokes, which . . . surprised me, and I haven't ever said anything. I always say to myself I should say something, but . . .

Emma's unwillingness to label herself as a non-racist stems directly from her own identity as white. She does not believe that she can fully tell whether she is racist, although her use of the term "they" to describe immigrants suggests at least a level of discomfort. However, she implies that there are moments in which her whiteness shields her from having to confront her brother's racist jokes. Her words were echoed by Frances, who implied that she was not qualified to comment on whether something or someone was racist because she was not black. Frances noted that when men denied sexism in things she felt to be sexist, she became annoyed. Both women experienced their white identities as disallowing them from commenting on race relations, even to the extent, in Emma's case, of not "say[ing] something" in the face of overt racism (although their reluctance came from their sense that their own racial identities would make their interventions inappropriate rather than from feeling that it had nothing to do with them). Others concurred with this point of view. They refused to consider their own racial identities at all but felt comfortable talking about the ways race relations affected black people, illustrating the by-now classic point that white people often do not see themselves as having a race or think of race relations as their problem.

A second group drew on their own experiences as immigrants to the U.S. to comment on their racial identities. In Chapter 3, Emily complained that Americans do not see white people as immigrants. Alex's experience seemed to be somewhat different, and her words suggest that being seen as an immigrant could be a "salutary" experience:

> All those dirty words attached to you. . . . You are an "immigrant," . . . a "sponger off the system," you are "coming in" [*all said in a tone of disdain*]. In [the English town where I lived], they used to have an expression for people who weren't from [there]—they were "offcomers." Well, you're an "offcomer." You're not "one of them" are you? . . . When you're in your own country, you think of "foreigners" [*with disdain*]. Now you are one.

Alex clearly sees how she is defined as different in the U.S., and she uses this experience to remember how people are defined as different in England. Her expressions of being "othered" here could almost be read as a symbolic coloring of her identity: Suddenly she understands what it feels like to be defined as not fitting in—although in this case, the "othering" is on the basis of her nationality rather than her racial identity. The experience of feeling as if she does not belong, however, enables her to see England from the perspective of those who are defined as outsiders.

Some of the other interviewees also made comparisons between their situations and those of immigrants or racial and ethnic minorities in England, with varying results. Nigel cited a situation in which children in a Nottingham school had been learning "Urdu nursery rhymes," which he thought was "horrendous."[43] Unlike Alex, who was able to see the world from the perspective of an outsider, he was adamant that immigrants should assimilate to the culture of their host country, whether they were in England or the U.S. He said, "If they want to speak their own [language,] they should fuck off back to their own country. . . . Yeah, don't lose your heritage, but learn to speak [the language of] wherever you're living." Nigel didn't seem to notice his privilege as an immigrant with an English accent as he derided those who do not give up their culture and language.

Craig was more self-aware about the issue of assimilation. He explained that, having moved himself, he was "very aware ... how it would be a comfortable thing to do [to] set up ... your own little [isolated] community where you carry on your own traditions to the extent that you exclude or alienate everybody else." However, he cited a couple of examples to show the complexity of the issue for him. One was the infamous "Tebbit test," whereby one's loyalty to England was shown by the country one supported in cricket matches,[44] which he said illustrated an attitude he deplored but, at the same time, could partly understand. The second involved non-Muslim people in a particular Midlands community who had objected to the slaughter of *halal* meat[45] in the streets, which, he said, gave him similar pause for thought. Although he could see "why it's important to maintain your belief systems," he was clearly uncomfortable that Muslims' practices in England might impinge on the feelings of non-Muslims. In light of this conversation, he defined Englishness by citing the numerous black people on English sports teams and by pointing out that the region of London in which he had lived was 54 percent non-white. "To be English, you don't have to be white. If you are born there and you identify with [that] country, if you participate in that country's development and ... culture, then you assimilate. [You] become part of that country." Craig's struggle to define national identity in keeping with his ideas about assimilation suggest that his national identity is infused with race: He wishes to be inclusive as long as people conform to a particular version of Englishness. In other words, he wants racial and ethnic minorities to adopt white English cultural norms and become "nice." (As Harriet said, "I can remember being horrified ... when [a former] boyfriend's father would say how nice Daley Thompson [a black British decathlete] was, and why weren't all black people like him."[46]) In different ways, both Craig and Nigel draw on the idea that members of a community must conform to a particular way of life—one that is defined as English but uses "culture" as a code for race to exclude people who do not conform. As Stuart Hall (1993b) asked, To whose way of life must people conform?[47] Gilroy (1992 [1987]: 69) takes up the theme, arguing, "What must be challenged is the way that these apparently unique customs and practices are understood as expressions of a pure and homogeneous nationality."

The attempts of these white English people to examine their own racial identities in relation to those of racial and ethnic minorities provide a more balanced account of the role of whiteness in their English national identities. Although they made unconscious assumptions about the intersections of their racial and national identities, complete with elisions and ellipses, they also had moments in which they engaged with the meaning of their white identities. In particular, when they took antiracist positions or thought about their own position as immigrants in relation to perceived outsiders in England, they provided a more complex picture of the workings of their white identities. However, underlying some of this is still the assumption that they are not qualified to talk about race or that the only people who belong in England are those who assimilate to particular (usually white) notions of culture.

A GENDER CONSCIOUSNESS OF ENGLAND

I have pointed in this chapter to the ways in which the people I talked to imagined England in gendered as well as raced terms. In particular, I noted the male icons they used to describe "typical" English people (unless they were women thinking about themselves). Here I develop the analysis of the relationship between their gender and national identities by showing how the interviewees sometimes drew on gender as a way to critique or reconceptualize dominant ideas about Englishness. Indeed, as they talked about gender relations, the majority of the interviewees implied that England should be more like the U.S. in this area of life.

In comparing the two countries in terms of gender relations, most of the interviewees argued that there was less sexism in the U.S. than in England. However, some saw only minor differences between the two countries, and a vocal few were highly critical of American gender relations. Indeed, as they did while discussing race, they sometimes contradicted themselves during the interviews, depending on which aspect of gender relations they were considering. Stephen, for instance, approvingly noted the pressure at his American university to hire a woman. Yet when confronted with an American woman who argued that England was more sexist than the U.S., he pointed to its maternity-leave policies and health system to dismiss her claims and paint England as more advanced in terms of gender relations.

The idea that England is more sexist than the U.S. emerged in a number of ways. Brad thought that his daughter was doing better academically at her new co-ed school than his son was, although the reverse had been true in England, when both children attended single-sex schools. He blamed American masculine culture, particularly the emphasis on sports, for this. Gordon and Diana aruged that it was marginally easier for women to get ahead in business in America, while Anne pointed to the lack of an "old boys' network" in the U.S. to corroborate this point of view. Antonia and Harriet found American men less sexist and more open in their relationships, while Tara said that English men were nonplussed by "strong" (American) women. Meanwhile, Gordon talked about being appalled when his family in England demanded that his wife take his last name when they married. (She didn't.) His American wife had found English women "weak" and "obsess[ed]" with "1950s . . . domesticity" when she worked there. For his part, he said that it would have been harder for him to break out of assigned roles if he had been a woman in England. Imogen agreed, saying that she felt much less pressure to do the "womanly thing" in the U.S. than she had in England.

These people thus used gender to criticize dominant understandings of Englishness, drawing on their experiences in the U.S. to suggest that there were other ways to think about relations between women and men. Gender, then, became a way for some of them to engage with alternative visions of national identity. It is also important that this group of people saw England as inferior to the U.S., something that was not particularly evident in their discussions of race relations.

On the other side of the spectrum, some interviewees were outraged at the treatment of women in the U.S., comparing it unfavorably to England. Craig was aghast that the equal-rights amendment had never been ratified, and he contrasted the "guarded" relations between the sexes in the U.S. with his experience of more acceptance of feminism and more women in positions of power in England. Dorothy felt that women in business in the U.S. were "tested" simply because of their gender and that her male boss treated her like an idiot. She also criticized her husband's family, who expected the women to wash the dishes on family occasions while the men watched sports. Frances, who was job hunting at the time, felt that some employers had tricked her into admitting that she had children, something she was sure they would not do to a man. She suggested that life in the U.S. was not "easier for women," although "lip-service" was paid to the idea of women's rights. She talked especially about the image of Hilary Rodham Clinton as a cookie-baking, stay-at-home mom that was prevalent in the media in the mid-1990s and compared that with the strong image of Margaret Thatcher while she was prime minister. She also derided the U.S. for not yet having elected a woman to the presidency.

Thus, although some interviewees used gender to criticize the U.S., England did not emerge as triumphant and flawless in these comparisons. Indeed, in this and the previous chapter, we have seen these English people struggling to rethink hegemonic understandings of Englishness as imperially benign, white, and harmonious in its race and gender relations. By spontaneously mentioning race or gender, or by critiquing the way that these categories work in England, they refused to see Englishness as embodying perfection. Indeed, they created images of England that were more nuanced than an exclusionary, all-white, all-male narrative, on the one hand, or a racial or gender utopia, on the other. The conceptual work they did to imagine England involved "policing" its borders (to use Schwalbe and Mason-Schrock's 1996 terminology) to make it a less idealized place. They used their experiences in the U.S. to redefine Englishness so that race and gender were not taken for granted. Rather, they were problematized, thereby challenging the dominant version of English identity as homogeneous.

CONCLUSION: IMAGINING ENGLAND

Having examined the relationship between imperialism and national identity, I turned in this chapter to the relationship between race and nation. I analyzed the how the interviewees conceptualized the U.S. as racially charged in a way that England was not. They argued that race relations were worse in the U.S., that Americans were more conscious of race, and, especially, that Americans took race and, to some extent, ethnicity too seriously. (Yet when they were confronted with pro-Republican Irish Americans, they often responded by drawing on their own nationality as English to assert their more authentic claims to understanding the Irish situation.) These comparisons enabled them to keep themselves separate from American racial discourses, finding fault as they looked in from the outside. They also found ways to excuse English racism, arguing that racism in England was unconscious or thoughtless and that England was simply older, smaller, and whiter. These arguments helped them to construct a benign version of English whiteness in which white people were simply set in their ways in England, whereas white Americans were more serious and racist. Indeed, Harry in particular showed how one can distance oneself from the racism of white Americans but not from the racism of white English people. In his case, his national identity seemed to override his concerns about racism. The people I talked to thus combined racial and national identities to distinguish themselves from Americans, implying that white Englishness was a less problematic identity than white Americanness.

I also examined the construction of English whiteness, first by analyzing the interviewees' unconscious racialized coding of Englishness, then by exploring how they did notice and respond to English race relations. Although the first part of this section was based on abstract questions in which interviewees were not asked explicitly about race, their comments provided useful data about how white people construct whiteness as normative and neutral. When I asked them to describe "typical" English people, they did so using mainly white (and male) icons. This may not seem surprising, as the majority of people in England are white and the interviewees themselves were white. But many of these people came from racially heterogeneous parts of England, and their tendency to see themselves or people like them as representative of Englishness is in keeping with the ways communities are imagined as homogeneous, despite evidence to the contrary.[48] More explicit questions about race encouraged some interviewees to focus on race relations in England. I noted the impact of anti-racist stances on white identity formation and how these people's experiences as immigrants in the U.S. had (or had not) given them insights into the problems of those classified as outsiders.

As the interviewees talked about their images of Englishness, gender also emerged as salient. Hence, the icons they unconsciously used to imagine Englishness tended to be male as well as white. When I encouraged them to talk more explicitly about gender relations, they did so by comparing England with the U.S. One group saw the attention paid to gender equality in the U.S. as little more than lip service, while the other group was more prepared to use gender as a way to critique England. These critiques show that they found it easier to find fault with gender relations in England than with race relations in that country. The question arises as to why this might be the case: While gender and race are equally important axes of difference, are racial identities more closely connected to national identity than gender identities? Is the image of a white England more of a touchstone than that of a male England? Or is racism perceived as more threatening than sexism by these interviewees, so that the nation needs to be protected from charges of the former but not the latter? These questions suggest the need for more work in the relationship between gender identities and national identities in order to tease out the connections.[49] They also suggest the complexities of the conceptual work involved in seeing oneself as a holder of more than one identity—in this case, national, gendered, and racial.

By analyzing the conceptual work that goes into imagining oneself as part of an identity, I have exposed the unconscious level on which interviewees sometimes drew to define Englishness. Using Frankenberg's notion of "discursive repertoires,"[50] I argued that as the interviewees imagined England, they responded to, exaggerated, downplayed, or rejected hegemonic narratives about Englishness. In so doing, I showed how individuals actively construct their own versions of particular identities, defining what the identity means to them and often acting in ways that enhance or perpetuate their particular version of the identity. Those who attempted to excuse English racism constructed Englishness differently from those who decried English racism. Likewise, those who critiqued gender relations in England refused to see England as benign and triumphant. Instead, they had a more realistic view of England that took into account its flaws and blemishes as well as its successes.

7   To Be English or Not?

Constructing Identities in the U.S.

There are certain things that you have to be British . . . to appreciate: Sooty,
Tony Hancock, *Bill and Ben the Flowerpot Men,* Marmite, skiffle music, the
Morecombe and Wise segment in which Angela Rippon shows off her legs by
dancing, . . . *Dixon of Dock Green,* HP sauce, salt cellars with a single large
hole, . . . making sandwiches from bread you've sliced yourself, really milky
tea, allotments, the belief that household wiring is an interesting topic for
conversation, steam trains, toast made under a gas grill, thinking that going
to choose wallpaper with your mate constitutes a reasonably good day out,
wine made out of something other than grapes, unheated bedrooms and
bathrooms, seaside rock [and] erecting windbreaks on the beach (why, pray,
are you *there* if you need a windbreak?) . . .

> Bill Bryson, *Notes from a Small Island*

DIFFERENT COMPONENTS OF IDENTITY

I BEGAN THIS BOOK by quoting Ken, who said that he wanted to
be able to be English when *he* wanted to be." Throughout, I have shown
how the English people I interviewed negotiated their national identities—asserting or denying them, noting others' definitions of them or
arguing for redefinitions of them. Their words have shown the ways
their identities are more or less relevant at different moments and in different aspects of their lives. As I examined how they understood their
identities, interactions emerged as the primary sites of identity construction. Within interactions, the people I talked to used various identity-constructing devices to make themselves feel more or less English:
culture and experiences, the perceptions they believed others had of
them, and identity work. However, woven through these interactional
modes of identity construction were the assumptions they made about
the naturalness of their national identities. Before discussing these different forms of identity construction, I briefly examine the strong need
these English people expressed for an identity.

THE NEED FOR AN IDENTITY ASSOCIATED WITH PLACE

The people I interviewed were sociological "strangers" in the U.S.,[1] people who were on unfamiliar terrain usually because they had grown up in England and then moved overseas (although a few had spent childhoods in both countries or in a third country). They showed fairly strong emotions during the interviews. Many became very animated, laughing and talking loudly; others seemed to become sad, sniffing or telling me about times that they had been tearful or homesick. Still others became angry or exasperated about their experiences in the U.S., swearing or shouting as they told their stories. The extent of emotion they were prepared to bare before a relative stranger is evidence of the strength of their feelings about England and their move to the U.S.

Their responses to my questions showed the strong need people have to claim an identity related to place. Even those who were uncomfortable with the concept of nationality, as I showed in Chapter 2, defined themselves as having come from somewhere (for example, from their region in England or, in a couple of cases, from the U.S. or Canada). To explain her need to stay connected with her friends in England and with English culture, Imogen made this point:

> The reason is not because I think England's great at all. It's OK, but everywhere is OK. The reason is just that I'm English and I've got an identity and I don't want to not have an identity. I don't envy all those international people that are here and have spent four years ... living in three different places.... It's interesting, but it comes at too high a price. I want to have an identity and roots.... I mean, if I have a family, ... I want it to ... know what it is and where it lives and where it comes from, and it doesn't matter where that is.

Imogen is adamant here that she needs to feel that she belongs somewhere, as her comment, "I want to have an identity and roots," suggests. Her need to be English comes from her desire to be settled so that she and her potential family can feel safe and secure about who they are and where they are from. Although she said that "it doesn't matter where that is" because "everywhere is OK," she obviously has chosen an English identity over an American one because she already feels English—even though she has a permanent job in the U.S. In addition, she does not consider the possibility of maintaining both identities simultaneously.

CONSTRUCTING IDENTITIES

The people I interviewed constructed their national identities as they lived their daily lives. They used discourses of naturalness, culture, and accountability (with both Americans and English people), as well as practices, to understand and assert their Englishness. They relied on a variety of practices to negotiate their identities. I identified unconscious or habitual practices and intentional practices that brought them psychological and material benefits. I also examined two kinds of cultural practices—playful or parodic practices and conceptual practices—that could deconstruct or undo identities. In the sections that follow, I examine each of these modes of identity construction in turn.

Discourses of Naturalness in Identity Talk

Defining identities often involves essentializing those identities—that is, treating them as if they were real or natural rather than as socially constructed and, often, as if they were stable or static.[2] Research on gender and racial identities shows the ways naturalness can be used to justify inequalities and create the assumption that differences exist.[3] In the case of national identities, people assume that the nation is a natural phenomenon, whether because of cultural similarities, the idea of a sovereign "people," or its territorial dimensions.[4]

> Every time the term nation is used to refer to a recognizable territory, belief in the existence and . . . legitimacy of the entity is reinforced. In this way, [territoriality] lends credence to culturally and politically derived definitions by grounding them in physical, and consequently, conceptual space. (Jackson and Penrose 1993: 8)

Simply talking about a group in national terms reifies the idea of a nation further, making it harder to see how nations are social constructions.

As with gender and race, conceptualizing one's national identity as natural encourages assertions of difference and inequality, as well as a belief in the immutability of that identity. When the people I interviewed relied on discourses of naturalness, they found conceptualizing themselves as different from, and sometimes as superior to, Americans easier. Hence, in Chapter 2 I showed that they thought reserve came naturally to them and that they used English history and landscape as evidence of their natural connection with the land. In Chapter 3, they assumed their "English" sense of humor to be natural, and in so doing defined themselves as better than Americans. Indeed, the idea that there was something natural in their experiences of England and Englishness cropped up again and again during the interviews. Important to these understandings of English identity was the idea of "roots." As Ken explained, when he returned to England he had a "visceral" reaction to it that felt "like seeing a very old friend." He would think, "Fuck! It's still here, and it's still part of me somehow." Vera agreed: "Whether I like it or not, I'm deeply rooted in England. I can't help not being, [so] I accept that I am." Both saw England as embedded in their selves, something that they could not deny and something that was rather indefinable. Indeed, it was usually as interviewees attempted to define Englishness that their use of a discourse of naturalness emerged. Thus, they saw their English identity as something "intangible" or "there in your core somehow," "in your heart," "something inside that is just there because you're English and it makes you want to be more English and not lose that," "just the way I am," "part of me and I'm not changing that," resulting from "instinctive leanings," or "It's you; it's your culture, and you're not going to lose it."[5]

Ken elaborated on these feelings when I asked what he did when he was homesick. He replied that he would "read a really English book." As I pressed him to define this, he explained:

> I certainly feel there is more to being English than living there and being a citizen. . . . For me, it's things like Gilbert and Sullivan that almost doesn't make any sense outside England. The jokes are English; the whole style of the thing is . . . inherently and unalterably English. . . . Something like the *Mikado* could [only] have been written . . . by an Englishman . . . in the 1880s. [It's] something that, for [some] reason . . . , seems to come out of whatever makes a country anything more than a collection of people, . . . but I don't know what that is.

Here Ken described the way he conceptualized English culture as rooted in England and English traditions such that it must be "inherently and unalterably English." Although he could not define what it was that "makes a country anything more than a collection of people," he used the natural discourses of inherence and unalterability to explain the formation of culture. By drawing on discourses of naturalness, Ken succeeded in creating an exclusionary definition of nationhood in which English culture made sense only within the context of England. Relying on naturalistic explanations for Englishness makes things English because they are from England, thereby denying human agency in the production of identities. In addition, the indefinable aura Ken found in Englishness was tautologous: The only method he could use to describe Englishness was to point to English culture, which he then defined as English.

Interviewees also used a discourse of naturalness to argue that taking an American identity would be "phony" compared with the "real" or true nature of their English identities.[6] As Frank explained, being English is "my real basic identity, I don't want to lose that because . . . I don't have a new one. I don't have an American identity to put on." Later, he criticized an English friend living in the U.S. who "loathe[d] everything English":

> You can't make yourself into an American. You're born it, and if you cast off your roots and say I don't want anything to do with them anymore, you're cutting off your nose to spite your face. . . . You need that to give you an anchor in life. It's something to hold on to, and it's something, if necessary, to go back to when you need help.

Remembering that Frank had been away from England for forty years and did not even carry a British passport anymore, we can see how committed he was to maintaining his English identity. He conceptualized his Englishness as something to hold on to. Although it might be possible to "cast off your roots," he said, "you can't make yourself into an American." For him, the accident of birth has stuck even though he moved away and created a life for himself in the U.S. Frank was almost implying that he could not help being English, something with which even an ardent critic of national boundaries like Harry concurred: "Americans will sort of decide that I'm English. And I *am* English, culturally. . . . I'm more English than I would like to admit in some ways." The sense from these people's words was that they were helpless to change their national identity; they simply *were* English, and that was all there was to it. In this way, they relied on a discourse of naturalness to help explain their national identification to themselves. This discourse of naturalness often encouraged them to emphasize the differences between them and Americans. In the next sections, I examine the impact of interactions on their national-identity formation. Even when they discussed acting in concert with others, however, these ideas about naturalness were not far away.

Identity as Constituted Through Culture

The respondents focused on their interactions with other English people to explain the importance of culture in their experiences of national identity. However, they believed that they brought their "roots" to these interactions, drawing on the ideas of naturalness outlined earlier. They used what they presumed were shared cultural understandings and shared experiences to reaffirm their similarity with other English people. As they talked about culture, it seemed that they often thought of culture as a natural, rather than constructed, phenomenon.

As they discussed their attitudes toward other English people, a number of contradictions arose that highlight the complexity of identity construction. Despite their propensity to use naturalistic conceptions of culture, they admitted that interacting with English people made them feel *more* English, suggesting the ways in which national identity varies from context to context. In addition, although at times they relished their connections with other English people, at other times, they found these connections threatening. In conjunction with this contradiction are the feelings they had toward their American partners.[7] Although the interviewees I quote here claim that English people understand them better than do Americans, Harry later suggests that his American partner understands him as well as any English person can. This raises the question of whether partners in cross-national relationships become "honorary English people" or whether the people I talked to found the differences in national identities between them and their partners a barrier. Although I witnessed a few joking moments about national differences between some interviewees and their partners, Harry was the only one to address the effect of his wife's national identity on their interactions. These issues all show the intricacies of national-identity construction, especially because those I spoke to defined their identities in one way at one moment and in other ways at other moments.

The interviewees explicitly talked about using interactions with other English people to maintain or enhance their Englishness, believing that these interactions sustained their Englishness ipso facto, or even that they became more English as they interacted with others. As Harriet said, "I'm more myself when I'm with English people . . . because the understanding goes deeper." She felt more like herself because she assumed that English people understood her in a way that was qualitatively different from the way she was understood by people of other nationalities. The interviewees found being with people who they felt understood their cultural references or shared their sense of humor "relaxing" and "restful."[8] Gary argued that other English people "automatically" knew what he meant when he referred to particular aspects of English culture, conceptualizing this in terms of the "common reference points" and linguistic "short cuts" he could use. Thus,

> I can say I was in the Young Socialists . . . and they can conjure up an image of approximately what I was like as a teenager. If I [were] to tell them . . . how I went to a comprehensive school . . . and I was into animal rights, and I listened to, name a band, *The Fall,* they can probably picture . . . that I wore woolly socks and desert boots, 'cause everybody did at that time who . . . had those other experiences. All those short cuts are right there. Whereas [with] an American, I have to cross a lot wider gap. I don't mean to sound clannish, but . . . I can get to more interesting issues quicker with English people than I can with Americans. I can skip all the preliminary cultural misunderstandings that might go on.

Here Gary draws on his cultural experiences, arguing that they produce a special bond between English people that enables them to understand one another in a way that outsiders cannot. Although Gary is a dual-national who spent some of his childhood in the U.S., the references to culture that he can make with other English people clearly are very meaningful to him. Obviously, he feels that he can understand English people, and they him, much more clearly than can Americans. The "gap" is "wider" with Americans.

Frances also conceptualized Americans as outsiders, including me as an insider in her national schema. She argued that she would have interacted differently with an American interviewer. "It's like you've been verified," she said. "I know where you're coming from. I can understand your . . . expressions, nuances, whatever . . . and you can understand what I'm saying." Frances assumes that she and I share common reference points and hence understand each other more closely than would an American and an English person. Her belief that we automatically understand each other draws on a homogeneous notion of Englishness[9] that assumes that English people can discern one another's essentials far more easily than they can relate to other nationalities. These individuals suggest the sense of safety and security that comes from interacting with other English people; they feel they know in fundamental ways what makes other English people tick and so can have more meaningful interactions with them than with others.

In making these claims, the interviewees did not dismiss the connections that other nationalities might have with one another. Thus, their conception of the importance of a shared cultural heritage extended beyond English people. They argued that Americans must also share common cultural ground with one another, as must every other nationality. They were concerned about pointing out that English people are not unique in this respect. As Gary said earlier, "I don't want to sound clannish."

The connections that they posited with other English people occurred on two fronts. On the first, as we have seen, they believed that all English people shared cultural experiences that set them apart from other people. Thus, they defined themselves as English because of the ways in which culture and experience emerged during their interactions with *any* English person. The second front that they mentioned was that of the English person abroad, or fellow expatriate or immigrant. Here they identified with English people who had similar experiences of moving. Thus, they often said to me, "You must have experienced this" or "You must know what I am talking about," as they recounted tales of interactions with Americans. Others explicitly mentioned bonding with other English people in America as they compared notes on their experiences abroad. Three women I interviewed were members of a British women's group, and they talked about this group as an important place for them to let off steam about the trials and tribulations of living in the U.S. Several men discussed finding other English men with whom to talk about "viewing the country as an outsider and being able to relate to things in a different way."[10] Peter found that he could "actually sit down and talk about stuff rather than just hang out" with one of his English friends:

> The fact that you have a lot of similar experiences of growing up and . . .
> of coming here and making your way over here [*brief pause*]. It's nice to
> have a mate . . . because he's pretty much gone through the same thing as
> I have, and I'm sure some of the things I can tell him [will] be helpful to
> him [and vice versa].

Likewise, Octavia would call an English friend who lived around the corner to say, "I knew *you* would understand!" when something had happened in her dealings with Americans or in interactions with her family back in England. These individuals, then, saw themselves as similar to two sets of people with different sets of experiences: those in England who had never lived in the U.S., and those English people who had moved to the U.S. In one case, it was the experience of Englishness that made them feel comfortable during interactions; in the other, it was the experience of having moved away from England. However, in both instances, they described their comfort as arising from a common heritage that emerged during interactions.

This idea that English people share a cultural bond on which they can draw led some of the interviewees to make naturalistic claims about the role of culture and experience in their identity formation. Vera pointed out that "you can see yourself in them, and they see themselves in you," suggesting the strong sense of identification she had with other English people. To "see [herself] in them," she had to believe that she and other English people were the same in fundamental ways. Indeed, the interviewees often talked about being on the same "wavelength"[11] as, or of not needing to explain themselves to, other English people—suggesting that they could almost communicate via telepathy. Diana, for instance, claimed that English people would receive her ideas "exactly as I give them out." She argued that she felt more English with other English people because "deep down . . . that's your real basic formation." The contradictory nature of this claim echoed the participants' use of culture to prove the naturalness of national identity. Diana felt that she was *more* English with other English people, implying that her national identity was mutable. Yet she defined that identity by suggesting that her "real basic formation" was naturally based. As she continued to explain, she oscillated between believing that this "formation" was natural and that it was socially constructed: "If you come here, let's say when you're twenty, . . . you'll never lose being [English]. It's too formative. They're your formative years. That's how you form your opinions, where you're taught your basic manners, and [how] you look upon people as other people." She implied that this "formation" would have occurred on the basis of being taught the "manners," "opinions," and mores of the culture for twenty years. She noted the contradictory sense of identity that this understanding gave her: "It's not like I feel like I'm [as] English [as] fellow English people in England. I really don't. But I'm closer to being that than I am to being anything else in the whole world." Although Diana wanted to distance herself from Englishness, her words implied that these formative years were set in stone and unchangeable because they were so deeply embedded within her. Despite the fact that she did not want to identify with a nationality, she felt close enough to her English background that she had to identify with it on some level.

Frank's words help to explain this sense: "The streets, the atmosphere, the connections to family, . . . the memories [are] all formative, and I think those things affect you more than you know when you're a child. . . . As a child, the things you learn [and] assimilate are instinctive and [that] makes them . . . stronger." Like Frank, others with whom I talked placed a high premium on their childhood years in England as having irrevocably formed them into the people they had become. Diana and Frank both believed that their connection with England was instinctive or something they could never lose, despite their efforts to explain it in terms of what they had been taught and had learned. Implicit in their discourse of the impact of culture and experiences on their identities was an understanding of their "formative years" as natural. Thus, although they may have defined their national identities using the ideas of shared culture and experiences, they often used a discourse of naturalness to make sense of this, perhaps to make it seem more real to them.

In this section, we have seen the contradictory nature of the interviewees' experiences of the cultural components of their national identities. Despite providing evidence of the ways in which national identity emerged during interactions with other English people on the basis of a shared culture, they often conceptualized this culture as natural, the result of their "roots" or "deep [and] basic formation." The implication is that their English nationality gave them an inherent and automatic connection with those who shared this accident of birth. Also, they pointed to the shared understandings that arose with other English immigrants or expatriates as a result of moving to the U.S. This, too, was the result of social experiences, but they implied that these experiences produced an almost naturalistic bond. Although they wanted to use the discourse of naturalness, the ways they highlighted their national identities as they moved from one interaction to another shows the socially constructed and contested nature of those identities.

Accountability as a Form of Identity Construction (with English People)

The third kind of identity construction occurred as a result of interviewees' feeling that they were defined by other people. This usually happened during interactions in which the interviewees believed that they were being held accountable for their identities.[12] In Chapters 3 and 4, I discussed how they felt Americans held them responsible for their Englishness, and how they in turn held Americans responsible for their Anglophilia. Here, however, I turn to the times that the interviewees experienced interactions with other English people as instances in which they were held accountable for their English identities. In these cases, they believed that others were defining their identities for them—a variation on Cooley's (1964 [1922]: 184) "looking glass self," whereby they began to see themselves as they believed others saw them.

The cultural communion with other English people noted earlier aroused contradictory feelings at different moments. Although they relished their bonds with other people from England, some felt constrained by English people they met while in the U.S. Gary, for instance, who said he felt culturally connected to English people also noted that interactions with them sometimes made him feel "less English" because he was reminded of his dual-nationality. He conceptualized these interactions with other English people as threatening because he worried that they might show up his lack of Englishness. Others had this sense when they returned to England and could not keep up with cultural references and current events. Imogen said that friends jokingly asked her, "[You] call yourself an Englishwoman?" when she admitted to not having heard about a new restaurant in England. Quentin also said he felt alienated when he returned to England: "I'm losing part of what it is to be English because I don't know what's been going on." Rather than feeling more English, these people worried that they became *less* English with other English people.

Others also responded with ambivalence and apprehension toward the English people they met while overseas. Quentin and Peter admitted to feeling a little cheated when a "limey" "invaded [their] turf" in the U.S., the former explaining that he would think, "Oh, damn it, I'm not as unique as I thought I was." Tara also noted the awkwardness with which English people sized one another up, establishing the kind of person each was (especially in terms of class background). Ken agreed, claiming that he did not like to meet other English people abroad because he worried that they would know "what I'm actually like." He felt that he might "modify [his] behavior slightly" as an "instinctive" thing. The fact that Ken thought his reactions to other English people were "instinctive" shows again the ways the interviewees assumed that some kind of natural bond existed between English people.

Harry also found it "very unnerving to talk to people who get you right away," and to whom he did not have to "explain the fundamentals." In contrast to Americans, who, he said, imagine that "the Queen is . . . my best friend," Harry described sitting down in a bar with a new English friend:

> Within two minutes, he knows exactly what I'm all about. He knows where I'm from, . . . he knows probably that I went to a public school, . . . I come from a middle-class family, . . . the kind of life, . . . what sort of friends I've got, the pubs I go to . . . He's got a three-dimensional picture of the kind of person I am.

Although exasperated by the assumptions Americans made about him, Harry was disconcerted by the fact that he didn't have to "explain [him]self" to other English people. To his mind, both sets of people made assumptions about him. Americans, he thought, made the wrong assumptions, whereas English people were able to make the right assumptions by drawing on shared cultural understandings. However, Harry was ambivalent about being pigeonholed by either set of people (although for different reasons). Like some of the other interviewees, who tried to distance themselves from an expatriate lifestyle, he felt uncomfortable interacting too much with English people. As he explained:

> I don't want to be about somebody who's English abroad. That isn't what I want to be. That's what everyone tries to define me as. . . . Even though culturally it's very easy for me, [and] it's in my nature to just feel comfortable around English people, I'd rather be an internationalist . . . who gets on well with all cultures.

In choosing not to interact with other English people, Harry attempted to limit the kind of connections he made and the way he defined himself. He did not want to be defined as "English abroad," preferring instead to be "an internationalist." By interacting with other English people, he would be laying himself open to definition by them, according to their standards, perhaps even modifying his behavior to fit the kinds of unwritten rules that accompany the routine summaries that English people can make about one another. Like Ken, Harry seemed to fear that English people could see through him, thereby keeping him in line. Talking to me (as a fellow English person), he said, was like talking to his wife because he did not have to "translate" for either of us. Interestingly, his wife is American, which calls his complaints about the assumptions made by Americans into question (unless she has become an "honorary English person").

The interviewees therefore had mixed responses to being defined during their interactions with English people. On the one hand, they relished the cultural communion that they believed occurred, seeing these interactions as opportunities to maintain or enhance their Englishness. On the other hand, they shied away from these interactions, either feeling that they were not English enough to engage with other English people or finding the sense that English people knew more about them than they would like unnerving. Interactions, then, were powerful sites of identity construction, maintenance, and deconstruction in these people's minds. Their experiences show how identity can be double-edged: People who hold a common identity may feel safe and secure with those who are similar to them, but, at the same time, they can also feel limited by the assumptions they believe fellow identity-holders make about them—either calling that identity into question or reminding them of an identity that they would prefer to disavow.

Accountability as a Form of Identity Construction (with Americans)

Many of the people I talked to also found the assumptions that Americans made about them constraining. In Chapters 3 and 4, we saw the ways they blamed Americans for their responses to Englishness. They held Americans accountable for what they saw as American Anglophilia, pointing to the numerous ways in which Americans commented on their national identities during interactions, especially on their accents. In many instances, interviewees placed the onus on Americans for understanding them or for overly valuing their English accents, complaining about the need to change the way they spoke. In other cases, they expressed a desire to avoid being a "celebrity," wishing simply to live their lives rather than having to engage in conversations about their nationalities or accents. Although some found the attention wearing, they did admit that Americans usually made these connections from a friendly and interested point of view. During these kinds of interactions with Americans, they learned how much particular Americans valued England and English culture: The Americans had visited England and enjoyed their trip, they relished English accents and warned the interviewee not to lose her or his accent, they treated the interviewee with more respect because of his or her national identity, or they used the Englishness of the interviewee as a status symbol in interactions with others (for example, the bosses who said, "This is my English-educated employee"). As Alex explained, English people in the U.S. learned to "shuffle inside" and to become adept at accepting compliments. In other words, although they might be cringing inwardly, they had to learn to be outwardly gracious about the attention they garnered.

The interviewees had mixed responses to these interactions. Although they joked about relishing the "celebrity status" they enjoyed in the U.S., they also said they sometimes felt constrained by the constant attention. In Chapter 4, I pointed to the loss of control some felt at being defined merely as an accent (although at other moments, interviewees defined themselves using their accents). Others felt limited by their interactions with Americans. Although Peter accepted his nickname in his town, "English Pete," with good humor, his words also suggested an undercurrent of resentment at being constantly defined by his nationality ("Oh, God, get over it already. I'm Pete, not 'English Pete'" [*the latter in an American accent*]). Others objected to the ways Americans defined English culture. A few noted that Americans were obsessed with English people's tea drinking and with the relationship between Englishness and rain, even though the interviewees did not see these as parts of their national identity. Some were annoyed by American's stereotypes of English people. As Harry commented, "I like to think I'm a lot more complex than that." They also worried about American's class- and region-specific versions of Englishness. Those who defined themselves as working-class or who were from the north of England, the Midlands, or the southwest found the emphasis on an upper-middle-class, southeastern version of Englishness particularly irritating. In these instances, they objected to the ways in which Americans reduced them to one-dimensional caricatures of Englishness. As with any identity, although one might take pride in the identity itself, when one is defined by others, the loss of control can be psychologically debilitating.[13]

Although these English people might have felt limited in some ways by Americans' definitions of them, they also felt that they received certain privileges from being English in the U.S. The Anglophilia they

noted among Americans often produced situations in which their Englishness was useful—when applying for jobs, for instance, renting apart-
ments, walking into singles bars, or talking their way out of parking tickets. Some found that Americans did not seem to think of them as
immigrants; the interviewees often conflated their nationality, race, class,
and sometimes gender to explain this phenomenon. Indeed, many
believed that they fit into the "mainstream" of American culture either
because of the assumed predominance of English culture in the U.S. or
because of their privileged class and racial backgrounds.

Despite the privileges that they believed came from being English in
the U.S., however, they were often critical of the ways Americans interacted with them. They held Americans accountable for their
Anglophilia, blaming them for the esteem in which they held English
people. Their thoughts reflect the problems that come with having an
identity—even a positive one—imposed on one. As Ann Snitow and
Denise Reily[14] point out, allowing others to define one's identity leaves
little sense of agency or control. Indeed, although the stigmatization as
English was generally one from which they benefited, interviewees
sometimes felt powerless and helpless as their identities were defined
by Americans. As they criticized the ideas of national identity held by
Americans, these English people wanted to be seen as more than simply English. They reminded me that there were real people underneath
their Englishness, an idea that they felt was often glossed over by Americans. Thus, they held Americans responsible for their attitudes toward
Englishness and saw Americans as the culprits for both the privileges
and the constraints they accrued from being English.

IDENTITIES AS CONTRADICTORY

In these four sections, we have seen the contradictions involved in identity construction. Although the people I talked to may have believed that
culture was important to their conceptions of national identity, they
drew on naturalistic definitions of both culture and identity to make this
point. Hence, they avoided thinking about the socially constructed
nature of their national identities. In addition, although they were often
explicit about feeling more or less English in different situations, they
ultimately fell back on the idea that national identity is immutable and
essential. Their contradictory feelings about being defined by their iden-

tities also show the vagaries of the role of interactions as identity-constructing devices. On the one hand, they relished the ability to commune
with other English people, but on the other, they were threatened by
these interactions when a chance existed that they might be defined as
more or less English than they wished to be. Echoing this dualism,
although being defined as English by Americans was freeing and sometimes brought the interviewees privileges, they also found being defined
simply as an English person constraining. Identities as they emerge during interactions, then, are slippery creatures. People want to be defined
according to the ways *they* define their identities—they "want to be able
to be English when [they] want to be," as Ken said, and they want to
control how their identity is interpreted. However, whether they were
interacting with other English people or with Americans, the interviewees found that their national identities could be defined in ways of
which they did not approve. Clearly, they preferred situations in which
they could retain control over their identities.

The dualisms expressed by these interviewees have implications
beyond the construction of English national identities. They show the
ways in which people make sense of socially constructed identities using
naturalistic discourses. They also show the pitfalls of engaging in interactions with others. In being held accountable for that identity,[15] one
risks not only being treated as a member of the identity, but also losing
control over the definition of that identity. Although identities emerge
during interactions with others, identity-holders are not always pleased
with the definitions of identity that result. Even with relatively privileged identities—for example, being white, middle-class, and English
in the U.S.—the holders of those identities felt limited and constrained
by others' assumptions.

PATTERNS OF IDENTITY CONSTRUCTION

I avoided constructing typologies about the interviewees' identity constructions because, as the contradictory evidence in the earlier sections
shows, they were often highly ambivalent about how to respond to
other English people and to Americans, and they drew on overlapping
but different discourses to conceptualize their relationships to Englishness. Indeed, as I showed in Chapter 5, interviewees such as Quentin,
Mike, and Craig could move from discourses in which they criticized

England's post-imperial arrogance at one moment to expressions of pride in its imperial legacy at another. The internal contradictions in many of the interviews illustrate the struggles of the people I spoke with to define a response to Englishness and Americanness that made sense to them. In a similar fashion to Frankenberg's findings,[16] few were able simply to draw on one discursive repertoire to understand their identities. Hence, I reported my analyses in a thematic way rather than attempting to account for differences among them. The latter task would have been hard to undertake because the same person's words often emerged on both sides of an issue.

Having said this, some general patterns did emerge. The length of time the interviewees had spent in the U.S. had some effect on how Americanized their accents were and, sometimes, on how willing they were to use American words and phrases. Also, the length of their time in the U.S. sometimes influenced the extent to which they saw themselves as immigrants: Those who had been away from England for a long time were more likely to adopt the "immigrant" label. By contrast, those who had arrived more recently were reluctant to see themselves as immigrants, as I showed in Chapter 3. A further finding was that the more highly educated interviewees sometimes evinced greater awareness about racism in the U.S. and England, although they were as likely as others to conceptualize Englishness in white terms.

A further general finding is the relationship of gender to national and racial identities. As I showed in Chapter 6, gender emerged less often than did race in the context of comparing the two countries because the interviewees often felt that gender relations in England and the U.S. were more similar than different. This is not to say that gender was not pertinent to the interviewees or to my analyses. Some interviewees were highly critical of American gender relations, while others decried sexism in England. Often, however, awareness of gender identities became relevant as interviewees talked about their experiences of immigration rather than of national identity. For instance, men sometimes argued that they would have found moving to another country more difficult if they had been women, and women with long-term partners sometimes alluded to the difficulties that married homemakers who had moved to the U.S. with their husbands faced in meeting people.

When it did emerge, gender tended to become apparent in relationship to other identities. For example, images of masculinity and femininity became relevant in conjunction with conceptualizations of normative versions of white, middle-class Englishness. In addition, some interviewees drew on gendered discourses of paternalism as they discussed imperialism—noting, for instance, how masculine their emphases on sport sounded. Thus, my evidence provides partial confirmation of the idea that gender identities are constructed and reproduced in relationship to other identities.

DOING IDENTITY WORK

Although most of those I talked to placed the blame for their identities squarely on the shoulders of Americans, we also saw them putting considerable identity work into being English. In Chapter 4, I examined the ways in which they played their accents up and down to suit situations, noting that they were more likely than not to play their accents up to gain privileges. In Chapter 2, we saw interviewees working to be "unflappable," "reserved," and "understated," frequently apologizing and projecting a "stiff upper lip" attitude—so much so that Alex wondered whether she became a "cartoon Brit."[17] In Chapter 3, I analyzed some of the ways in which English people "did" their Englishness. From holding a beer glass in a certain way to having a particular sense of humor, shopping at particular stores, wearing particular clothes, or watching English television programs, the interviewees used cultural practices to assert their sense of themselves as English. Chapters 5 and 6 provided examples of interviewees doing conceptual work as they engaged with hegemonic definitions of Englishness, sometimes concurring with them, and sometimes imagining their own versions of English national identity. Many other examples of identity work emerged during the interviews. Some people purposely ate English food, drank English tea, read English novels, watched English sports, followed English current events and politics by reading English newspapers, celebrated English holidays such as Guy Fawkes' Night, or followed English traditions at Christmastime. Some people even believed that they ironed in an English way or ate their breakfast the way other English people did. These were all ways that they maintained their Englishness.

These cultural practices show the agency individuals have in asserting, enhancing, maintaining, and reconstructing their identities. My analyses have shown three different ways to do this identity work: through habitual or unintentional practices; through intentional practices (which include two, sometimes overlapping elements—practices that ensure material benefits and those that ensure psychological benefits); and through playful or parodic practices. Thus, in Chapter 4, I noted the ways in which identity-constructing practices can become so habitual that they are unconscious or unintentional, seeming to be "natural" rather than produced by individuals. Because I relied on the interviewees' self-reports, I do not have many examples of these kinds of habitual practices (although I have discussed many ways that interviewees rely on discourses of naturalness to justify their national identities). My analyses of the ways that English people's accents varied did suggest some examples of these kinds of practices, however. Although some people claimed not to vary their accents, I heard their accents changing during the interviews or noted inconsistencies in their statements about whether they intended to keep their English accents or not. Also, in Chapter 6, I analyzed how interviewees unconsciously imagined England as white, and sometimes as male and upper-middle-class.

Another form of identity work I discussed in Chapters 3 and 4 was that arising from intentional practices—the practices that individuals carry out in response to what they believe other people think of them. There, I refined Erving Goffman's (1959: 252) conception of "self-presentation" by suggesting that there are two levels to the work that people do to influence the definition of a situation. One occurs in order to derive material benefits, and the other occurs to derive psychological benefits. In Chapter 3, I showed how interviewees responded to Americans' Anglophilia by asserting their Englishness in different situations, usually to gain benefits. I argued that this was an example of their holding Americans accountable for their perceived Anglophilia. For example, as Diana said, "If people are going to be so dumb as to run a system where it goes totally on appearances or how you sound, then . . . I'm going to play them at their own game." Diana's experiences, combined with those of the other people I talked to, suggest that actions such as "play[ing] them at their own game" contain two elements. The first involves acting in ways that achieve material benefits. For instance, Diana decided to act deliberately in certain ways—for instance, by playing up her English accent to get an apartment—to enhance her own prestige or power. Thus, the interviewees might accentuate their Englishness in specific situations to obtain concrete material benefits, such as torn-up parking tickets, free subway tokens, or any of the other privileges they mentioned. Overlapping in some ways, but distinct in others, is the idea that Diana expressed elsewhere when she aimed to "consider [Americans] shit"[18] by playing up her accent. In this situation, the psychological benefits she derived from emphasizing her English accent were distinct from the material benefits she aimed to achieve in the first example (although her use of the word "dumb" does suggest that she felt superior while playing the system). Thus, in addition to (or instead of) scheming to achieve concrete material benefits, they may self-consciously assert their Englishness to enhance their own self-esteem and derive personal satisfaction. This may or may not result in enhanced prestige or power (although one could argue that by acting in ways that boost their self-esteem, they make interactions more enjoyable and beneficial for themselves). The way Gary held his beer glass and cigarette spring to mind as examples of this kind of identity work. Gary claimed that he had been told he held his glass in an English manner, so he purposely did this to present himself as English in the nightclub. It is not clear from his description whether he received any benefits from this behavior (or, indeed, whether anybody noticed his actions). However, his practices helped him feel superior in the situation. Thus, individuals may intentionally do identity in order to receive both tangible material benefits and intangible psychological benefits from their Englishness.

The third type of identity work I examined is that arising from playful practices (or "performative" practices, to use Butler's (1990: 25) term. The playfulness and humor of the English people I studied came through in all the interviews: Although they took the interviews seriously, a substantial amount of laughter, self-parody, and playfulness was also present. I have tried to give a sense of this throughout the book, especially in Chapter 4, where some of the participants played with their accents for their own and my amusement. I have also analyzed their stance on humor, pointing especially to their unfavorable comparisons with Americans, who, they said, take themselves too seriously. We saw this in Chapter 3 when I discussed the interviewees' ideas of an English sense of humor; in Chapter 5 when I discussed how the interviewees regarded Americans as too serious about race, ethnicity, and identity politics; and in Chapter 2, when I showed the interviewees' critiquing American displays of national identity as too serious.

In contrast to their stereotype of the serious American, the English people I interviewed believed that they were witty, sarcastic, and ironic. Conventional beliefs about humor and playfulness that stem from Freudian analyses posit that humor masks more serious messages.[19] As Barrie Thorne reminds us, playfulness is often used to "frame" events apart from everyday life so that threatening themes such as sexuality, power, and aggression can be negotiated in a safe space.[20] Certainly, I have taken most of the interviewees' jokes as indicative of a deeper meaning. Gary said that his beer-glass holding made him feel superior but that he was only "half-serious"; when discussing the impact of British imperialism on India with Indian friends, Quentin said he sounded like a participant in a *Monty Python* film; Andy hung Union Jack bunting out of his window on the Fourth of July. All of these actions I took seriously. Along with Thorne, I assumed that they all evidence how the boundaries between English people and Americans were solidified.[21]

A potentially different reading emerges if we view these and other actions simply as evidence of parody and playfulness. As Judith Butler's analysis of gender identity reminds us, to see identity as constituted through practices, as a "performative accomplishment" (1990: 141), is to recognize the possibilities for transformation. In her words, gender performance is "a parodic repetition that exposes the phantasmatic effect of abiding identity as a politically tenuous construction" (1990: 141). She uses the examples of drag and cross-dressing to point to the possibilities of subversion because they show the ways in which gender is socially constructed. Because drag parodies something that has no essence, "it is an imitation without an origin" (1990: 138). And because every iteration of gender will be slightly different, the potential remains for gender identity to be undermined. In a similar way, these interviewees could be parodying a particular kind of English identity. The playfulness that sometimes emerges as they assert feelings of superiority suggests that they wished to mock these feelings of superiority as they assert them. Thus, as I show in Chapter 2, these interviewees could be criticizing the "rule Britannia and fuck the rest of the world"[22] attitude of nationalism. Alex, walking through U.S. customs with her head held high, thinking, "This is the voice of the British Empire," playfully asserted the idea of English superiority. However, she can also be seen to be drawing attention to the irrelevance of British imperialism in the American context. Likewise, Harry, complaining about the way "Johnny Foreigner" plays soccer, also drew on a stereo-type of xenophobic English people. Because he said this laughingly, he could have been parodying rather than affirming this stereotype. As Barrie Thorne and Judith Butler suggest, playfulness and parody might look like identity assertion on the surface, but in pointing to the con-structed nature of such assertions, social actors may also be engaged in transforming or deconstructing that identity.[23] The question remains open as to how serious the interviewees were when they played with the idea of superiority. Certainly, humor allowed them simultaneously to assert and yet negate their sense of superiority; however, their play-fulness might also toy with a xenophobic version of English identity in order to deconstruct it. In some ways, their use of humor in these instances mirrored the ways in which they asserted their national iden-tities—doing identity at the same time that they undermined it. Fol-lowing up on the possibility of identity deconstruction, I turn now from the ways the interviewees did identity work to examine the ways they chose not to do it.

WORKING TO UNDO IDENTITY

Identities are not essences. Therefore, they do not exist outside the minds of those who invoke them. That is not to say that identities are not relevant and important for individuals as they live their lives (and it is certainly not to ignore the fact that they can have real and damag-ing consequences for people's lives). It is to say, however, that identi-ties are human constructions, with all the mutability, impermanence, instability, and historical and spatial variation that this implies.[24] By focusing on the practices individuals use to construct identities and showing how their experiences of identities as natural are discursively constructed, I wanted to point to the ways in which identities can be downplayed and undone as well as asserted and reconstructed. R. W. Connell's analysis of the relationship between practice and structure reminds us that structures contain the seeds of their own transforma-tion in the shape of practices.[25] By repeatedly acting in different ways (within the constraints or enablements of structures), individuals ulti-mately may change those structures.[26] It was to this end that I examined the identity projects of those who refused to accept, or attempted to redefine, the identity "English."

As we saw in Chapter 2, some of the people I talked to were explicit that they did not want to identify themselves as English. Instead, they called on English regional identities or on other national, political, or ideological identities. Many equated claiming a national identity with being nationalistic, something that they were concerned to avoid. Meanwhile, others attempted to avoid "doing" their English identities. Antonia talked about working at being less cynical, perceiving cynicism as a particularly English trait, and Ken and Peter worked to move beyond the feelings of constraint that came with a perceived English attitude of "It's just not cricket!" Ken, in particular, said he would not return to live in England until he had learned to stand up to that attitude. Frances noted that her American husband was trying to encourage their children to be more outgoing, while others worked hard to leave what they saw as their English reserve or "stiff upper lip" behind. Quentin even implied that he was not "truly British" because he was not reserved enough. Others tried to change their English vocabularies so that Americans would not mark them as different and to learn about American sports or politics. Stephen wanted to distance himself from Englishness when he saw how other English people played up their accents or their cultural identities in the U.S.

Still others pointed to how their experiences in the U.S. challenged their definition of "properly" English. As Emily said, "You are different because you left. . . . Once you have . . . made your way by yourself, it has to change you. . . . There's something not me about England. I think I'm better off somewhere else." Emily explicitly denies a link to England here—saying that England is "not [her]"—because she no longer feels she belongs there. These people argued that they were different from other English people because they had moved away. They felt that they had a more detached perspective from which to view England and could now see the country's good and bad characteristics. Many commented that things that had never struck them as particularly English now did so, because they could see these things as outsiders. In noting how they had changed their views of England, they implied that they were not as English as they used to be.

In addition, in Chapters 2, 5, and 6, we saw interviewees doing conceptual work by engaging with images of England. In Chapter 5, I analyzed how the interviewees responded to hegemonic definitions of Englishness as they considered the post-imperial moment, and in Chapter

6 the impact of race on their national identities became clear. As they reacted to hegemonic narratives about England, they accepted, manipulated, exaggerated, downplayed, or rejected them, attempting to construct versions of English identity that made sense to them. For instance, although some responded to what they knew about the imperial legacy with shame and guilt, others felt proud of colonization, either because of its "civilizing" mission or because of the forms of culture that it helped to disseminate. These very different responses are evidence of the broad range of conceptual work that enabled interviewees to challenge or maintain particular kinds of English identities. By focusing on their conceptual work, we see the potential for them to "undo" as well as "do" identity within the constraints of structures.[27]

In Chapter 2, many interviewees criticized images of England as falsely nostalgic, unrepresentative, or stereotypical. Although I ultimately showed that a naturalistic conception of England as a green historical theme park may have prevailed, the interviewees criticized the emphases on history and tradition and the idea that England is a rural paradise. They struggled with their own ideals of Englishness, trying to avoid clichés and criticizing the parodic and cartoonlike images of England they saw around them in the media and popular culture.

In distancing themselves from England and Englishness, these people engaged in a form of identity work that involved reconceptualizing prevailing ideas about national identity. This, I suggest, has implications that reach far beyond these interviewees' imaginations. If the interviewees seem to be refusing to do national identity—or are even *undoing* national identity in some cases—then we can see them as social actors who act in ways to challenge or reconstruct the broader structures and institutions within which they operate.[28] Identity-creating practices have the potential not only to re-create structures, but also to undo them. Although individuals may be acting in response to a situation or particular structural configuration, they are working to challenge that situation in some way. Thus, interviewees who refused to self-identify using their nation, learned to use American terminology, or criticized the images of England they saw in the media as unrepresentative were attempting to take their national identities into their own hands. As Denise Reily and Ann Snitow show,[29] there are times that people do not want the particular identities that are foisted upon them. Scholars in gender and ethnicity have also shown the potential for people to escape from, undo, or redo their identities.[30]

The people who refuse to cave in to stereotypical conceptions or who challenge the hegemonic definitions of their identity are on the front line of redefining identities. Their experiences teach us that identity is not natural, immutable, or inherent. Rather, identity is a social product. For this reason, there are different versions of identities throughout time and space.

UBIQUITOUS DISCOURSES OF NATURALNESS

Although these interviewees' experiences suggest that they can avoid doing identity in some situations, powerful mechanisms for reinforcing identity remain in place. Chief among these is the organization of the world according to identities. Clearly, one cannot meaningfully give up being English when national boundaries exist that construct England as a country within the United Kingdom and when citizenship involves not only privileges, rights, and responsibilities, but also participation in rituals, symbols, and myths. These macro forces keep identities in place. Individuals are constrained by particular definitions of Englishness and by their own degree of privilege in the U.S. to construct their identities in particular ways. Even on the level of interactions, individuals continue to treat one another as if certain identities are important. As the interviewees argued in the case of accountability, other people provide the means for keeping their national identities in place.

A further problem remains in the propensity of individuals themselves to believe in the naturalness of their identities. Harriet suggested how deep the ideology of naturalness can run. She recalled trying to change to fit in with what she thought of as American styles of behavior. Thus, she went through

> a stage when I [thought], "OK, I'm going to be strident, and I'm going to be American, and I'm going to complain." I didn't enjoy it . . . , and in fact my [American] boyfriend told me I was rude and I wasn't doing it the right way . . . because I get very cross with tea here because they do not know how to serve tea. They make it with tepid water. . . . He said I was complaining about the wrong things and I wasn't doing it properly, so I don't complain.

Harriet's belief that she was not able to complain in "the right way" and the corroboration by her boyfriend, who said she was complaining improperly about "the wrong things," is illuminating. Many people, of course, perceive tea as quintessentially English, which adds weight to the boyfriend's claim that Harriet had not chosen the right topic about which to complain. More important, however, Harriet was quick to see her boyfriend as right—that she really did not know how to complain "properly" in America. The implication is that this inability comes from her Englishness. This example shows the pitfalls of attempting to change behavior that one associates with identity. Although Harriet worked to try to be what she thought of as American, when her behavior did not meet with approval, she presumed that she was naturally unable to complain and gave up. Likewise, in Chapter 4, I showed how easily Imogen and Vera spoke with American accents in some situations but refused to use them in everyday life because they seemed fake. They used the discourse of naturalness to justify an inability to change. They are stuck in a version of reality in which natural forms of Englishness and Americanness exist, and they cannot move from the former to the latter, or even bridge the two.

Thus, when we think about moving beyond or challenging identities—especially identities based on gender, race, and nation that privilege some at the expense of others—it is important to remember the powerful discourses of naturalness on which people draw to keep identitites in place. Believing that identities are natural enables people to see themselves as different from, and sometimes as superior to, other people. People believe that they cannot act in certain ways because of their identities, but the issue may be that they do not want to change because change would ruin the image they have of themselves. Attending to the work that goes into identity construction shows us the agency that individuals have, but it also alerts us to the work those individuals do to keep identity in place.

CONCLUSION: CONSTRUCTING ENGLISHNESS

In this project, I set out to explore what Englishness is and how it is constructed. The answer to the first question is based in part on the second. Although we have seen some people defining Englishness in terms of a green historical theme park, a naturally sarcastic sense of humor, or a homogeneous white national grouping, other evidence has pointed to the ways in which these notions of Englishness are essentialized stereotypes. Indeed, the interviewees have actively engaged with simplistic definitions of Englishness to reinterpret them, reject them, or reinvoke them. The work that they do to construct their national identities involves supplementing hegemonic definitions of Englishness (as portrayed, for example, in the media or by elites) with their own, more individualized versions. This study has shown that no one way exists to define English identity, and attempting to find one would be reductive in the extreme.

Although the study focused on one group of immigrants, my findings about the construction of identity are important for other groups. Methodologically, using the experiences of "outsiders within" or "strangers" to the U.S. provided data that captured the identity negotiations of those whose marginality attuned them to the question of who they thought they were.[31] In theoretical terms, I have developed a practice-based approach to national identity that shows how it intersects with other kinds of identities in the lives of individuals. I have also analyzed how individuals carry out identity work to help construct their identities, and I have developed an understanding of the sense of entitlement and privilege that comes with an assumption of superiority. Most important, I have investigated the emergent status of identities, pointing to their dynamic, contested, and contradictory characteristics, despite the discourses of naturalness that surround them.

Appendix
Descriptions of Interviewees

ALEX had moved to the U.S. with her husband, Andy, two years before the interviews were conducted. She was waiting for her green card so that she could find a job. Meanwhile, she cared for their daughter and belonged to various social groups, including a British women's group. She was in her early thirties and was originally from the southeast of England. She held a master's degree.

ANDY had moved to the U.S. with his wife, Alex, two years earlier because he was unhappy with his job in the United Kingdom. He said that Alex claimed they had moved because of his "midlife crisis" but that his English job really had involved too much traveling. Andy was originally from the southeast of England and was in his late thirties. He had a Ph.D. and was working as a professor at a large university on the East Coast of the U.S.

ANNE was from the southeast of England and had moved to the U.S. three years earlier with her English husband after he had been offered a job there. They conceptualized their move as permanent: He had been unable to find work in his academic field in the United Kingdom and had worked in other European countries while looking for a permanent position. Anne had a green card and worked in a management position. She was in her forties.

ANTONIA had moved to the U.S. two years before the interview and was married to an American lawyer. She had attended a public school in England and had done part of her undergraduate studies in the U.S. She had changed careers when she moved to the U.S. She and her husband planned eventually to settle in England. Antonia had traveled extensively in Europe before moving to the U.S. and had an upper-class background. She was from the southeast of England and was in her twenties.

BRAD was in his forties and was originally from the north of England. He had moved to the U.S. three years prior to the interview. He had been educated at Cambridge and now worked as a corporate manager. He had met his American wife while living in Eastern Europe, and they had agreed that they would spend the first ten years of their children's lives in the United Kingdom and the next ten years in the U.S. Brad hoped that he and his family would one day return to England. During the interview, his wife popped in and out, offering me English foods that she had bought at the local English shop.

CATRIONA had lived in the U.S. for fourteen years. She and her Irish husband had two children, and they had lived in Ireland before moving to the U.S. Catriona worked part-time and belonged to a British women's group. She held dual-nationality, having recently become an American citizen. She defined herself as upper-middle-class. Catriona was from the southeast of England and was in her forties.

CRAIG had recently moved to the U.S. to live with his American girlfriend. He initially had problems with his visa but at the time of the interview was working as a physician in a large city on the East Coast. He had been educated at an English public school, was originally from the southwest of England, and had traveled as a child because of his parents' jobs. He was in his late twenties.

DIANA had recently moved to the U.S. in search of work, having saved money to make the transition from England. She was a dual-national because her father was American and her mother, English. Before she moved, she had spent time abroad as part of her job with an international organization. She had been educated at an English public school, held an undergraduate degree from Oxford, and had done graduate work in the U.S. She was originally from East Anglia and had an upper-middle-class background. Diana was in her late twenties.

DOROTHY had moved to the U.S. with her American husband after their marriage seven years earlier, because he did not want to live in England. She had a green card and worked as a secretary for a large electronics firm. Dorothy also had a young daughter in day care and was involved with the British women's group. She was in in her late twenties. She was from the southeast of England but, as a result of her parents' travels, had been born in Africa.

EMILY was in her forties and had moved to the U.S. six years earlier. She had also spent much of her adulthood in Canada, and she and her English husband had returned to England two years before their move to the U.S. They did not settle there, however, because Emily did not feel that she could fit in. In fact, she defined herself as Canadian, not as English or American. Emily was taking graduate classes when the interview was conducted. She was originally from the southeast of England.

EMMA had been in the U.S. for seven years but had also spent part of her childhood there. She was married to an American man she had met in England, and many of her siblings had also married Americans. She had two young children, and she ran a day-care center in her home. She was originally from East Anglia and was in her thirties.

FRANCES had moved to the U.S. with her American husband and their two children shortly before the interview was conducted. Although her husband had come in response to a job offer, she was searching for employment at the time of the interview. Frances employed an English nanny to look after her children while she hunted for a job. She had spent some time working abroad, particularly in the Caribbean. She was from the southeast of England and was in her thirties.

FRANK had immigrated to Canada on an assisted passage forty years earlier and had moved to the U.S. twenty years later. His wife was American, and they had three children. He had worked as a corporate manager for many years, then pursued a career as an actor. He was one of the few interviewees who saw himself as an immigrant, and he very clearly defined himself as working-class, despite his social mobility. He was originally from London and was nearing retirement age.

GARY had moved to the U.S. eight years before the interview but had spent his childhood in both England and the U.S., because his father was American and his mother, English. After completing a degree at Cambridge, he had married an American woman, who was expecting their first child. When I spoke to him, he was working on his doctorate degree. He was originally from the southwest of England and was in his late twenties.

GORDON had been in the U.S. for five years and described his background as working-class. When the interview was conducted, he was combining graduate school with a full-time professional job and hoped to return to England to teach American Studies. As a young man, he had been traveling around the U.S. and had met his American wife when she sat next to him on a bus. He saw his life revolving around that chance encounter on the bus. He was from the Midlands in central England and was in his thirties.

HARRIET had been in the U.S. for four years. She had an American boyfriend and planned to stay in the States. Harriet worked for an international organization and had traveled extensively in the Far East and Latin America. Her job also enabled her to visit England frequently, so she still shopped for all her clothing there. Harriet held a master's in business administration. She was from the southeast of England and was in her late twenties.

HARRY had left England five years before the interview because, he said, he was disgusted with Thatcherism. He was working as a journalist in the U.S. and lived with his American girlfriend and her family. He had attended a public school, embraced the label "trashy tabloid Brit," and defined himself as very left-wing. He was from the southwest of England and was in his early thirties.

HUGH and his wife, Zoe, had recently moved to the U.S. because he had been offered a job. He conceptualized his move to the States as permanent and expressed bitterness about his experience on the job market in England during the 1980s and 1990s. He classified his background as upper-middle class, and he held a doctorate degree. Hugh was from the southeast of England and was in his forties.

IAN had moved to the U.S. to attend graduate school four years before the interview after completing a bachelor of arts degree in England. In addition to working toward his Ph.D., he was setting up a company in the U.S. Ian was very politically active, and cited Thatcherism as one of his reasons for leaving England. He had traveled extensively before moving to the U.S., especially in Australia and Latin America. Ian was from the north of England and was in his early thirties.

IMOGEN had been in the U.S. for three years, but planned to return to England eventually. She had, however, recently had her belongings shipped to the U.S. as a symbol that she would be staying a while. Imogen worked for an international organization and had visited many parts of the world, including Africa and Latin America. She had an Oxford education and classified her class status as *nouveau riche*. She was originally from the Midlands and was in her late twenties.

KEN had been living on the East Coast for about four years. He had given up a lucrative job in business in London to move to the U.S. to become an actor. He had traveled extensively before moving to the States, particularly in Australia, and had been educated at an elite public school. He was upper-middle-class. Ken was from the southeast of England and was in his mid-thirties.

LUCINDA's family had moved to the U.S. ten years before, and she attended school in the U.S., working toward an undergraduate degree at the time of the interview. She enjoyed reminiscing about the English countryside near her grandparents' home, and she hoped to return to England one day. Lucinda was originally from the Midlands and was in her late teens.

MIKE had been in the U.S. for five years. He was finishing a Ph.D. at a prestigious university the Northeastern U.S., having done his undergraduate work at Cambridge. Despite his educational background, he defined himself as working class. Having accepted a job offer, he was the only interviewee who had concrete plans to return to England. He was originally from the Midlands and was in his late twenties.

NIGEL had arrived in the U.S. two years earlier, having fallen in love with an American woman he met through friends in England. After conducting a long-distance relationship, he had left his job in England as a skilled craftsman and moved to the U.S. to marry her. Initially, he did not hold a job; instead, he took care of his wife's two children. At the time of the interview, he was working as a traveling salesman and defined himself as working-class. Nigel was from the southeast of England and in his forties.

OCTAVIA had moved to the U.S. nine years before the interview. She had met her American husband while working as a camp counselor in Vermont after finishing high school in the United Kingdom and had worked as a secretary after she moved to the U.S. At the time of the interview, she was pregnant with their second child and had given up her job. Her bathroom was full of English beauty products, and she prided herself on the fact that her house was decorated in an English style. She was from the southeast of England and was in her thirties.

PETER had been in the U.S. for eight years; prior to his move, he had traveled widely, particularly in Australia. He had a green card and worked as a stockbroker. He planned to stay in the U.S. and said he thoroughly enjoyed his life in what he characterized as a town full of young people, where he went out every night and enjoyed being outdoors when he was not working. His apartment walls were decorated with pictures of English landscapes, which he proudly showed me. Peter defined himself as upper-middle-class. He was from the southeast of England and was in his thirties.

PIERS had been in the U.S. for eight years and hoped to stay. He was in graduate school at the time of the interview and had been educated at an elite English public school. His room was full of evidence of his Englishness—for instance, videotapes of British comedies and a Union Jack clock. Piers had one of the more Americanized accents in my sample. He was from the Midlands and was in his twenties.

QUENTIN had been based in the U.S. for five years and had a green card. His job took him away from the States a lot, so he considered himself a professional nomad. He also had a public-school education and an Oxford degree. He was upper-middle class from the southeast of England and was in his thirties.

ROWENA had had been in the U.S. for less than a year. She had obtained qualifications as a nanny from a prestigious institution in London and had moved to the U.S. to look after the children of a very wealthy family. She defined her background as middle-class. Rowena was from the north of England and was in her early twenties.

STEPHEN had come to the U.S. to attend graduate school four years earlier, having completed a bachelor of arts degree at Oxford. He hoped to remain in the U.S. once he had completed his Ph.D. Although he claimed to have an Americanized accent, it sounded very English to my ear. He identified his background as lower-middle-class. Stephen was from the north of England and he was in his late twenties.

TARA had been in the U.S. for five years and she was taking a break from graduate school by working for a large international organization when I interviewed her. She was from an Anglo-American family: One of her grandparents was American. She had a public-school education and a Cambridge degree, and she planned to return to England when she completed her Ph.D. She classified herself as having an upper-middle-class background. She was from East Anglia and was in her early thirties.

VERA had lived in the U.S. for nine years. Before their most recent move to the States, she and her husband, William, had moved back and forth among the U.S., England, and Australia because of his work. Vera was about to embark on a second graduate degree; she was very active in a local international women's organization and in volunteer work. Vera hoped to return to England one day. She was from the southeast of England and was nearing retirement age.

WILLIAM, who was married to Vera, also had been in the U.S. for nine years after many years of traveling among the U.S., Australia, and England. He worked as a university professor in the U.S. Both he and Vera held dual British–American citizenship, and their adult children lived in the U.S. William expressed bitterness about his experiences with the lack of funding in English universities in the 1980s. He was from the southeast of England and was also nearing retirement age.

Zoe and her husband, Hugh, had recently arrived in the U.S. Zoe had a college degree, but her green card had not come through when the interview was conducted, so she was not working outside the home. She was very involved in the lives of her three children and volunteered at their church. She planned to get a part-time job once her green card arrived. She was from East Anglia and was in her late thirties.

Notes

CHAPTER ONE

Epigraphs: Pat Barker, *The Eye in the Door* (New York: Dutton, 1994); *A New England,* words and music by Billy Bragg, copyright BMG Music Publishing Ltd. All rights reserved. Used by permission. Electra/Asylum Records, 1987.

1. I assigned each interviewee a pseudonym.

2. In England, "public" schools are private, fee-paying high schools.

3. On the brain drain, see Bown 1991; Coghlan 1993; Duff 1990; Ryan 1989; Turney 1993; Watson 1989; but see also Dickson 1993; Spicer 1989.

4. *Economist* 1990; United Nations Economic Commission for Europe 2001. Available from: <http://www.unece.org/stats>.

5. Haseler 1996: 80.

6. Nairn 1977. See also Bogdanor 1999; Hechter 1999; Nairn 2000a, 2000b.

7. See, for instance, Aslet 1997; Barnes 1998; Billig 1995; Buruma 1998; Colley 1992; Dodd 1995; Haseler 1996; Heffer 1999; Hitchens 2000; Kushner 1992; Leonard 1997; Lloyd 1998; Marr 2000; Newman 1987; Paxman 1998; Redwood 1999; Samuel 1998. See also Taylor 1991: 146, however, on the lack of attention paid to English nationalism.

The Union Jack dominated the stadium during the final match of the 1966 World Cup Soccer Final, which England won. Today, England's supporters are more likely to fly the St. George's Cross (cf., Paxman 1998:21). Englishness, it seems, is being rediscovered.

8. The election of Tony Blair's New Labour forced a rethinking of British national identity. In contrast to the previous Conservative governments that emphasized the "heritage industry," Blair has attempted to update the country's old-fashioned, tradition-bound image by "rebranding" Britain—building the infamous millennium dome and launching "millennium products" in order to emphasize Britain's technological sophistication. His government has also started the process of reforming the House of Lords by abolishing the powers of hereditary peers. The phenomenon of "Cool Britannia," a phrase coined in 1997 to suggest the revitalization of Britain, particularly in the realm of popular culture, is another indication of how interested Blair is in redefining Britishness away from an antiquated image and encouraging people to be proud of new representations of Britain (see Paxman 1998: 238–240 on rebranding and "Cool Britannia"). This evidence all shows that the establishment is interested in defining what it means to be British and even, perhaps, in reinventing British identity.

The death of Diana, Princess of Wales, and the mourning that followed also shows that Britons are beginning to see themselves as unlike the generations who preceded them. One interpretation, played up in the media, involved Britain as a multicultural society, whose different races, classes, and sexualities were united in grief by her death. The aftermath of Princess Diana's death also provided an occasion for some commentators to point to a new way of being British, one that rejected repression and a "stiff upper lip" and was openly emotional. Although there have been critiques of this position since then—especially about the lack of attention paid to those who did not share in the public outpouring of grief— the situation after Diana's death appeared to reach crisis proportions as people (fueled by the media) moved from shock and disbelief to grief and finally anger as they attempted to understand the roles of the media, the royal family, and themselves in the tragedy and how this affected what it meant to be British.

9. The term "Little Englander" was first used in Victorian times to criticize those who opposed imperialism and overseas expansion (Room 1999 [1959]). More recently, it refers to a strain of domestic parochialism that is frequently directed against the European Union.

10. Bogdanor 1999; Hechter 1999; Nairn 1977, 2000a, 2000b.

11. A recent study by the National Centre for Social Research confirmed the importance of studying English people. This research showed that whites were more likely than blacks to classify themselves as English than as British and that the number of people identifying as English has more than doubled in the past two years. In addition, those who identified as English were more likely than those who preferred the label "British" to admit to being racially prejudiced and to think that English people should be born in England or have English parents (Carvel 2000; National Centre for Social Research 2000).

12. See Chambers (1993: 147) and Taylor (1991: 147) on the ways that the label "England" often subsumes "Britain" in nationalist discourse. Taylor points to the late change of title from "England" to "Britain" in a series on patriotism (Samuel 1989a, 1989b, 1989c) as evidence that the "English/British" don't seem to know who they are. Haseler (1996: 31) also documents this slippage.

13. Simmel 1950.

14. Although I had intended to sample middle-class and upper-middle-class people, as I discuss in detail in Chapter 3, some of my interviewees self-identified as working-class. My sample was highly educated—twenty of the thirty-four had a professional or graduate degree, and a further nine had a college degree or a technical or vocational qualification. Hence, a large number of interviewees had professional or managerial jobs (thirteen) or were in graduate school (seven). Six women did not do paid work—two of them were unemployed, looking for professional jobs, and four stayed home and took care of their homes and children. Two other women worked full time taking care of other people's children. Of the remaining seven, two were actors who had given up lucrative careers in business, two worked part-time in sales, one was a traveling salesman, and one was a secretary. Thus, although varied, my sample consisted mostly of middle- and upper-middle-class professionals. The

majority of the interviewees had come to the U.S. for one of three reasons: for employment, for education, or to be with an American partner. I interviewed an equal number of women and men, and my interviewees ranged in age from those in their twenties to those in their sixties or seventies (twenty-three of the interviewees were in their twenties or thirties). They came from different regions of England, although the largest number—nineteen—were from the southeast of the country.

The majority of the interviewees (twenty) had traveled elsewhere—mostly in Europe and the Commonwealth—before coming to the U.S., sometimes on business, sometimes on extended vacations, and sometimes on one- or two-year postings; two had lived in Canada for extended periods of time. Six of the other interviewees had moved back and forth between the U.S. and England before settling in the U.S. semi-permanently. This sometimes made it hard to count the number of years that they had lived in the States. Based on their current stay, the interviewees were fairly equally divided between those who had been in the U.S. for less than two years, those who had been there between three and five years, and those who had been there between six and ten years. One other had lived in the U.S. for fourteen years, and another had been there for twenty years. Fourteen of my sample had American partners; for these people, this relationship was often the rationale for moving to the U.S., although not in all cases. Eight others had British partners; six of these formed three couples, and I interviewed each partner in these six cases. Three other interviewees had partners whose nationality was neither American nor British.

15. See Jones 1998 for the interview schedule and a discussion of other methodological issues.

16. I am also white, which may have affected their responses to my questions about their racial identities.

17. Acker et al. 1983: 424–5; Frankenberg 1993: 29–32; Reinharz 1989 (1983): 181, 1992: 27–34.

18. Acker et al. 1983: 427; Harding 1991; Smith 1987.

19. For examples of "top-down" approaches, see, for example, Bendix 1964; Boli-Bennett 1979; Edelman 1964; Gellner 1983; Ramirez 1987; Tilly 1975; Zelinsky 1988. An exception is Greenfeld 1992. See Schlesinger 1987 for an overview. By asking open-ended questions, I hoped to obtain data about what was important to the interviewees about English identities in their own words: see Glaser and Strauss 1967 for a theoretical justification of this idea.

20. Erikson 1980 (1959).

21. See Anderson 1983. See Anthias and Yuval Davies 1992 on nations and Cooley 1964 (1922); Mead 1934; Weigert et al. 1986; and Widdicombe and Wooffitt 1995 on identities.

22. See Anderson 1983; Anthias and Yuval Davies 1992; Billig 1995; Deutsch 1966 (1953); Goulbourne 1991; Hobsbawm and Ranger 1983; Isaacs 1975 (on nation); Gilroy 1992 (1987); Hall 1990; Jackson and Penrose 1993; Omi and Winant 1994 (1986) (on race); Kessler and McKenna 1978 (on gender); DeMott 1990; West and Fenstermaker 1995 (on class).

23. Garfinkel 1992 (1967): 122–8; Kessler and McKenna 1978: 113.

24. See also Berger and Luckmann 1967: 89.

25. Schwalbe and Mason-Schrock 1996: 124; see also Anderson 1983.

26. See Garfinkel 1992 (1967); Goffman 1959; Heritage 1986 (1984); Mead 1934. See Kessler and McKenna 1978; West and Fenstermaker 1995; and West and Zimmerman 1987 for analyses of how gender is constructed through everyday interactions. See Bucholtz 1995; Frankenberg 1993; Gilroy 1992 (1987); Hall 1986; Omi and Winant 1994 (1986); and Ware 1992 for evidence of how race and ethnicity emerge during interactions. See Bucholtz 1995; Rodríguez 1994; Waters 1990; and Williams 1991 for analyses of how people are held accountable for their perceived race and ethnicity. And see DeMott 1990; Langston 1992; and West and Fenstermaker 1995 for evidence showing how people are held accountable on the basis of class.

27. Garfinkel 1992 (1967); Goffman 1959; Heritage 1986; Smith 1987; West and Fenstermaker 1995; West and Zimmerman 1987.

28. See Schwalbe and Mason-Schrock 1996: 114 for other work in this tradition.

29. West and Zimmerman 1987.

30. See Banks 1988; Bhavnani and Phoenix 1994; Butler 1990; Hall 1987; Lather 1991; Pratt 1984; Schwalbe and Mason-Schrock 1996; Widdicombe and Wooffitt 1995.

31. However, particular identities can also be forced on people. See Reily 1988; Rodríguez 1994; Snitow 1990.

32. West and Fenstermaker 1995.

33. Connell 1987, 1995; Foucault 1972 (1971); Gerson and Peiss 1985; Giddens 1984; Lather 1991; Parker 1992; Smith 1987; Widdicombe and Wooffitt 1995. My use of the term "discourse" suggests the importance of language and representation in supporting and reproducing structures.

34. Cohen 1989; Connell 1987; Giddens 1984; Parker 1992.

35. Connell 1987, 1995.

36. Hewitt 1992.

37. See, for instance, Collins 1991; Jones 1982; Jordan 1992; King 1988; Scott 1992.

38. For example, Anthias and Yuval Davies 1992; Gilroy 1992 (1987); C. Hall 1993; Lake 1992; McClintock 1995; Willis 1990; WING 1985.

39. McClintock 1995; Pratt 1992; Ware 1992.

40. Mackenzie 1986.

41. I generally use "black" as an inclusive term to refer to people living in Britain whose ancestors originated in Africa or Asia (including the Indian Subcontinent). Although "black" is not a perfect term, it is often used in Britain to describe Asian Britons, African-Caribbean Britons, and African Britons. I would prefer to avoid the term "people of color," which reproduces the idea that white is not a color; however, as I move back and forth between Britain and the U.S., I may use this term. It emerged in the 1990s as an antidote to the use of "minorities" to describe people classifed as "racial others" in the U.S. This problem with terminology illustrates the socially constructed nature of race (Omi and

Winant 1994 [1986]). Because I describe how race is imagined by my interviewees, I take for granted its constructed status.

42. See C. Hall 1993; McClintock 1993, 1995; Said 1978; Ware 1992.

43. Frankenberg 1994.

44. McClintock 1995; Ware 1992.

45. Pajaczkowska and Young 1992: 204.

46. Pratt 1991.

47. See Ware 1992 on discourses of imperialism in British popular culture; Gilroy 1992 (1987) on the links between race and nation; and Hall 1990 on the use of the "other" to construct identities.

48. Gilroy 1992 (1987); Paul 1997. See also Carvel 2000; National Centre for Social Research 2000.

49. Cocks 1989; Pateman 1998.

50. Anthias and Yuval Davies 1992: 114–5, 125–8; Mostov 1998.

51. WING 1985.

52. Greenhill 1992.

53. For example, Athearn 1953; Berthoff 1953; Erickson 1972; Fischer 1989.

54. All statistics in this paragraph are from the Current Population Survey of January 1995. Available from: <http://ferret.bls.census.gov/cgi-bin/ferret>. This nationally representative survey is conducted monthly. The statistics cover those born in England and living in the U.S. Although there are statistics for those born in Britain and living in the U.S., I did not use this data set so as to be as conservative as possible in my estimates.

55. 7.59 percent were classified as "black," 2.03 percent as "Asian," and 4.42 percent as "other."

56. People born in England but living in the U.S. were also employed as service workers (6.85%); in production, craft, or repair industries or as operators (19.38%); and in farming, forestry, and fishing (1.45%).

57. Cf., Harding, who calls this "reinventing ourselves as the other" (1991: chap. 11).

58. Alba 1990; Brodkin 1998; Frankenberg 1993, 1997; Ignatiev 1995; Jacobson 1998; Reed 1982; Roediger 1991; Ware 1992; Williams 1990.

59. McIntosh 1992: 78; see also Frankenberg 1993.

60. See, for instance, Lipsitz 1998; Stefancic and Delgado 1996; Waters 1998. See also Brimelow 1995 for an anti-immigrant tract written ironically by a white Englishman.

61. Frankenberg 1994.

62. See Gilbert and Mulkay 1984 and Mulkay and Gilbert 1982 on the expectation of contradictions within narratives.

63. To some extent, the tenuous visa status of some of the interviewees mediated their otherwise privileged status, especially in an era of anti-immigrant sentiment.

64. Naficy 1993: 16–7.

65. Guy Fawkes was a Catholic conspirator whose plot to blow up the Houses of Parliament in the reign of James I was foiled. His torture and death

are still celebrated in parts of Britain as "Bonfire Night" on 5 November, with fireworks, bonfires, and the burning of a "guy" (an effigy of Fawkes).

66. See di Leonardo 1984; Hondagneu-Sotelo 1994; Kibria 1993 for studies of immigrants that examine their communities.

67. Naficy 1993: 29. In his analysis of Iranian culture in Los Angeles, Naficy found that the relative class privilege of Iranian exiles enabled them to avoid creating an "Irantown" in Southern California.

68. Among those who used these terms were Harry, Quentin, Tara, Ian, Andy, Brad, and Harriet.

69. Menlo Consulting 1999. See Chapter 3 for more evidence of Anglophilia.

70. Bourdieu 1997 (1972).

71. West and Zimmerman 1987.

72. Swidler 1986: 277; see also Geertz 1973.

73. Frankenberg 1993: 14.

74. Schwalbe and Mason-Schrock 1996.

CHAPTER TWO

Epigraph: William Wordsworth, "I Travelled Among Unknown Men," in M. H. Abrams, ed., *Norton Anthology of English Literature,* 5th ed. (W. W. Norton, 1986); Nick Hornby, "Introduction," in Georgina Henry, ed., *The Guardian Year '96* (Fourth Estate, 1996).

1. Hobsbawm and Ranger 1983.

2. See also Anderson 1983; Halbwachs 1980 (1950); Wright 1985.

3. Anderson 1983; Hall 1990: 232.

4. See also Haseler 1996; Porter 1992; Samuel 1998; Wright 1985.

5. Hobsbawm 1983: 5; Porter 1992: 1; Wright 1985: 19–22.

6. I refer here to the debate about a proportionally representative voting system, recent evidence of miscarriages of justice, and controversy over the abolition of the monarchy and the House of Lords.

7. Lowenthal 1991; Porter 1992.

8. Samuel 1989a; Wright 1985.

9. Wright 1985: 69–71.

10. See also Haseler 1996; Lowenthal 1991: 222.

11. See also Haseler 1996: 106; Howkins 1986: 71.

12. Howkins 1986: 62; Lowenthal 1991: 221.

13. Hobsbawm 1983: 10.

14. Lowenthal 1991: 215–6.

15. Ibid.: 220; see also Wright 1985: 51–6.

16. Wright 1985: 15.

17. Anderson 1983; Schwalbe and Mason-Schrock 1996.

18. Naficy 1993.

19. *Four Weddings and a Funeral* was a popular British film released around the time I conducted the interviews.

20. Howkins 1986; Lowenthal 1991.

21. As I discussed in Chapter 1, although I asked the interviewees about England and their English identities, some of them responded by talking about Britain and their British identities. Sometimes this was a conscious decision on their part to be more inclusive of the other countries within the United Kingdom. More often, however, they simply conflated England and Britain as they spoke.

22. See Howkins 1986; Lowenthal 1991; and Wright 1985: 81–7 for examples.

23. Connell 1995.

24. Anderson 1983.

25. These quotations are from Harriet, Frances, Emily, Imogen, and Andy.

26. Wright 1985: 86.

27. Hobsbawm and Ranger 1983; Lowenthal 1991; Porter 1992; Wright 1985.

28. Hobsbawm and Ranger 1983; Porter 1992; Wright 1985.

29. Howkins 1986.

30. The advertisement for Carling Black Label beer had a rowdy chorus sung by men, reminiscent of the "shouting and jeering" that he mentions.

31. However, this may be changing with the current crop of more diverse films about Britain hitting the U.S.—for instance, *Trainspotting*, *Twin Town*, *Secrets and Lies*, *Bhaji on the Beach*, *The Full Monty*, *Nil by Mouth*, and *My Son the Fanatic*.

32. See Wright 1985: 73, 168.

33. See Lowenthal 1991: 217–20; Porter 1992: 2; Wright 1985: chap. 1, chap. 2.

34. I have changed the names of towns to protect the confidentiality of the interviewees. In this case, "Stourbridge" is an upper-middle-class suburb on the outskirts of a large city in England.

35. This is one of the reasons it is hard to classify this group of people as immigrants or expatriates, as I discussed in Chapter 1. My initial assumption was that immigrants would stay, and expatriates would one day return home. However, even those who had U.S. citizenship sometimes talked longingly of returning to England.

36. Brad, Andy, Imogen, Tara, Piers, Diana, Frank, Harry, and Alex were among the interviewees who made these comments.

37. For instance, Lewis 1997.

38. Several interviewees noted the benefits of a more open approach to feelings and interactions. Emily, Imogen, Harriet, Gordon, Emma, and William all said that they had become more outgoing, self-confident, and assertive since they had moved to the U.S. Other interviewees were critical of the "psychological[ly] repressed nature" of life in England. Vera and Emily criticized the "horrible secrecy [where] . . . nanny will tell you what should be done."

39. See McDaniel 2000 for more on the relationship between class and levels of reserve both historically and in the present day. Billig's study, *Banal Nationalism* (1995: 119), also points to class differences in displays of nationalism: whereas the tabloids he examined engaged in brazen flag-waving, the broadsheet newspapers were far more subdued, although still nationalistic.

40. These comments are from Ian, Quentin, Imogen, and Frank.

41. Billig 1995; Colls and Dodd 1986; Jackson and Penrose 1993; Nairn 1977, 1988; Taylor 1991.

42. See also Nairn 1977: 293, 1988: 128. An exception is Newman 1987. There has, however, been an upsurge of interest in Englishness as concerns have grown about the influence of the European Union and the new devolved assemblies in Belfast, Cardiff, and Edinburgh. See Aslet 1997; Barnes 1998; Billig 1995; Buruma 1998; Colley 1992; Dodd 1995; Haseler 1996; Heffer 1999; Kushner 1992; Lloyd 1998; Marr 2000; Nairn 2000b; Paxman 1998; Redwood 1999; Samuel 1998.

43. Jackson and Penrose 1993: 9.

44. Taylor 1991: 146.

45. Ibid.: 147.

46. Ibid.:148.

47. However, this applies only when they are in England. He admits that it is harder to do once one has left the country.

48. Although it could be argued that public displays of the flag are patriotic and, hence, are less problematic than displays of nationalist sentiments, the interviewees tended to use both "patriotic" and "nationalistic" as pejorative terms when discussing Americans' pride in their nation.

49. See critiques of this position by Colley 1992 and Haseler 1996.

50. See Chapter 6 for more on this.

51. Imogen and Mike commented on the class system; Zoe commented on washing machines; Craig, Tara, and Catriona commented on Northern Ireland; and Harriet commented on English television.

52. See the epigraph at the beginning of this chapter for the full stanza. It is noteworthy that Craig used the word "foreign" instead of "unknown," perhaps reflecting his feelings of alienation in the U.S.

53. Harry, Piers, and Gary were among those who felt this way.

54. Tara and Gordon made this critique.

55. Antonia, Octavia, Craig, Emily, and Frank expressed this point of view.

56. Tara, Harry, Imogen, Mike, Octavia, Quentin, Rowena, Anne, Catriona, Craig, and Dorothy felt that the social life in England was better than in the U.S., whereas Diana and Peter found English people dull.

57. Among the former were Tara, Piers, Brad, Craig, Emily, Nigel, and Octavia. Anne and Ken shared the latter perspective.

58. The assignation of students to groups or classes based on their grades or perceived academic potential.

CHAPTER THREE

1. Bourdieu 1997 (1972).

2. See Wright 1996, 1997.

3. See Goldthorpe 1983, 1984; Stanworth 1984.

4. DeMott 1990 and Kelley and Evans 1995 suggest that this is also applicable in England.

5. The U.S. Army advertising slogan was "Be All That You Can Be—in the Army."

6. Indeed, they both felt pressure in England to change their upper-class RP accents in favor of more middle- and working-class modes of speech. Despite the privileges associated with being upper class, as "Estuary English" spreads across classes and the political rhetoric of classlessness takes hold in England, it is not necessarily beneficial to have an upper class accent in daily interactions. See Rosewarne 1994a; Snedegar 1996; Wales 1994. RP, also known as BBC English, stands for Received Pronunciation. It is an ostensibly regionless accent that is characteristic of members of the upper and upper-middle classes who have been educated at fee-paying schools. Estuary English is an accent associated with the area around the Thames estuary. Its proponents argue that it is spreading throughout southeastern England and growing in importance as a "classless" accent. See Rosewarne 1994a, 1994b. I discuss RP and Estuary English accents in more detail in Chapter 4.

7. Note that Diana uses "he" as the generic term to describe people from England. I analyze the interviewees' propensity to imagine English people as male in Chapter 6.

8. "The City" refers to the City of London, the financial and business district in the center of London.

9. For more on this, see Chapter 2.

10. See also McIntosh 1992; Pratt 1984.

11. Because he had not been able to get into a university immediately after he had finished his secondary education, but now had his Ph.D., he felt that the English educational system had given him a second chance.

12. Goldthorpe and Lockwood 1996: 26; Lamont 1992. But cf. Langston 1992: 146; West and Fenstermaker 1995: 27.

13. Lipsitz 1998; Stefancic and Delgado 1996. See also Brimelow 1995.

14. The implication here is that English people do not have accents.

15. This quote is from Diana.

16. The *Beano* is a children's comic book.

17. English as a Second Language.

18. Hugh asserts his children's national identities in the context of complaining that the rest of the world is more prone to disease than England, perhaps unconsciously drawing on the island mentality in Britain that obsesses about diseases such as rabies spreading from other countries. This obsession reached dizzying heights in the days before the Channel Tunnel opened, as people worried that rats from continental Europe would bring rabies through the tunnel. This is now ironic in light of continental Europe's stance against British meat because of Bovine Spongiform Encephalopathy (BSE), swine fever, and foot and mouth disease.

19. Feagin 1997; Frost and Shea 1986; Wright 1940. See also Baltzell 1964 for more recent privileging of WASP status.

20. British men in particular were seen as weak and effeminate. See Kimmel 1996.

21. Cogan 1989: 23; Haltunnen 1982: 93.

22. Beisel 1993: 149; DiMaggio 1986; Fussell 1983; Gans 1974. However, Cogan 1989 argues that during the nineteenth century, "real womanhood"—an alternative to the cult of true womanhood—was evident in the northeastern U.S. This vision of womanhood rejected imported English manners as artificial, preferring instead home-grown American values such as self-reliance.

23. Brandon 1980; Hitchens 1991: 121–3; MacColl and Wallace 1989.

24. Beisel 1993: 148; Higham 1988 (1955); Levine 1988; Schlesinger 1946.

25. Higham 1975, 1988 (1955). See also Feagin 1997; Horsman 1997; and Jacobson 1998 on nativism.

26. Higham 1988 (1955): 96.

27. Ibid.: 147.

28. Ibid.: 154–6; Brodkin 1998. During World War I, the "Teuton" was eliminated from Anglo-Saxonism to explain away U.S. support of Britain: see Higham 1988 (1955): 201.

29. Higham 1975: 56. See also DeConde 1992 and Hitchens 1991 for other historical evidence of Anglophilia, and Buruma 1998 for evidence of European "Anglomania." However, Moser 1998 argues that Anglophobia has also been a factor in U.S. history.

30. Baltzell 1964.

31. See, for example, analyses by Cameron 1997; Nunberg 1997; Santoro 1999; Stefancic and Delgado 1996; Tatalovich 1995.

32. Bloom 1987.

33. See Levine 1988 for a critique of Bloom 1987. See also Hu-DeHart 1994 on the origins of the backlash against multiculturalism.

34. I used Lexis-Nexis and limited my search to the Northeastern U.S.

35. House music is a popular type of electronic dance music.

36. Lavelle 1997.

37. Asimov 1997; Billera 1999; Grimes 2000; Groening 1999; Julian 1997; McKinley 1999.

38. Like the interviewees, Americans do not often distinguish between Britain and England. I use "Britain" here to emphasize this and the fact that many of the films, television programs, artists, and so on mentioned in these articles are Welsh, Scottish, or Northern Irish, as well as English.

39. McKinley 1999.

40. Auerbach 1996. See also Keating 2000; Merrill 2000; Poniewozik 2000.

41. See Hipsky 1994; Joyner 1998; and Taitz 1999 on British or Anglophilic films. See Gener 1999; McGough 1997; and Wolf 1995 on British stage and film actors and their impact in the U.S. See Duffy et al. 1993; Farber 1998; and Rosen 1996 on the British influence in music. See Campagna 1996; Haas 1995; and Winks 1998 on Anglophilia among the book-buying public. See Epstein 1997 and Wheatcroft 1990 on Anglophilia in the U.S. See Buruma 1998 on "Anglomania" among Europeans. See Morais 1997 on the "snob appeal" of the London *Financial Times*. See McCabe 1997 and Editorial 1994 on Anglophilic offerings on U.S. public television. See Sullivan 1999 on the Anglophilic appeal of the British

newsmagazine *The Economist*. See Martinez 1998 on cricket. On the effect of Princess Diana, see Hagen 1997 on buying her dresses at an auction; George and Shin 1997 on mourning her death in New York City; and Curran 1998 on "Diana studies."

42. "Surfacing" 1994; "Nobles" 1995.

43. For some of these sites, see <http://www.britishinamerica.com>; <http://www.british-expats.com>; <http://www.britsabroad.co.uk>; <http://www.essentially-english.com>; Queen 2001; Reed 2001; and <http://www.ukgoods.com>.

44. See <http://www.bbc.co.uk>; <http://www.beeb.com>; <http://www.itn.co.uk>.

45. See <http://www.football365.co.uk>; <http://www.footballunlimited.co.uk>; <http://www.sky.com/sports>.

46. Mano 1995; Queenan 1990; Sullivan 1999; Wheatcroft 1990.

47. Foreman 1998; Goodman 1997; Lloyd 1998.

48. Foreman 1998.

49. Fussell 1983; Hitchens 1991.

50. Farber 1998; Rosen 1996.

51. See, for instance, Alibhai-Brown 2000.

52. Among those who noted these television programs were Mike, Imogen, Piers, Peter, Lucinda, Harry, and Emma.

53. These quotes are from Harriet, Alex, Catriona, and Emily.

54. Lieberson 1985; Waters 1990.

55. See Bartlett 1992; Clark 1957; Danchev 1997; DeConde 1992; Hitchens 1991.

56. See Bourdieu 1997 (1972) for more on the idea of cultural capital and how it functions as a resource on which individuals can draw to enhance their prestige.

57. Garfinkel 1992 (1967); Heritage 1986 (1984); Kessler and McKenna 1978; West and Zimmerman 1987. See also Schwalbe and Mason-Schrock 1996 on identity work.

58. Heritage 1986 (1984): 135–78; West and Fenstermaker 1995: 21; West and Zimmerman 1987: 136.

59. The interviewees also noted the hostile responses they sometimes received from Irish Americans who are critical of British policies in Northern Ireland. I explore this in detail in Chapter 6.

60. This is exemplified by the Englishman "Preedy" in the Sansom novel Goffman cites (1959: 4–5).

61. Marks and Spencer is a chain store found on the main street of most towns in Britain. It sells food, clothes, and toiletries. As Tara explained, "Marks and Spencer is . . . reasonably priced, but everything [is] of a certain quality, and that's very British."

62. The Criminal Justice Act of 1994 comprehensively extended police powers to detain and search people traveling in groups of six or more and to prevent gatherings with amplified music. It was primarily directed at convoys of "New Age" travelers, squatters, hunt saboteurs, and attendees at "raves." Its passage

caused riots and was opposed by many human-rights groups in the United Kingdom.

63. These quotes are from Anne, Gary, Alex, Harry, Diana, Antonia, Andy, Tara, Mike, Quentin, Imogen, Catriona, Craig, and Emily.

64. These quotes are from Catriona, Peter, and Hugh.

65. Both of these quotes are from Alex.

66. Goffman 1986 (1974).

67. Peter, Gary, Harry, Alex, Andy, Frances, and Quentin made these comments.

CHAPTER FOUR

1. Although people usually refer to the speech style of the United Kingdom as "British English," I call it "English English" because I am studying only people from England.

2. I use the terms "language" and "accent" conterminously. The literatures that consider change in language see it as encompassing not just the variety of language spoken, but also the dialect, accent, tone, vocabulary, and speech style used. I consider accent and vocabulary changes to be a subset of linguistic change more generally. Since the interviewees are monolingual in everyday life, with English as their primary language, there are no instances in which they move from one language to another. Instead, I focus on how they modify or maintain their accents or vocabulary while in the U.S.

3. Garfinkel 1992 (1967); Goffman 1959; Heritage 1986 (1984); West and Fenstermaker 1995.

4. See, for instance, Banks 1988; Bhavnani and Phoenix 1994; Butler 1990; Hall 1987; Lather 1991; Pratt 1984; Widdicombe and Wooffitt 1995.

5. Reily gives an example of the contradictory nature of gender identity. She argues that "while it's impossible to thoroughly be a woman, it's also impossible never to be one" (1988: 113–4).

6. See Widdicombe and Wooffitt 1995 for a review of the relationship between language and identity.

7. Goffman 1959.

8. We also see this negotiation and choice in ethnic and gender identity: Bucholtz 1995; Gans 1979; Garfinkel 1992 (1967); Kessler and McKenna 1978; Nagel 1994; Reily 1988; Snitow 1990; Waters 1990.

9. For more examples, see Gilbert and Mulkay 1984; Mulkay and Gilbert 1982.

10. This is similar to the idea that gender-constructing practices are so habitual that individuals do not notice them, or would find them hard to change if they did: Frye 1983: 37.

11. Butler 1990.

12. Because I am focusing on England, I describe the meaning of accents in England only. Scotland, Wales, and Northern Ireland have their own accents, dialects, and languages.

13. Trudgill 1983, 1984, 1990; Wells 1982: 5.

14. Wells 1982: 9; Snedegar 1996.

15. See Wells 1982: 13. However, see Burke 1987 for examples of the intersections of class and accent in other countries. Also, Labov's classic 1966 work finds social stratification of accent in New York City.

16. The term was coined by Daniel Jones in 1926, according to Rosewarne 1994a: 6. RP is also known as BBC English. The use of the word "received" to describe this accent, suggesting something generally accepted or approved as good (*Oxford English Dictionary* 1987 [1971]), is evidence of its hegemonic status in England (see Crowley 1989:35).

17. Wells 1982: 14.

18. Trudgill and Hannah 1994 (1982): 2.

19. Together with this hierarchy goes a long history of prescriptivism, with the most infamous example being Alan Ross and Nancy Mitford's coinage of "U" to describe upper-class speech and "non-U" to characterize everyone else's speech in 1956: Buckle 1978; Mitford 1956. See also Milroy and Milroy 1991 (1985) for a review of the prescriptive tradition; Crowley 1991 for selected readings in this tradition; Crowley 1989 and Mugglestone 1995 for histories of accent as a social symbol; and Alford 1866 (1864) for another example of prescriptivism.

20. A government-funded high school.

21. Bourhis et al. 1981; Chapman et al. 1977; Giles 1970, 1973; Giles and Sassoon 1983.

22. Cheyne 1970; Giles 1971; Strongman and Woosley 1967.

23. Chapman et al. 1977: 142.

24. This vignette also provides a telling comparison between the different workings of class in Britain and the U.S. Gary explained that, unlike him, his (American) wife was able to talk to anyone as an equal and was not able to understand his crisis of confidence.

25. See Chapman et al. 1977.

26. Milroy and Milroy 1991 (1985): 110.

27. For instance, Joyce 1991.

28. Rosewarne 1994a, 1994b; Wales 1994.

29. Diana, Princess of Wales, is said to have taken elocution lessons to demote her RP accent to Estuary English: Wales 1994: 6. One hallmark of this accent is the glottal stop, a sound made in place of a *t* or *d* in speech. The sound presumably originates in the glottis, the opening at the upper part of the windpipe and between the vocal chords (*Oxford English Dictionary* 1983). Examples would be glottal stops in place of the *t* in words such as Sco(?)land, ga(?)eway, sta(?)ement, ne(?)work. Estuary English speakers use more glottal stops than RP speakers but fewer than do "cockney" speakers: Rosewarne 1994a: 5.

30. Snedegar 1996; Wales 1994.

31. Rosewarne 1994a: 7.

32. See also Snedegar 1996; Wales 1994.

33. Language choice is a continual process rather than an all-or-nothing decision, and individuals may vary their language on many different levels, such

as dialect; tone of voice; choice of accent, pitch, and subject matter; and degree of formality: Coupland 1985; Giles 1979: 258; Giles and Coupland 1991: 63; Gumperz 1982, 1992. See also Giles 1973 and Giles et al. 1973 on communication accommodation theory, and Burke and Porter 1991 for examples of language choice in literature.

34. An XR3-I was a sporty fuel-injection Ford car sometimes used as a status symbol by upwardly mobile lower-middle-class British men.

35. "Spurs" refers to Tottenham Hotspurs, a London football (soccer) club.

36. This raises the issue of the extent to which my speech patterns influenced my interviewees' accents: see Giles 1973; Giles and Coupland 1991; Trudgill 1986. Although this obviously did occur, I have no way of knowing the extent of it, nor can I control for it in my analysis. In addition, my own characterizations of the interviewees' accents are biased by my class and regional background. Having spent my formative years in the southeast of England, with English parents, attending public (private) schools, my original accent is upper-middle-class RP. However, I had lived in the U.S. for seven years at the time of the interviews and had picked up some American intonations. Unlike the sociolinguistic and social-psychological literatures, I did not use scientific methods such as the matched-guise technique (see Hogg and Abrams 1988: 197 for a description) to determine the extent to which the interviewees' accents changed or became Americanized during an interview, or whether a particular accent was "really" an RP accent. The claims I make about their accents are based on my own ear. Thus, as I transcribed Peter's interview, for instance, I marked the places where I heard his accent changing. Someone else might have found more or fewer instances of accent change. However, because I am more concerned with the words my interviewees used to talk about accents than how they said those words, this should not provide too much cause for concern.

37. See the various British American dictionaries on the market for more examples: Horwill 1939; Moss 1984; Schur 1973.

38. Giles and Coupland 1991. See Brown and Levinson 1987 (1978) for a theoretical review of this idea.

39. Giles 1973; Giles et al. 1973.

40. Ibid.; Giles and Coupland 1991: 71, 74.

41. Trudgill (1986: 23) explains, for instance, that he learned to pronounce his first name, Peter, with an American accent so that people would not think that he was ordering a pizza.

42. Trudgill (1986: 20) suggests that, although there is no way to predict how quickly or how much English English speakers will accommodate to American English, they will follow approximately the same route. He argues that they will converge to the features of American English that are most prominent in the consciousness of English English speakers (ibid.: 12; see also idem 1983: chap. 8), although they may resist the change if they hear themselves sounding too American (Trudgill 1986: 18). He suggests that, first, English people's *t*s will change to *d*s (as in "butter"); next, the *a* in, for example, "dance" will become longer, to sound like "romance"; third, the *o* in "hot" and "pot" may change so that

"hot" almost rhymes with an English English accent pronouncing "heart," or "pot" rhymes with "part" (although this is a more complex change to make); and finally, the non-prevocalic r may be acquired (that is, the r in "girl" will be pronounced) (Trudgill 1986: 13–20).

43. Milroy and Milroy 1991 (1985): 59. In general, most in my sample spoke with an English accent, occasionally veering into American intonation or pronunciation and more often using American words. Emma, Gary and Lucinda had lived in the U.S. as children for various lengths of time, and Emily and Frank had both been away from England for more than twenty years. All five spoke with more Americanized accents. No clear pattern emerges from the data as to whether women or men were more likely to pick up American accents or whether the age of the interviewee affected the Americanness of her or his accent. In addition, the region or type of original English accent of each interviewee had little bearing on the degree of Americanization of her or his accent at the time of the interview, and whether the interviewee was married to or living with an English or American partner or single also had no effect. One variable that did have some effect on the accent is the length of time an interviewee has been in the U.S. None of the interviewees who had lived in the U.S. for fewer than two years had noticeably American or Anglo-American accents (apart from Rowena, who had a slight American intonation). The interviewees with the most Americanized accents had all been here between six and ten years. There were others who had been here for longer periods of time who had retained more of an English accent. William and Vera, for instance, had each been in the U.S. for eleven years.

44. Cameron 1997; Giles et al. 1995; Nunberg 1997; Sebastian and Ryan 1985; Stefancic and Delgado 1996; Tatalovich 1995.

45. Gladwell 1996; Waters 1999: 67, 81.

46. This quote is from Gordon.

47. Bourdieu 1997 (1972).

48. The novelty value of English pronunciations in the U.S. may be greater than that of American pronunciations in Britain because of the larger proportion of American television shows and movies that are exported to Britain (although watchers of PBS, BBC America, and Merchant–Ivory productions in the U.S. might find English accents less wondrous). The English people I interviewed also suggested that Britain is less insular than the U.S., which is implicit in Mike's comments here.

49. Goffman 1963.

50. However, it is true that "bloody" is not a swear word commonly used in the U.S., so the salesman might have misunderstood the depth of her frustration.

51. The social-psychological literature shows that speech maintenance or divergence is likely to occur as an identity-maintaining device. For example, Labov's study of speech styles in Martha's Vineyard showed that young men were moving away from the standard New England norm and toward a more conservative and characteristically "Vineyard" speech (1972). They adopted this

accent as a way to differentiate themselves from what they perceived as encroachers on the island—the wealthy summer tourists. Indeed, one of the broadest Vineyard accents came from a young man who had spent time away from the island. Other studies have shown similar relationships between ethnic identity and language. In Quebec, those with the strongest attachment to the French ethnic group spoke English with the heaviest French accents (Gatbonton-Segalowitz 1975 cited Ryan 1979: 148; see also Taylor et al. 1973). In Victorian England, dialect literature in Lancashire and Yorkshire helped to consolidate northern working- and middle-class identities to contrast with "the effete and privileged south": Joyce 1991: 168. Research into Welsh and Belgian "ethnolinguistic identity" (Giles and Johnson 1987) showed maximum divergence away from the outgroup language when participants felt ethnically or nationally threatened (Bourhis and Giles 1977; Bourhis et al. 1979).

52. Joe Strummer and Mick Jones. CBS Records, 1977.

53. Popular during the late 1970s and early 1980s, The Clash played at Rock Against Racism concerts, and their lyrics are often overtly left-wing, anti-racist, and anti-imperialist. See Gilroy 1992 (1987): 115–35 and Hebdige 1979 for more on Rock against Racism.

54. When I asked Quentin why he had used such a strong word, he said he thought it was probably an accurate description because he had "walked out of Britain saying this place is too arrogant, too resting on its own laurels, too parochial in its view, [too] bigoted," suggesting that he did not agree with their abhorrence of the U.S. See Chapters 2 and 5 for more on interviewees' critiques of English xenophobia.

55. Social-identity theory explains the desire to maintain one's accent in intergroup situations by arguing that individuals are searching for a positive self-image: see Hogg and Abrams 1988: chap. 2 and Widdicombe and Wooffitt 1995 for reviews. Drawing on the idea that individuals categorize themselves and one another to enhance their self-esteem, the theory posits that group members will compare themselves with members of other groups (outgroups) to maximize their distinctiveness, positively evaluating themselves and members of their ingroup in comparison with these outgroup members (Tajfel 1974; Tajfel and Turner 1979; Tajfel and Turner 1986). When individuals see themselves as members of their ingroup, then, they will aim for linguistic distinctiveness from the outgroup, accentuating their speech differences. This theory predicts that English people in America will maintain or accentuate their speech styles as a way to create distinctions between themselves and Americans and to boost their own self-esteem and morale. One implication of this is that English people will positively evaluate their own speech and negatively evaluate that of Americans.

56. These quotes are from Gordon and Tara.

57. Giles and Coupland 1991: 69; Gumperz 1982, 1992.

58. Goffman 1959.

59. Having said this, I am reliant for my data on what the interviewees told me and on the accents I heard during the interviews. Unsurprisingly, because we were talking about an issue that raises hard questions about similarity, dif-

ference, and privilege, there were contradictions in what the interviewees said. See Gilbert and Mulkay 1984 and Mulkay and Gilbert 1982 on contradictions in interviews and texts.

60. These are Quentin's words.

61. Giles and Coupland 1991: 70.

62. In contrast to this, other interviewees pointed out that Americans were often unable to distinguish among English accents.

63. Drag queens, for instance, undermine the idea that gender is an essence because their anatomy is distinct from their gender identity and the gender of the performance: Butler 1990: chap. 3; see also Weston 1993.

64. See Hogg and Abrams 1988: chap. 4 for a review of stereotyping literature.

65. Reily (1988) uses the example of the sexual harassment of women by men in the street as a time that gender identity is forced on women.

66. Garfinkel 1992 (1967); Heritage 1986 (1984); West and Fenstermaker 1995; West and Zimmerman 1987.

67. Imogen explained that she was visiting a friend in New York who had found out that his plumber was a staunch supporter of the Irish Republican movement. Other interviewees were scathing about the problems they had interacting with Irish Americans who defined them as the oppressors in the conflict in Northern Ireland. I consider this in more detail in Chapter 6.

68. Goffman 1986 (1974).

69. "Blow it" is an exclamatory remark and Alex uses it here instead of swearing.

CHAPTER FIVE

Epigraph: Sinéad O'Connor, *Black Boys on Mopeds,* Ensign Records Ltd., 1989.

1. Daniel Defoe, *Selected Writings* (Cambridge, 1975 [1701]).

2. Anderson 1983: 204–5.

3. See Cohen 1985; Halbwachs 1980 (1950); Hobsbawm 1983; Schwartz 1990; Smith 1986; Zerubavel 1994.

4. See Leith 1983: chap. 1 for a short linguistic history of the various tribes who invaded and inhabited the British Isles. See also Hilton 1989. Another instance of motivated forgetting is that the Angles and Saxons of that beloved "Anglo-Saxon" couplet were actually Germanic tribespeople. One wonders how easily anti-German sentiment could be whipped up in Britain, historically and in the present day, if this were common knowledge.

5. Cohen 1985: 21; Pratt 1993: 451.

6. See MacLeod 1992.

7. Jackson Lears 1985.

8. WING 1985; see also Paul 1997.

9. Britannia is an image of a helmeted woman, carrying a shield and trident, used to personify Britain. She was first used on coins in Roman times and again in the reign of Charles II. Britannia is the Roman name for Britain: Room 1999 (1959).

10. The Falklands Islands (also known as Las Malvinas) in the South Atlantic became the site of a war between Argentina and Britain in 1982 after Argentina claimed sovereignty over the islands. Argentina later surrendered its claim to sovereignty.

11. See Dresser 1989; Porter 1992; Samuel 1989c; and Surel 1989 for more examples.

12. See also Schwalbe and Mason-Schrock 1996: 119–20.

13. I use the term "imperial mind-set" to suggest a sense of self-importance resulting from the experience of being colonizers.

14. Gilroy 1992 (1987): 51–69.

15. Frankenberg 1994: 63–4; Mohanty 1991a, 1991b; Said 1978.

16. C. Hall 1993; McClintock 1993: 67, 1995: 21–75; Pajaczkowska and Young 1992: 13.

17. McClintock, 1993, 1995; Mohanty 1991a, 1991b.

18. WING 1985; see also Paul 1987.

19. "Patrials" were defined under the 1971 Act as citizens of the United Kingdom and its colonies born, adopted, registered, or naturalized in the United Kingdom, or U.K. citizens born abroad with a parent or grandparent who had obtained U.K. citizenship by one of those means; U.K. citizens born abroad who had been settled in the United Kingdom for five years or more; and Commonwealth citizens born to or adopted by U.K. citizens who had been born in the United Kingdom. The act lifted settlement restrictions on Commonwealth citizens with British-born grandparents, who were mainly Canadians and Australians, but did not allow many U.K. citizens without British ancestry (such as U.K. passport holders in East Africa and Malaysia) to settle in Britain: ibid.: 35–8.

20. Ibid.: 42.

21. Ibid.: 36.

22. Ibid.: 45; Anthias and Yuval-Davis 1992: 125–7.

23. Agulhon 1981; Warner 1985.

24. Cocks 1989; Pateman 1988.

25. Anthias and Yuval-Davis 1992: 127–8.

26. This quote is from Vera. In the early 1990s, Britain's gross domestic product did fall behind that of Italy, to the consternation of some in Britain: *Economist* 1990, United Nations Economic Commission for Europe 2001.

27. This terminology is inspired by Frankenberg's use of "race-cognizant" discursive repertoires in her analyses of her interviews. These are discourses that acknowledge racial differences and the structural and institutional inequalities that characterize race relations in the U.S. The interviewees in her study who drew on these discourses were usually cognizant of their own location in these systems of inequality: Frankenberg 1993: 157–76; see also idem, 1994.

28. This raises the issue that people who leave a country may be more critical than those who stay. My sample, then, may consist of people who are especially disdainful of English arrogance. An alternative reading is that the criticism of England seen in this section may be a form of *post hoc* justification as to

why they left. It may be that seeing their departure as a form of protest enhances their self-esteem.

29. A feminist analysis suggests that the distinction Gary draws here between people and institutions ignores the idea that "the personal is political," suggesting that the relationship between the two is much more complex than he admits: Hanisch 1969.

30. See also Dyer 1997: 10–1 on white guilt.

31. Frye 1983; Lorde 1984; Moraga and Anzaldúa 1983 (1981); Pratt 1984; Rich 1986: 136–55; Russo 1991; Spelman 1988. See also Ignatiev and Garvey 1996.

32. Rorty 1996. See also Ellison 1996.

33. Abdel Nour 1997.

34. Frankenberg 1993: 174–87.

35. It is interesting that both Harry and Diana turned to the issue of Ireland to express their feelings that England needed to take responsibility for its actions. In Chapter 6 I examine the interviewees' feelings about the conflict in Ireland by examining their interactions with Irish Americans. Here it is important to note that they considered Ireland to be a colonized country and relevant to discussions of imperialism.

36. Halbwachs 1980 (1950).

37. Eric Idle, *Always Look on the Bright Side of Life*, Virgin Records, 1989.

38. Frankenberg 1993: 14.

39. See McClintock 1995 for more examples of this idea.

40. Pajaczkowska and Young 1992.

41. See also Pratt 1992.

42. One example of this is the "World Series" baseball competition.

43. A rugby scrum or scrummage occurs when the forward players from both sides hunch down together and push against each other while the hooker tries to heel the ball back.

44. Numerous commentators have discussed the violence among some English football fans both at home and abroad. Some point to the racism, xenophobia, and nationalism embedded in such behavior; others point to the ways the violence expresses aggressive masculinity. See Buford 1993 (1991); Dodd 1995; Hornby 1992; Lloyd 1998; Paxman 1998; Ware 1997. For fictionalized accounts of football violence, see King 1997, 1999 (1998), and Sampson 1999 (1998).

45. Billig 1995: 124–5.

46. See McClintock 1995; Ware 1992.

47. This was a soccer match that took place in no-man's land between British and German soldiers during the Christmas truce of 1914: Walvin 1975:113. See also "In Brief" 2000.

48. Ian also insisted that the "only" time he was nationalistic was when he was watching soccer.

49. For example, before the England–Germany game in the 2000 European Championships, writers for the British tabloid *The Sun* proudly announced to their readers that England's squad was staying in Waterloo, reminding them that

"Iron Duke" Wellington's "stunning defeat of Napoleon" had occurred on the battlefield there in 1815. Earlier in the article, they had summoned up images of Richard the Lionheart (King of England in the twelfth century) leading his troops into battle, proclaiming that England's "lionhearts will be roaring into battle against Germany tonight": Parker and Darvill 2000. Meanwhile, the London *Daily Mail* also used warlike imagery: "Let the Battle Commence," it commanded: "England versus Germany" 2000.

50. Hornby 1992; but see also Hornby 1996.

51. Clearly, as a British citizen, she has never been exposed to U.K. immigration restrictions so has no basis for comparison.

52. This is in contrast to Britain, where most police officers do not carry guns.

53. These quotations are from Diana, Lucinda, and Piers.

54. Now, with the advent of "Cool Britannia," the interviewees might feel differently again.

CHAPTER SIX

Epigraph: A. S. Byatt, *Still Life* (London: Vintage, 1995 [1985]), 89.

1. Ansell 1997; Billig 1997; Cohen 1997; Gilroy 1992 (1987); Phoenix 1997; Small 1994; Ware 1992, 1997.

2. See Dyer 1997; Frankenberg 1993, 1997; and McIntosh 1992 on the unmarked status of whiteness. See Allen 1994; Babb 1998; Barrett and Roediger 1997; Brodkin 1998; Feagin 1997; Ignatiev 1995; Ignatiev and Garvey 1996; Jacobson 1998; McClintock 1995: 52–6; Roediger 1991; and Williams 1990 for historical treatments of how certain groups were included and excluded from the construct the "white race."

3. See C. Hall 1993; McClintock 1995; Said 1978; Ware 1992.

4. This is exemplified by two *Sun* newspaper reports within a space of two years. In the first report, the writers opined that black Britons protesting the favorable treatment accorded Zola Budd, a white South African runner, by the immigration authorities should "return to their original homelands. There is no place for them in Britain" (27 April 1984, as quoted in Gilroy 1992 [1987]: 63). A year and a half later, *The Sun* proudly commented that "this country has always involved a reputation as a tolerant, welcoming haven for refugees and immigrants" (24 October 1985, as quoted in ibid.: 229).

5. See Fryer 1984; McClintock 1995: 112–3; Ranger 1996: 6; Ware 1992: 37.

6. The title of the book is *The Empire Strikes Back:* CCCS 1982.

7. In 1991, there were 3,015,100 racial and ethnic minorities in Britain out of a total population of 54,888,800. Racial and ethnic minorities therefore represented nearly 5 percent of the population. These statistics are from the 1991 Census of the Population, Local Base Statistics, Crown Copyright; ESRC/JISC purchase: "Population" 1991.

8. Gilroy 1992 (1987). See also Carvel 2000; National Centre for Social Research 2000.

9. Enoch Powell, a Conservative Party Member of Parliament, was notorious in the 1960s for his strong racist stance against immigration from former colonies.

10. See Ansell 1997; Billig 1997; Cohen 1997; Phoenix 1997; Small 1994; and Ware 1992, 1997, for more examples of this.

11. I also asked men to consider how their experiences would have differed if they had been women, and vice versa, to encourage them to think about their gender identities. The data I collected from this question had more to do with the interviewees' experiences of immigration than with the interrelationships between their national and gender identities. However, later in the chapter, I report on the ways their gender identities surfaced as they talked about their national identities.

12. Dorothy, Frances, Imogen, Craig, and Gary made this argument.

13. Ian uses the terms "Indian" and "Pakistani" interchangeably here.

14. This quote is from Imogen, whom an English friend accused of lacking a sense of humor.

15. See Gans 1979; Lieberson 1985; Waters 1990.

16. This quote is from Craig.

17. The first quote is also from Craig. The second is from Peter, who used racial and ethnic epithets liberally throughout his interview. Indeed, the company he and his Dutch partners had set up was called FCL, short for "Four Cloggies and a Limey."

18. These quotes are from Tara, Frank, and Craig.

19. Gilroy 1992 (1987); see also Carvel 2000 and National Centre for Social Research 2000 on racism and Englishness, and Runneymede Trust 2000 on racism and Britishness.

20. See Layton-Henry 1992: 15.

21. Ian noted this whitewashing tendency when he tried to buy a book on the history of race relations in Britain. At a bookstore in London, he was sent to the sociology section rather than to the history section. He took this to imply that even *histories* of racial and ethnic minorities are expected to begin relatively recently: cf. Fryer 1984; McClintock 1995; Ranger 1996.

22. In the U.S., white people are much more willing to talk about their ethnic identity. See, for example, Waters 1998.

23. Frankenberg 1993: 32–5.

24. For instance, Billig 1997; Clark and O'Donnell 1999; Cohen 1997; Delgado and Stefancic 1997; Dyer 1997; Ferber 1998; Fine et al. 1997; Frankenberg 1993, 1994, 1997; Hartigan 1999; hooks 1989; Jacobson 1998; Kincheloe et al. 1998; Lipsitz 1998; McIntosh 1992; Morrison 1997; Pratt 1984; Roediger 1991; Ware 1992, 1997.

25. See Ignatiev and Garvey 1996; Stowe 1996.

26. Dyer 1997; Frankenberg 1993; Waters 1990. It is important to remember, however, that not all white identities are the same. Hartigan's 1999 study of whites living in Detroit is a good example of how class intersects with whiteness to produce heterogeneous attitudes, and how whiteness is not the norm in all situations in the U.S. Hartigan's work, together with Frankenberg's 1993

study of the "social geography of race," also suggests how localized experiences and understandings of race are.

27. Essed 1991: 193–213; McIntosh 1992.

28. This is similar to one of the stages Thompson 1999: 67 discusses.

29. See Faludi 1991.

30. Frankenberg 1993.

31. Ibid.

32. It should be noted, however, that other interviewees explicitly refused to make generalizations about "typicals."

33. Frankenberg 1993: 14.

34. McIntosh 1992.

35. An example of this is the infamous illustration "New Yorker's View of the United States": Gould and White 1986 (1974): 20.

36. Gilroy 1992 (1987): 55.

37. Harry admitted this in the previous section. See Lipsitz 1998 on the "possessive investment" white people have in seeing their whiteness as harmless and Ignatiev and Garvey 1996 on being a race traitor. See hooks 1989; Russo 1991; and Thompson 1999 on doing anti-racist work. See Carvel 2000 and National Center for Social Research 2000 on the relationship between Englishness and racial prejudice.

38. "Sloane Ranger" is a social label given to some people who have public-school accents and may congregate in Sloane Square in Chelsea, London (hence the name). Among the stereotypes associated with Sloane Rangers are that they own black labrador dogs, drive Range Rovers, and wear waxed "Barbour" jackets and striped shirts. Lady Diana Spencer, before her marriage to Prince Charles, was a good example of a Sloane. For more information, see Room 1999 (1959).

39. McIntosh 1992.

40. Frances, Ken, and Emma made these critiques.

41. Emily, Quentin, and Gary had these complaints.

42. Others who did this included Mike, Imogen, and Gary.

43. See Gilroy 1992 (1987): 60–1 and Ware 1992: 12–3 for their analyses of similar controversies in education.

44. Norman Tebbit, then chairman of the Conservative Party, said that English people who supported non-English cricket teams in test matches did not really belong in England. He implied that English people of South Asian or West Indian ethnicity would meet this criterion for exclusion.

45. *Halal* meat conforms to the rules laid down by Islamic dietary requirements for the ritual slaughter of animals.

46. Daley Thompson won many medals for the decathlon in the 1980s. Ironically, in light of Harriet's story, he refused to carry the Union Jack at the 1982 Commonwealth Games: Gilroy 1992 (1987): 62.

47. S. Hall 1993; see also Gilroy 1992 (1987): 60–9.

48. Anderson 1983; Cohen 1985; Pratt 1993.

49. See, however, Agulhon 1981; Dresser 1989; Warner 1985.

50. Frankenberg 1993.

CHAPTER SEVEN

Epigraph: Bill Bryson, *Notes from a Small Island* (London: Doubleday Books, 1995), 117.

1. Simmel 1950.
2. Schwalbe and Mason-Schrock 1996: 124.
3. See, for example, Kessler and McKenna 1978 on gender and Omi and Winant 1994 on race.
4. See Jackson and Penrose 1993: 7–9. See also Anderson 1983; Anthias and Yuval Davies 1992; Goulbourne 1991; Hobsbawm and Ranger 1983.
5. Imogen, Lucinda, Octavia, Zoe, Ken, and Alex made these comments.
6. This quote is from Frank.
7. Fourteen of the thirty-four interviewees had American partners.
8. Quentin and Vera made these comments.
9. As we saw in Chapter 6, the interviewees sometimes unconsciously assumed that all English people were the same as them—white and middle- or upper-middle-class.
10. This quote is from Stephen.
11. This quote is from Vera.
12. Garfinkel 1992 (1967); Heritage 1986 (1984).
13. As Reily 1988 points out in the case of the sexual harassment of women, having an identity imposed on one can also be harmful and oppressive.
14. Snitow 1990; Reily 1988.
15. Garfinkel 1992 (1967); Heritage 1986 (1984); West and Fenstermaker 1995; West and Zimmerman 1987.
16. Frankenberg 1993.
17. These quotations are from Hugh, Quentin, Dorothy, Craig, and Tara.
18. Although her comment is somewhat vague, it is clear that she tried to belittle Americans.
19. Freud 1960 (1905).
20. Thorne 1993: 79–87.
21. Ibid.: chap. 5.
22. This quote is from Piers.
23. Butler 1990: 141; Thorne 1993: 88.
24. Hall 1996: 4; Lather 1991.
25. Connell 1987, 1995.
26. Connell 1987; Giddens 1984.
27. Connell 1987.
28. Ibid.
29. Reily 1988; Snitow 1990.
30. Bucholtz 1995; Butler 1990; Kessler and McKenna 1978; McElhinny 1995; Thorne 1993; West and Zimmerman 1987.
31. Collins 1986; Simmel 1950.

References

Abdel Nour, Farid. 1997. "'Dead to Us': Richard Rorty and the Wrong of Ethnocentrism." Unpublished ms., Rutgers University, New Brunswick, N.J.

Acker, Joan, Kate Barry, and Joke Esseveld. 1983. "Objectivity and Truth: Problems in Doing Feminist Research." *Women's Studies International Forum* 6, no. 4: 423–35.

Agulhon, Maurice. 1981. *Marianne into Battle*. Trans. J. Lloyd. Cambridge: Cambridge University Press.

Alba, Richard D. 1990. *Ethnic Identity: The Transformation of White America*. New Haven, Conn.: Yale University Press.

Alford, Henry. 1866 (1864). *A Plea for the Queen's English: Stray Notes on Speaking and Spelling*. London: A. Strahan.

Alibhai-Brown, Yasmin. 2000. "A Magic Carpet of Cultures in London." *New York Times* (25 June), sec. 2, 1, 32.

Allen, Theodore. 1994. *The Invention of the White Race. Volume I. Racial Oppression and Social Control*. London and New York: Verso.

Anderson, Benedict. 1983. *Imagined Communities: Reflections on the Origins and Spread of Nationalism*. London: Verso and New Left Books.

Ansell, Amy Elizabeth. 1997. *New Right, New Racism: Race and Reaction in the United States and Britain*. New York: New York University Press.

Anthias, Floya, and Nira Yuval Davies (with Harriet Cain). 1992. *Racialized Boundaries: Race, Nation, Gender, Colour and Class and the Anti-Racist Struggle*. London: Routledge.

Asimov, Eric. 1997. "To Go: Name a Food and You Can Have It Delivered." *New York Times* (3 December), F5. Available from: Lexis-Nexis.

Aslet, Clive. 1997. *Anyone for England? A Search for British Identity*. London: Little, Brown.

Athearn, Robert G. 1953. *Westward the Briton*. New York: Charles Scribner's Sons.

Auerbach, Jon. 1996. "Boston's New Accent: British, Anglophilia Is All the Rage." *The Globe* (Boston) (11 August), A1. Available from: Lexis-Nexis.

Babb, Valerie. 1998. *Whiteness Visible: The Meaning of Whiteness in American Literature and Culture*. New York and London: New York University Press.

Baltzell, E. Digby. 1964. *The Protestant Establishment: Aristocracy and Caste in America*. New York: Random House.

Banks, Stephen P. 1988. "Achieving 'Unmarkedness' in Organisational Discourse: A Praxis Perspective on Ethnolinguistic Identity." In *Language and Ethnic Identity*, ed. William B. Gudykunst. Clevedon, U.K., and Philadelphia: Multilingual Matters.

Barnes, Julian. 1998. *England, England*. London: Jonathon Cape.

Barrett, James R., and David Roediger. 1997. "How White People Became White." Pp. 404–6 in *Critical White Studies: Looking Behind the Mirror*, ed. Richard Delgado and Jean Stefancic. Philadelphia: Temple University Press.

Bartlett, C. J. 1992. *"The Special Relationship": A Political History of Anglo-American Relations since 1945*. London and New York: Longman.

BBC. 2000. "BBC Online Homepage." Available from: <http://www.bbc.co.uk>.

BBC Worldwide Ltd. 2000. "Your Starting Point for Shopping on the Web." Available from: <http://www.beeb.com>.

Beisel, Nicola. 1993. "Morals Versus Art: Censorship, the Politics of Interpretation, and the Victorian Nude." *American Sociological Review* 58: 145–62.

Bendix, Richard. 1964. *Nation-Building and Citizenship: Studies of Our Changing Social Order*. New York: John Wiley and Sons.

Berger, Peter L., and Thomas Luckmann. 1967. *The Social Construction of Reality: A Treatise on the Sociology of Knowledge*. New York: Doubleday.

Berthoff, Rowland Tappan. 1953. *British Immigrants in Industrial America, 1790–1950*. Cambridge, Mass.: Harvard University Press.

Bhavnani, Kum-Kum, and Ann Phoenix. 1994. "Shifting Identities, Shifting Racisms: An Introduction." In *Shifting Identities, Shifting Racisms: A Feminism and Psychology Reader*, ed. Kum-Kum Bhavnani and Ann Phoenix. London: Sage Publications.

Billera, Leslie. 1999. "True Brit." *New York Daily News* (28 December), 37. Available from: Lexis-Nexis.

Billig, Michael. 1995. *Banal Nationalism*. London and Thousand Oaks, Calif.: Sage.

———. 1997. "Keeping the White Queen in Play." Pp. 149–57 in *Off White: Readings on Race, Power and Society*, ed. Michelle Fine et al. New York and London: Routledge.

Bloom, Allan. 1987. *The Closing of the American Mind*. New York: Simon and Schuster.

Bogdanor, Vernon. 1999. *Devolution in the United Kingdom*. Oxford: Oxford University Press.

Boli-Bennett, John. 1979. "Ideology of Expanding State Authority in National Constitutions." In *National Development and the World-System*, ed. J. Meyer and M. Hannon. Chicago: University of Chicago Press.

Bourdieu, Pierre. 1997 (1972). *Outline of a Theory of Practice*. Trans. Richard Nice. Cambridge: Cambridge University Press.

Bourhis, Richard Y., and Howard Giles. 1977. "The Language of Intergroup Distinctiveness." In *Language, Ethnicity and Intergroup Relations*, ed. Howard Giles. London: Academic Press.

Bourhis, Richard Y., Howard Giles, and Wallace E. Lambert. 1981. "The Social Consequences of Accommodating One's Style of Speech: A Cross-National Investigation." *International Journal of the Sociology of Language* 6: 55–72.

Bourhis, Richard Y., Howard Giles, J.P. Leyens, and H. Tajfel. 1979. "Psycholinguistic Distinctiveness: Language Divergence in Belgium." In *Language and Social Psychology*, ed. H. Giles and R. St Clair. Oxford: Basil Blackwell.

Bown, William. 1991. "Football and the Brain Drain." *New Scientist*, vol. 132 (30 November), 59–60. Available from: Infotrac.

Brandon, Ruth. 1980. *The Dollar Princesses: Sagas of Upward Mobility, 1870–1914*. New York: Alfred A. Knopf.

Brimelow, Peter. 1995. *Alien Nation: Common Sense about America's Immigration Disaster*. New York: Random House.

Britishinamerica.com. 2000. "Britishinamerica.Com: Uniting the British Community in America." Available from: <http://www.britishinamerica.com>.

Brits Abroad. 2000. "Brits Abroad." Available from: <http://www.britsabroad.co.uk>.

Brodkin, Karen. 1998. *How Jews Became White Folks and What That Says about Race in America*. New Brunswick, N.J., and London: Rutgers University Press.

Brown, Penelope, and Stephen C. Levinson. 1987 (1978). *Politeness: Some Universals in Language Usage*. Cambridge: Cambridge University Press.

Bryson, Bill. 1995. *Notes from a Small Island*. London: Doubleday Books.

BSkyB. 2000. "Sky Sports." Available from: <http://www.sky.com/sports>.

Bucholtz, Mary. 1995. "From Mulatta to Mestiza: Passing and the Linguistic Reshaping of Identity." Pp. 351–75 in *Gender Articulated*, ed. Mary Bucholtz. New York and London: Routledge.

Buckle, Richard, ed. 1978. *U and Non-U Revisited*. London: Debrett's Peerage.

Buford, Bill. 1993 (1991). *Among the Thugs*. New York: Vintage Departures.

Burke, Peter. 1987. "Introduction." In *The Social History of Language*, ed. Peter Burke and Roy Porter. Cambridge: Cambridge University Press.

Burke, Peter, and Roy Porter. 1991. *A Social History of Language*. Cambridge: Polity Press.

Buruma, Ian. 1998. *Anglomania: A European Love Affair*. New York: Random House.

Butler, Judith. 1990. *Gender Trouble: Feminism and the Subversion of Identity*. New York and London: Routledge.

Byatt, A. S. 1995 (1985). *Still Life*. London: Vintage.

———. 1996. *Babel Tower*. New York: Random House.

Cameron, David Rutz. 1997. "How the Garcia Cousins Lost Their Accents: Understanding the Language of Title VII Decisions Approving English-Only Rules." *California Law Review* 85, no. 5 (October): 1347–93. Available from: Infotrac.

Campagna, Darryl. 1996. "Ardent for Austen." *Times Union* (Albany, N.Y.) (14 April), G1. Available from: Lexis-Nexis.

Carvel, John. 2000. "The Rise of Little Englanders: Xenophobic Views Are Increasing, Says Survey, as Figures Reveal Widening Gap on Nationality, Race and Foreign Affairs." *The Guardian* (London) (28 November), 4. Available from: Lexis-Nexis.

CCCS (Centre for Contemporary Cultural Studies). 1982. *The Empire Strikes Back: Race and Racism in '70s Britain*. London: Hutchinson, Centre for Contemporary Cultural Studies, Birmingham.

Chambers, Iain. 1993. "Narratives of Nationalism: Being "British." In *Space and Place: Theories of Identity and Location*, ed. Erica Carter, James Donald, and Judith Squires. London: Lawrence and Wishart.

Chapman, A. J., J. R. Smith, and H. C. Foot. 1977. "Language, Humour and Intergroup Relations." In *Language, Ethnicity and Intergroup Relations*, ed. Howard Giles. London: Academic Press.

Cheyne, W. M. 1970. "Stereotyped Reactions to Speakers with Scottish and English Regional Accents." *British Journal of Social and Clinical Psychology* 9: 77–9.

Clark, Christine, and James O'Donnell, eds. 1999. *Becoming and Unbecoming White: Owning and Disowning a Racial Identity*. Westport, Conn., and London: Bergin and Garvey.

Clark, William. 1957. *Less than Kin: A Study of Anglo-American Relations*. Boston: Houghton-Mifflin.

Cocks, Joan Elizabeth. 1989. *The Oppositional Imagination; Feminism, Critique, and Political Theory*. New York and London: Routledge.

Cogan, Frances B. 1989. *All-American Girl: The Ideal of Real Womanhood in Mid-Nineteenth Century America*. Athens: University of Georgia Press.

Coghlan, Andy. 1993. "High-Fliers Still Leaving Britain." *New Scientist*, vol. 140 (20 November), 7. Available from: Infotrac.

Cohen, Anthony. 1985. *The Symbolic Construction of Community*. Chichester, U.K.: Ellis Horwood.

Cohen, Ira J. 1989. *Structuration Theory: Anthony Giddens and the Constitution of Social Life*. New York: St. Martin's Press.

Cohen, Phil. 1997. "Laboring under Whiteness." Pp. 244–82 in *Displacing Whiteness: Essays in Social and Cultural Criticism*, ed. Ruth Frankenberg. Durham, N.C., and London: Duke University Press.

Colley, Linda. 1992. *Britons: Forging the Nation 1707–1837*. New Haven, Conn., and London: Yale University Press.

Collins, Patricia Hill. 1986. "Learning from the Outsider Within: The Sociological Significance of Black Feminist Thought." *Social Problems* 33, no. 6: 14–32.

———. 1991. *Black Feminist Thought: Knowledge, Consciousness and the Politics of Empowerment*. New York: Routledge.

Colls, Robert, and Philip Dodd. 1986. *Englishness: Politics and Culture, 1880–1920*. London and Dover, N.H.: Croom-Helm.

Connell, R. W. 1987. *Gender and Power: Society, the Person and Sexual Politics*. Stanford, Calif.: Stanford University Press.

———. 1995. *Masculinities*. Berkeley and Los Angeles: University of California Press.

Cooley, Charles. 1964 (1902). *Human Nature and Social Order*. New York: Schoken.

Coupland, Nikolas. 1985. "'Hark, Hark, the Lark': Social Motivations for Phonological Style-Shifting." *Language and Communication* 5, no. 3: 153–71.

Crowley, Tony. 1989. *The Politics of Discourse: The Standard Language Question in British Cultural Debates*. Basingstoke, Hants., and London: Macmillan Education.
————. 1991. *Proper English? Readings in Language, History and Cultural Identity*. London and New York: Routledge.

Curran, Bob. 1998. "In the Ivory Tower, Diana Lives On." *Buffalo News* (N.Y.) (4 August), 2C. Available from: Lexis-Nexis.

Current Population Survey. 1995. Available from: <http://ferret.bls.census.gov/cgi-bin/ferret>.

Danchev, Alex. 1997. "On Friendship: Anglo-America at Fin de Siècle." *International Affairs* 73, no. 4: 747–61.

DeConde, Alexander. 1992. *Ethnicity, Race, and American Foreign Policy*. Boston: Northeastern University Press.

Defoe, Daniel. 1975 (1701). *Selected Writings*. Cambridge: Cambridge University Press.

Delgado, Richard, and Jean Stefancic, eds. 1997. *Critical White Studies: Looking Behind the Mirror*. Philadelphia: Temple University Press.

DeMott, Benjamin. 1990. *The Imperial Middle: Why Americans Can't Think Straight about Class*. New York: William Morrow.

Deutsch, Karl W. 1966 (1953). *Nationalism and Social Communication: An Inquiry into the Foundations of Nationality*. Cambridge, Mass., and London: Massachusetts Institute of Technology Press.

Dickson, David. 1993. "UK Brain-Drain 'No Worse.'" *Nature*, vol. 366, no. 6452 (18 November), 197. Available from: Infotrac.

di Leonardo, M. 1984. *Varieties of Ethnic Experience*. Ithaca, N.Y., and London: Cornell University Press.

DiMaggio, Paul. 1986. "Cultural Entrepreneurship in Nineteenth Century Boston: The Creation of an Organizational Base for High Culture in America." In *Media, Culture and Society: A Critical Reader*, ed. Richard Collins et al. London: Sage Publications.

Dodd, Philip. 1995. "A Mongrel Nation (England)." *New Statesman and Society*, vol. 8, no. 341 (24 February), 26–7. Available from: Infotrac.

Dresser, Madge. 1989. "Britannia." In *Patriotism: The Making and Unmaking of British National Identity, Volume III. National Fictions*, ed. Raphael Samuel. London and New York: Routledge.

Duff, Michael. 1990. "Britain's Brain Drain Is Not a Myth." *New Scientist*, vol. 127, no. 1736 (29 September), 14. Available from: Infotrac.

Duffy, Thom. 1993. "The British Invasion Continues." *Billboard*, vol. 105, no. 7 (13 February), B4–B6. Available from: Infotrac.

Dyer, Richard. 1997. *White*. London and New York: Routledge.

Easthope, Antony. 1998. *The English Nation: The Great Myth*. Stroud, U.K.: Sutton Publishing.

Economist Book of Vital World Statistics. 1990. London: Hutchinson/Economist Books.

Edelman, Murray. 1964. *The Symbolic Uses of Politics*. Urbana: University of Illinois Press.

Editorial. 1994. "Veddy British PBS." *Providence Journal-Bulletin* (28 May), 8A. Available from: Lexis-Nexis.

Ellison, Julie. 1996. "A Short History of Liberal Guilt." *Critical Inquiry* 22, no. 2: 344–71.

"England versus Germany 2000: Let the Battle Commence." 2000. *Daily Mail* (17 June), 48–9. Available from: Lexis-Nexis.

Epstein, Joseph. 1997. "Anglophilia, American Style." *American Scholar* 66 (Summer). Available from: Dialog Web.

Erickson, Charlotte. 1972. *Invisible Immigrants: The Adaptation of English and Scottish Immigrants in Nineteenth-Century America.* Coral Gables, FL: University of Miami Press.

Erikson, Erik H. 1980 (1959). *Identity and the Life Cycle.* New York: W. W. Norton.

Essed, Philomena. 1991. *Understanding Everyday Racism.* Newbury Park, London, New Delhi: Sage Publications.

Essentially English. 1997. "Quality English Gifts and Collectibles." Available from: <http://www.essentially-english.com>.

Faludi, Susan. 1991. *Backlash.* New York: Crown Publishers.

Farber, Jim. 1998. "Bands Across the Water: In All Sorts of Genres, Britannia Rules These Days." *Daily News* (New York) (6 December), p. 20). Available from: Lexis-Nexis.

Feagin, Joe R. 1997. "Old Poison in New Bottles: The Deep Roots of Modern Nativism." Pp. 348–53 in *Critical White Studies: Looking Behind the Mirror,* ed. Richard Delgado and Jean Stefancic. Philadelphia: Temple University Press.

Ferber, Abby. 1998. *White Man Falling: Race, Gender and White Supremacy.* Lanham, Md.: Rowman and Littlefield.

Fine, Michelle, Linda Powell, Lois Weis, and L. Mun Wong, eds. 1997. *Off White: Readings in Race, Power and Society.* London and New York: Routledge.

Fischer, David Hackett. 1989. *Albion's Seed: Four British Folkways in America.* New York and Oxford: Oxford University Press.

"Football365." 2000. 365 Corporation PLC. Available from: <http://www.football365.co.uk>.

Foreman, Jonathon. 1998. "Big Bad Brits (and Other Myths)." *National Review,* vol. 50, no. 7 (20 April), 56–8. Available from: Proquest.

Foucault, Michel. 1972 (1971). *The Archaeology of Knowledge and the Discourse on Language.* New York: Pantheon Books.

Frankenberg, Ruth. 1993. *White Women, Race Matters: The Social Construction of Whiteness.* Minneapolis: University of Minnesota Press.

———. 1994. "Whiteness and Americanness: Examining Constructions of Race, Culture and Nation in White Women's Life Narratives." Pp. 62–77 in *Race,* ed. Steven Gregory and Roger Sanjek. New Brunswick, N.J.: Rutgers University Press.

———. 1997. "Introduction: Local Whiteness, Localizing Whiteness." Pp. 1–33 in *Displacing Whiteness: Essays in Social and Cultural Criticism,* ed. Ruth Frankenberg. Durham, N.C., and London: Duke University Press.

Freud, Sigmund. 1960 (1905). *Jokes and Their Relation to the Unconscious*, ed. and trans. James Strachey. New York: W. W. Norton.

Frost, David and Michael Shea. 1986. *The Rich Tide: Men, Women, Ideas and Their Transatlantic Impact*. London: Collins.

Frye, Marilyn. 1983. *The Politics of Reality: Essays in Feminist Theory*. Freedom, Calif.: Crossing Press.

Fryer, Peter. 1984. *Staying Power: The History of Black People in Britain*. London: Pluto Press.

Fussell, Paul. 1983. *Class: A Guide Through the American Status System*. New York: Summit Books.

Gans, Herbert J. 1974. *Popular Culture and High Culture: An Analysis and Evaluation of Taste*. New York: Basic Books.

———. 1979. "Symbolic Ethnicity: The Future of Ethnic Groups and Cultures in America." *Ethnic and Racial Studies* 2, no. 1: 1–20.

Garfinkel, Harold. 1992 (1967). *Studies in Ethnomethodology*. Cambridge: Polity Press.

Gatbonton-Segalowitz, E. 1975. "Systematic Variables in Second Language Speech: A Sociolinguistic Study." Ph.D. diss., McGill University, Montreal.

Geertz, Clifford. 1973. *The Interpretation of Cultures*. New York: Basic Books.

Gellner, Ernest. 1983. *Nations and Nationalism*. Ithaca, N.Y.: Cornell University Press.

Gener, Randy. 1999. "The Coaches Speak: Accents R Us (or Ah Us, If You Like)." *New York Times* (21 February), sec. 2, 10. Available from: Lexis-Nexis.

George, Tara, and Paul H. B. Shin. 1997. "The City Weeps with Britons." *Daily News* (New York) (7 September), 17. Available from: Lexis-Nexis.

Gerson, Judith, and Kathy Peiss. 1985. "Boundaries, Negotiation and Consciousness: Reconceptualizing Gender Relations." *Social Problems* 32: 317–31.

Giddens, Anthony. 1984. *The Constitution of Society: Outline of the Theory of Structuration*. Berkeley and Los Angeles: University of California Press.

Gilbert, C. Nigel, and Michael Mulkay. 1984. *Opening Pandora's Box: A Sociological Analysis of Scientists' Discourse*. Cambridge: Cambridge University Press.

Giles, Howard. 1970. "Evaluative Reactions to Accents." *Educational Review* 22, no. 3: 211–28.

———. 1971. "Patterns of Evaluation in Reactions to RP, South Welsh and Somerset Accented Speech." *British Journal of Social and Clinical Psychology* 10: 280–1.

———. 1973. "Accent Mobility: A Model and Some Data." *Anthropological Linguistics* 15, no. 2: 87–105.

———. 1979. "Ethnicity Markers in Speech." In *Social Markers in Speech*, ed. Klaus Scherer and Howard Giles. Cambridge: Cambridge University Press.

———. 1995. "Reactions to Anglo- and Hispanic-American Accented Speakers: Affect, Identity, Persuasion, and the English-Only Controversy." *Language and Communication* 15, no. 2: 107–20.

Giles, Howard, Richard Y. Bourhis, and D. M. Taylor. 1977. "Towards a Theory of Language in Ethnic Group Relations." In *Language, Ethnicity and Intergroup Relations*, ed. H. Giles. London: Academic Press.

Giles, Howard, and Nikolas Coupland. 1991. *Language: Contexts and Consequences.* Milton Keynes: Open University Press.

Giles, Howard, and P. Johnson. 1987. "Ethnolinguistic Identity Theory: A Social Psychological Approach to Language Maintenance." *International Journal of the Sociology of Language* 68: 66–99.

Giles, Howard, and Caroline Sassoon. 1983. "The Effect of Speaker's Accent, Social Class Background and Message Style on British Listeners' Social Judgements." *Language and Communication* 3, no. 3: 305–13.

Giles, Howard, Donald M. Taylor, and Richard Y. Bourhis. 1973. "Towards a Theory of Interpersonal Accommodation Through Language: Some Canadian Data." *Language in Society* 2: 177–92.

Gilroy, Paul. 1992 (1987). *There Ain't No Black in the Union Jack: The Cultural Politics of Race and Nation.* London: Routledge.

Gladwell, Malcom. 1996. "Black Like Them." *New Yorker* (29 April, 6 May), 74–81.

Glaser, Barney, and Anslem Strauss. 1967. *The Discovery of Grounded Theory: Strategies for Qualitative Research.* New York: Aldine.

Goffman, Erving. 1959. *The Presentation of Self in Everyday Life.* Garden City, N.Y.: Doubleday Anchor Books.

———. 1963. *Stigma: Notes on the Management of Spoiled Identity.* New York: Simon and Schuster.

———. 1986 (1974). *Frame Analysis: An Essay on the Organization of Experience.* Boston: Northeastern University Press.

Goldthorpe, John. 1983. "Women and Class Analysis: In Defense of the Conventional View." *Sociology* 17: 465–99.

———. 1984. "Women and Class Analysis: A Reply to the Replies." *Sociology* 18: 491–9.

Goldthorpe, John, and David Lockwood. 1996. "Affluence and the British Class Structure." In *Class: Critical Concepts, Volume IV*, ed. John Scott. London and New York: Routledge.

Goodman, John. 1997. "No More Mr. Nice Guy." *Sunday Times Magazine* (London) (16 March), 17–22.

Goulbourne, Harry. 1991. *Ethnicity and Nationalism in Post-Imperial Britain.* Cambridge: Cambridge University Press.

Gould, Peter, and Rodney White. 1986 (1974). *Mental Maps.* Winchester, Mass.: Allen and Unwin.

Greenfeld, Leah. 1992. *Nationalism: Five Roads to Modernity.* Cambridge, Mass., and London: Harvard University Press.

Greenhill, Pauline. 1992. "English Immigrants' Narratives of Linguistic and Cultural Confusion: Examples of Ethnic Expression from Ontario." *Ethnic and Racial Studies* 15, no. 2: 236–65.

Grimes, William. 2000. "On This Side of the Pond." *New York Times* (22 March), F6. Available from: Lexis-Nexis.

Groening, Tom. 1999. "What on Earth? Why Maine Needs Official State Soil." *Bangor Daily News* (17 March). Available from: Lexis-Nexis.

Guardian Newspapers. 2000. "Football Unlimited." Available from: <http://www.footballunlimited.co.uk>.

Gumperz, John J. 1982. *Discourse Strategies*. Cambridge: Cambridge University Press.

———. 1992. "Contextualization Revisited." In *The Contexualization of Language*, ed. Peter Auer and Aldo di Luzio. Amsterdam and Philadelphia: John Benjamin Publishing.

Haas, Al. 1995. "Little Things That Make Britain Great." *The Record* (Bergen County, N.J.) (9 April), T02. Available from: Lexis-Nexis.

Hagen, E. A. 1997. "To Di For." *Sunday News* (13 July), G1. Available from: Lexis-Nexis.

Halbwachs, Maurice. 1980 (1950). *The Collective Memory*. New York: Harper Colophon.

Hall, Catherine. 1993. "'From Greenland's Icy Mountains . . . to Afric's Golden Sand': Ethnicity, Race and Nation in Mid-Nineteenth Century England." *Gender and History* 5, no. 4: 236–65.

Hall, Stuart. 1986. "Gramsci's Relevance for the Study of Race and Ethnicity." *Journal of Communication Inquiry* 10, no. 2: 5–27.

———. 1987. "Minimal Selves." In *The Real Me: Postmodernism and the Question of Identity*. London: ICA Documents 6.

———. 1988. "New Ethnicities." *Black Film British Cinema*. ICA Conference. ICA Documents (February), 27–31.

———. 1989. "Ethnicity: Identity and Difference." *Radical America* 23, no. 4: 9–20.

———. 1990. "Cultural Identity and Diaspora." Pp. 222–37 in *Identity: Community, Culture, Difference*, ed. Jonathon Rutherford. London: Lawrence and Wishart.

———. 1993. "The Dialogics of Identity in an Age of Globalization." Paper presented at the Center for the Critical Analysis of Contemporary Culture (CCACC), Rutgers University, New Brunswick, N.J.

Haltunnen, Karen. 1982. *Confidence Men and Painted Women: A Study of Middle Class Culture in America, 1830–1870*. New Haven, Conn., and London: Yale University Press.

Hanisch, Carol. 1969. "The Personal Is Political." *Feminist Revolution* (March), 204–5.

Harding, Sandra. 1991. *Whose Science? Whose Knowledge? Thinking from Women's Lives*. Ithaca, N.Y.: Cornell University Press.

Harris, Andrew S. 1998. "Britannia.Org." Available from: <http://www.britannia.org>.

Hartigan, John, Jr. 1999. *Racial Situations: Class Predicaments of Whiteness in Detroit*. Princeton, N.J.: Princeton University Press.

Haseler, Stephen. 1996. *The English Tribe*. Basingstoke, Hants., and New York: Macmillan and St. Martin's Press.

Hebdige, Dick. 1979. *Subculture: The Meaning of Style*. London: Methuen.

Hechter, Michael. 1999. *Internal Colonialism: The Celtic Fringe in British National Development*. New Brunswick, N.J., and London: Transactions Publishers.

Heffer, Simon. 1999. *Nor Shall My Sword: The Reinvention of England.* London: Weidenfeld and Nicholson.

Heritage, John. 1986 (1984). *Garfinkel and Ethnomethodology.* Cambridge: Polity Press.

Hewitt, Nancy. 1992. "Compounding Differences." *Feminist Studies* 18: 313–26.

Higham, John. 1975. *Send These to Me: Jews and Other Immigrants in Urban America.* New York: Atheneum Press.

———. 1988 (1955). *Strangers in the Land: Patterns of American Nativism 1860–1925.* New Brunswick, N.J., and London: Rutgers University Press.

Hilton, Rodney. 1989. "Were the English English?" In *Patriotism: The Making and Unmaking of British National Identity, Volume I. History and Politics,* ed. Raphael Samuel. London and New York: Routledge.

Hipsky, Martin A. 1994. "Anglophil(m)Ia: Why Does America Watch Merchant–Ivory Movies?" *Journal of Popular Film and Television* 22: 98–107.

Hitchens, Christopher. 1991. *Blood, Class and Nostalgia: Anglo-American Ironies.* London: Vintage.

Hitchens, Peter. 2000. *The Abolition of Britain: From Winston Churchill to Princess Diana.* San Francisco: Encounter Books.

Hobsbawm, Eric. 1983. "Introduction: Inventing Traditions." Pp. 1–14 in *The Invention of Tradition,* ed. Eric Hobsbawm and Terence Ranger. Cambridge: Cambridge University Press.

Hobsbawm, Eric, and Terence Ranger, eds. 1983. *The Invention of Tradition.* Cambridge: Cambridge University Press.

Hogg, Michael A., and Dominic Abrams. 1988. *Social Identifications: A Social Psychology of Intergroup Relations and Group Processes.* London and New York: Routledge.

Hondagneu-Sotelo, Pierrette. 1994. *Gendered Transitions: Mexican Experiences of Immigration.* Berkeley: University of California Press.

hooks, bell. 1989. "Critical Interrogation: Talking Race, Resisting Racism." *Art Forum* (May), 18–20.

Hornby, Nick. 1992. *Fever Pitch.* London: Victor Gollancz.

———. 1996. "Introduction." Pp. ix–xi in *The Guardian Year '96,* ed. Georgina Henry. London: Fourth Estate.

Horsman, Reginald. 1997. "Race and Manifest Destiny: The Origins of American Radical Anglo-Saxonism." Pp. 139–44 in *Critical White Studies: Looking Behind the Mirror,* ed. Richard Delgado and Jean Stefancic. Philadelphia: Temple University Press.

Horwill, H. W. 1939. *An Anglo-American Interpreter.* Oxford: Clarendon Press.

Howkins, Alan. 1986. "The Discovery of Rural England." Pp. 62–88 in *Englishness: Politics and Culture,* ed. Robert Colls and Philip Dodd. London and Dover, N.H.: Croom-Helms.

Hu-DeHart, Evelyn. 1994. "PC and the Politics of Multiculturalism in Higher Education." In *Race,* ed. Steven Gregory and Roger Sanjek. New Brunswick, N.J.: Rutgers University Press.

Ignatiev, Noel. 1995. *How the Irish Became White.* New York and London: Routledge.

Ignatiev, Noel, and John Garvey. 1996. *Race Traitor.* New York and London: Routledge.

"In Brief: Wartime Match Remembered." 2000. *The Guardian* (London) (17 June). Available from: Lexis-Nexis.

Isaacs, Harold R. 1975. *Idols of the Tribe: Group Identity and Political Change.* New York: Harper and Row.

Jackson, Peter, and Jan Penrose. 1993. "Introduction: Placing 'Race' and Nation." Pp. 1–2 in *Constructions of Race, Place and Nation,* ed. Peter Jackson and Jan Penrose. London: University College London Press.

Jackson Lears, T. J. 1985. "The Concept of Cultural Hegemony: Problems and Possibilities." *American Historical Review* 96: 596-3.

Jacobson, Matthew Frye. 1998. *Whiteness of a Different Color: European Immigrants and the Alchemy of Race.* Cambridge, Mass., and London: Harvard University Press.

Jones, Jacqueline. 1982. "My Mother Was Much of a Woman: Black Women, Work and the Family under Slavery." *Feminist Studies* 8: 235–70.

Jones, Katharine W. 1998. "Accent on Privilege: Negotiating English Identities in an American Context." Ph.D. diss., Rutgers University, New Brunswick, N.J.

Jordan, June. 1992. "Report from the Bahamas." In *Race, Class and Gender: An Anthology,* ed. Margaret Andersen and Patricia Hill Collins. Belmont, Calif.: Wadsworth.

Joyce, Patrick. 1991. "The People's English: Language and Class in England c. 1840–1920." In *Language, Self and Society: A Social History of Language,* ed. Peter Burke and Roy Porter. Cambridge: Polity Press.

Joyner, Will. 1998. "Signs of Renewal in the Latest British Invasion." *New York Times* (20 December), sec. 2, 13. Available from: Lexis-Nexis.

Julian, Sheryl. 1997. "Tea's Time; Move Over, Coffee. Caffeine Drinkers Are Turning a New Leaf." *The Globe* (Boston) (12 March), E1. Available from: Lexis-Nexis.

Keating, Stephen. 2000. "Cable's British Invasion, but with a Target of 25 Million, BBC America May Have Waited Too Long." *Advertising Age,* vol. 71 (10 April), S10. Available from: Infotrac.

Kelley, Jonathon, and M.D.R. Evans. 1995. "Class and Conflict in Six Western Nations." *American Sociological Review* 60, no. 2: 157–78.

Kessler, Suzanne J., and Wendy McKenna. 1978. *Gender: An Ethnomethodological Approach.* New York: John Wiley and Sons.

Kibria, Nazli. 1993. *Family Tightrope: The Changing Lives of Vietnamese Americans.* Princeton, N.J.: Princeton University Press.

Kimmel, Michael. 1996. *Manhood in America: A Cultural History.* New York: Free Press.

Kincheloe, Joe L., Shirley R. Steinberg, Nelson M. Rodriguez, and Ronald E. Chennault, eds. 1998. *White Reign: Deploying Whiteness in America.* New York: St. Martin's Press.

King, Deborah. 1988. "Multiple Jeopardy, Multiple Consciousness: The Context of a Black Feminist Ideology." *Signs* 14, no. 1: 265–95.

King, John. 1997. *The Football Factory.* London: Vintage.

————. 1999 (1998). *England Away.* London: Vintage.

Kirk, Russell. 1993. *America's British Culture.* New Brunswick, N.J., and London: Transaction Publishers.

Kushner, Tony, ed. 1992. *The Jewish Heritage in British History: Englishness and Jewishness.* London and Portland, Ore.: Frank Cass.

Labov, W. 1966. *The Social Stratification of English in New York City.* Washington, D.C.: Center for Applied Linguistics.

Labov, William. 1972. *Sociolinguistic Patterns.* Philadelphia: Pennsylvania University Press.

Lake, Marilyn. 1992. "Mission Impossible: How Men Gave Birth to the Australian Nation: Nationalism, Gender and Other Seminal Acts." *Gender and History* 4, no. 3: 305–22.

Lamont, Michèle. 1992. *Money, Morals and Manners: The Culture of the French and American Upper Middle Class.* Cambridge: Cambridge University Press.

————, ed. 1999. *The Cultural Territories of Race: Black and White Boundaries.* Chicago: University of Chicago Press, Russell Sage Foundation.

Langston, Donna. 1992. "Tired of Playing Monopoly?" Pp. 110–20 in *Race, Class and Gender: An Anthology,* ed. Margaret Andersen and Patricia Hill Collins. Belmont, Calif.: Wadsworth.

Lather, Patti. 1991. *Getting Smart: Feminist Research and Pedagogy With/in the Postmodern.* New York and London: Routledge.

Lavelle, Louis. 1997. "Shop Caters to Anglophiles; a Crumpet with Your Tea? British Outpost Gains Foothold in Ridgewood." *The Record* (Bergen County, N.J.) (20 August), B01. Available from: Lexis-Nexis.

Layton-Henry, Zig. 1992. *The Politics of Immigration.* Oxford and Cambridge, Mass.: Basil Blackwell.

Leith, Dick. 1983. *A Social History of English.* London and Boston: Routledge and Kegan Paul.

Leonard, Mark. 1997. *Britain: Renewing Our Identity.* London: Demos.

Levine, Lawrence W. 1988. *Highbrow/Lowbrow: The Emergence of Cultural Hierarchy.* Cambridge, Mass., and London: Harvard University Press.

Lewis, Michael. 1997. "Royal Scam." *New York Times Magazine* (9 February), 22.

Lieberson, Stanley. 1985. "Unhyphenated Whites in the United States." *Ethnic and Racial Studies* 8, no. 1: 158–80.

Lipsitz, George. 1998. *The Possessive Investment in Whiteness from Identity Politics.* Philadelphia: Temple University Press.

Lloyd, John. 1998. "The Making of Cruel Britannia." *New Statesman,* vol. 11, no. 510 (26 June), 8–10. Available from: Proquest.

Lorde, Audre. 1984. *Sister Outsider.* Freedom, Calif.: Crossing Press.

Lowenthal, David. 1991. "British National Identity and the English Landscape." *Rural History* 2, no. 2: 205–30.

MacColl, Gail, and Carol McD. Wallace. 1989. *To Marry an English Lord: Or How Anglomania Really Got Started.* New York: Workman Publishing.

Mackenzie, John M., ed. 1986. *Imperialism and Popular Culture.* Manchester: Manchester University Press.

MacLeod, Arlene Elowe. 1992. "Hegemonic Relations and Gender Resistance." *Signs: Journal of Women in Culture and Society* 17, no. 3: 533–57.

Mano, D. Keith. 1995. "Why Americans Feel Inferior to the British . . . and Why We Shouldn't." *Forbes,* vol. 155, no. 6 (13 March), S123. Available from: Dialog Web.

Marr, Andrew. 2000. *The Day Britain Died.* London: Profile Books.

Martinez, Soljane. 1998. "No Spitting in the Dugout: It Wouldn't Be Cricket." *Providence Journal-Bulletin* (5 October), 1B. Available from: Lexis-Nexis.

McCabe, Bruce. 1997. "PBS Returns with Another 'Masterpiece.'" *The Globe* (Boston) (12 October), Television Week, 3. Available from: Lexis-Nexis.

McClintock, Anne. 1993. "Family Feuds: Gender, Nationalism and the Family." *Feminist Review* 44: 61–80.

———. 1995. *Imperial Leather: Race, Gender and Sexuality in the Colonial Conquest.* New York and London: Routledge.

McDaniel, Patricia A. 2000. "Shrinking Violets and Caspar Milquetoasts: Shyness, Power and Intimacy in the United States, 1950–1995." Ph.D. diss., Rutgers University, New Brunswick, N.J.

McElhinny, Bonnie. 1995. "Challenging Hegemonic Masculinities." Pp. 217–43 in *Gender Articulated,* ed. Mary Bucholtz. New York: Routledge.

McGough, Michael. 1997. "A Trade Gap in Accents of English." *The New York Times* (17 August), sec. 2, 11. Available from: Lexis-Nexis.

McIntosh, Peggy. 1992. "White Privilege and Male Privilege: A Personal Account of Coming to See Correspondences Through Work in Women's Studies." In *Race, Class and Gender: An Anthology,* ed. Margaret Andersen and Patricia Hill Collins. Belmont, Calif.: Wadsworth.

McKinley, Jesse. 1999. "The British Invasion? Surrender." *New York Times* (21 May), E1. Available from: Lexis-Nexis.

Mead, George Herbert. 1934. *Mind, Self and Society.* Chicago: University of Chicago Press.

Menlo Consulting. 1999. "Americans as International Travellers." Independent research commissioned for the British Tourist Authority Research Department. New York (August).

Merrill, Cristina. 2000. "Absolutely Fabulous." *American Demographics,* vol. 22, no. 1 (January), 27–9. Available from: Proquest.

Milroy, James, and Lesley Milroy. 1991 (1985). *Authority in Language: Investigating Language Prescription and Standardization.* London and New York: Routledge.

Mitford, Nancy. 1956. *Noblesse Oblige.* London: Hamish Hamilton.

Mohanty, Chandra Talpade. 1991a. "Introduction: Cartographies of Struggle. Third World Women and the Politics of Feminism." Pp. 1–47 in *Third World Women and the Politics of Feminism,* ed. Chandra Talpade Mohanty, Ann Russo, and Lourdes Torres. Bloomington: Indiana University Press.

———. 1991b. "Under Western Eyes: Feminist Scholarship and Colonial Discourses." Pp. 51–80 in *Third World Women and the Politics of Feminism,* ed. Chandra Talpade Mohanty, Ann Russo, and Lourdes Torres. Bloomington: Indiana University Press.

Moraga, Cherrie, and Gloria Anzaldúa, eds. 1983 (1981). *This Bridge Called My Back: Writings by Radical Women of Color.* New York: Kitchen Table Women of Color Press.

Morais, Richard C. 1997. "'The U.S. Is a Very Noisy Place.'" *Forbes,* vol. 159, no. 12 (16 June), 54. Available from: Dialog Web.

Morrison, Toni. 1997. "Playing in the Dark: Whiteness and the Literary Imagination." Pp. 79–84 in *Critical White Studies: Looking Behind the Mirror,* ed. Richard Delgado and Jean Stefancic. Philadelphia: Temple University Press.

Moser, John E. 1999. *Twisting the Lion's Tail: American Anglophobia Between the World Wars.* New York: New York University Press.

Moss, Norman. 1984. *British/American Language Dictionary.* Lincolnwood, Ill.: Passport Books.

Mostov, Julie. 1998. "'Our Women'/'Their Women': Symbolic Boundaries, Territorial Markers, and Violence in the Balkans." Pp. 327–36 in *Women, Culture and Society: A Reader,* ed. Barbara J. Balliet and Patricia McDaniel. Dubuque, Iowa: Kendall/Hunt Publishing.

Mugglestone, Lynda. 1995. *"Talking Proper": The Rise of Accent as Social Symbol.* Oxford: Clarendon Press.

Mulkay, Michael, and C. Nigel Gilbert. 1982. "Accounting for Error: How Scientists Construct Their Social World When They Account for Correct and Incorrect Belief." *Sociology* 16: 165–83.

Naficy, Hamid. 1993. *The Making of Exile Cultures: Iranian Television in Los Angeles.* Minneapolis and London: University of Minnesota Press.

Nagel, Joanne. 1994. "Constructing Ethnicity: Creating and Recreating Ethnic Identity and Culture." *Social Problems* 41, no. 1: 152–76.

Nairn, Tom. 1977. *The Break-up of Britain: Crisis and Neo-Nationalism.* London: New Left Books.

———. 1988. *The Enchanted Glass: Britain and Its Monarchy.* London: Chandos.

———. 2000a. *After Britain: New Labour and the Return of Scotland.* London: Granta Books.

———. 2000b. "Ukania under Blair." *New Left Review* 1, no. 1: 69–103.

National Centre for Social Research. 2000. "British Social Attitudes: Focusing on Diversity," 17th report, 2000–01 ed. Available from: <http://www.natcen.ac.uk/news/news_bsa_pr2000.htm>.

Newman, Gerald. 1987. *English Nationalism: A Cultural History, 1740–1830.* New York: St. Martin's Press.

"Nobles: Get Ready for Ethelred." 1995. *New York Times* (23 July), sec. 6, 6. Available from: Lexis-Nexis.

Nunberg. Geoffrey. 1997. "Lingo Jingo: English-Only and the New Nativism." *American Prospect,* vol. 33 (July/August), 40–7. Available from: Wilson Web.

Omi, Michael, and Howard Winant. 1994 (1986). *Racial Formations in the United States from the 1960s to the 1980s.* New York and London: Routledge and Kegan Paul.

Oxford English Dictionary, The Compact. 1987 (1971). Oxford: Oxford University Press.

Oxford English Dictionary, The Shorter. 1983. Oxford: Guild Publishing by arrangement with Oxford University Press.

Pajaczkowska, C., and Lola Young. 1992. "Racism, Representation, Psychoanalysis." Pp. 198–219 in *Race, Culture and Difference*, ed. James Donald and Ali Rattansi. Newbury Park, Calif.: Sage Publications.

Parker, Ian. 1992. *Discourse Dynamics: Critical Analysis for Social and Individual Psychology.* London and New York: Routledge.

Parker, Nick, and Mike Darvill. 2000. "England Stay in Waterloo 185 Years After Iron Duke's Win." *The Sun* (London) (17 June), 10.

Pateman, Carole. 1988. *The Sexual Contract.* Stanford, Calif.: Stanford University Press.

Paul, Kathleen. 1997. *Whitewashing Britain: Race and Citizenship in the Postwar Era.* Ithaca, N.Y., and London: Cornell University Press.

Paxman, Jeremy. 1998. *The English: Portrait of a People.* London: Michael Joseph.

Phoenix, Ann. 1997. "'I'm White! So What?' The Construction of Whiteness for Young Londoners." Pp. 187–97 in *Off White: Readings on Race, Power and Society*, ed. Michelle Fine et al. New York and London: Routledge.

Poniewozik, James. 2000. "Anarchy from the U.K. A Different British Invasion is Under Way as BBC America Imports Shows That Are Anything but Stuffy." *Time*, vol. 155, no. 23 (5 June), 81. Available from: Infotrac.

"Population by Ethnic Group." 1991. Available from: <http://www.warwick.ac.uk/~errac/tab1.htm>.

Porter, Roy. 1992. *Myths of the English.* Cambridge and Oxford: Polity Press.

Pratt, Mary Louise. 1991. *Imperial Eyes: Travel Writing and Transculturation.* London and New York: Routledge.

————. 1993. "Arts of the Contact Zone." Pp. 442–56 in *Ways of Reading: An Anthology for Writers*, ed. D. Bartholomae and A. Petrosky. Boston: St. Martin's Press.

Pratt, Minnie Bruce. 1984. "Identity: Skin, Blood, Heart." In *Yours in Struggle: Three Feminist Perspectives on Anti-Semitism and Racism*, ed. Minnie Bruce Pratt, Barbara Smith, and Elly Bulkin. New York: Long Haul Press.

Queen, Rob. 2001. "Living in North America." Available from: <http://expatlife.webjump.com>.

Queenan, Joe. 1990. "The Four Bikers of the Apocalypse." *New York Times* (7 October), sec. 7, 27.

Ramirez, F. 1987. "Global Changes, World Myths and the Demise of Cultural Gender: Implications for the U.S." In *America's Changing Role in the World-System*, ed. T. Boswell and A. Bergesen. New York: Praeger.

Ranger, Terence. 1996. "Introduction." Pp. 1–25 in *Culture, Identity and Politics*, ed. Terence Ranger, Yunas Samad, and Ossie Stuart. Aldershot, U.K., and Brookfield, Vt.: Averbury.

Redwood, John. 1999. *The Death of Britain? The UK's Constitutional Crisis.* Basingstoke, Hants., London, and New York: Macmillan and St. Martin's Press.

Reed, John Shelton. 1982. *One South: An Ethnic Approach to Regional Culture.* Baton Rouge: Louisiana State University Press.

Reed, Nigel. 2001. "Britnet." Available from: <http://www.british-expats.com>.

Reily, Denise. 1988. *Am I That Name? Feminism and the Category of "Women" in History.* Minneapolis: University of Minnesota Press.

Reinharz, Shulamit. 1989 (1983). "Experiential Analysis: A Contribution to Feminist Research." In *Theories of Women's Studies*, ed. G. Bowles and R. Duelli Klein. New York: Routledge.

Reinharz, Shulamit, with Lynn Davidman. 1992. *Feminist Methods in Social Research.* New York: Oxford University Press.

Rich, Adrienne. 1986. *Blood, Bread and Poetry.* New York and London: W. W. Norton.

Rodríguez, Clara E. 1994. "Challenging Racial Hegemony: Puerto Ricans in the United States." In *Race*, ed. Stephen Gregory and Roger Sanjek. New Brunswick, N.J.: Rutgers University Press.

Roediger, David. 1991. *The Wages of Whiteness: Race and the Making of the American Working Class.* London and New York: Verso.

Room, Adrian. 1999 (1959). *Brewer's Dictionary of Phrase and Fable*, rev. ed. London: Cassell.

Rorty, Richard. 1996. "Who Are We? Moral Universalism and Economic Triage." *Diogenes* 44/1, no. 173: 5–15.

Rosen, Craig. 1996. "Britpop Acts on Invasion Alert." *Billboard*, vol. 108, no. 6 (10 February), 1–2. Available from: Infotrac.

Rosewarne, David. 1994a. "Estuary English: Tomorrow's RP?" *English Today* 10, no. 1 (37): 3–7.

———. 1994b. "Pronouncing Estuary English." *English Today* 10, no. 4 (40): 3–8.

Runnymede Trust. 2000. *The Future of Multi-Ethnic Britain.* Report of the Commission on the Future of Multi-Ethnic Britain. London: Profile Books.

Russo, Ann. 1991. "We Cannot Live Without Our Lives: White Women, Anti-Racism and Feminism." Pp. 297–313 in *Third World Women and the Politics of Feminism*, ed. Chandra Talpade Mohanty, Ann Russo, and Lourdes Torres. Bloomington: Indiana University Press.

Ryan, Alan. 1989. "Scholar Slip: Britain's Painful Brain Drain." *New Republic*, vol. 201, no. 23 (4 December), 14–16. Available from: Infotrac.

Ryan, Ellen Bouchard. 1979. "Why Do Low-Prestige Language Varieties Persist?" In *Language and Social Psychology*, ed. Howard Giles and Robert N. St Clair. Baltimore: University Park Press.

Said, Edward. 1978. *Orientalism.* New York: Vintage Books.

Sampson, Kevin. 1999 (1998). *Awaydays.* London: Vintage.

Samuel, Raphael. 1989a. "Introduction: Exciting to Be English." Pp. xviii–lxvii in *Patriotism: The Making and Unmaking of British National Identity. Volume I. History and Politics*, ed. Raphael Samuel. London and New York: Routledge.

———. 1989b. "Introduction: The 'Little Platoons.'" Pp. ix–xxviii in *Patriotism: The Making and Unmaking of British National Identity. Volume II. Minorities and Outsiders*, ed. Raphael Samuel. London and New York: Routledge.

———. 1989c. "Introduction: The Figures of National Myth." Pp. ix–xxxvi in *Patriotism: The Making and Unmaking of British National Identity, Volume III. National Fictions*, ed. Raphael Samuel. London and New York: Routledge.

———. 1998. *Island Stories: Unravelling Britain.* London and New York: Verso.

Santoro, Wayne A. 1999. "Conventional Politics Takes Center Stage: The Latino Struggle Against English-Only Laws." *Social Forces* 77, no. 3 (March). Available from: Infotrac.

Schlesinger, Arthur M. 1946. *Learning to Behave: A Historical Study of American Etiquette Books.* New York: Macmillan.

Schlesinger, Philip. 1987. "On National Identity: Some Conceptions and Misconceptions Criticized." *Social Science Information* 26, no. 2: 219–64.

Schur, Norman W. 1973. *British Self-Taught: With Comments in American.* New York: Macmillan.

Schwalbe, Michael L., and D. Mason-Schrock. 1996. "Identity Work as Group Process." *Advances in Group Processes* 13: 113–47.

Schwartz, Barry. 1990. *George Washington: The Making of an American Symbol.* Ithaca, N.Y.: Cornell University Press.

Scott, Joan. 1992. "Experience." Pp. 22–40 in *Feminists Theorize the Political*, ed. Judith Butler and Joan Scott. New York and London: Routledge.

Sebastian, Richard J., and Ellen Bouchard Ryan. 1985. "Speech Cues and Social Evaluation: Markers of Ethnicity, Social Class and Age." In *Recent Advances in Language, Communication and Social Psychology*, ed. Howard Giles and Robert N. St. Clair. London: Lawrence Erlbaum Associates.

Simmel, Georg. 1950. *The Sociology of Georg Simmel.* Glencoe, Ill.: Free Press.

Small, Stephen. 1994. *Racialised Barriers: The Black Experience in the United States and England in the 1980s.* London and New York: Routledge.

Smith, Anthony. 1986. *The Ethnic Origins of Nations.* London: Basil Blackwell.

Smith, Dorothy. 1987. *The Everyday World as Problematic: A Feminist Sociology.* Boston: Northeastern University Press.

Snedegar, Jean. May 2, 1996. *Report on Accents and Class in Britain.* "The World" Radio Show. London: British Broadcasting Corporation and Public Radio International.

Snitow, Ann. 1990. "A Gender Diary." In *Conflicts in Feminism*, ed. Marianne Hirsch and Evelyn Fox Keller. New York and London: Routledge.

Spelman, Elizabeth V. 1988. *Inessential Woman: Problems of Exclusion in Feminist Thought.* Boston: Beacon Press.

Spicer, Andi. 1989. "Brain-Drained." *Geographical Magazine*, vol. 61, no. 3 (March), 55. Available from: Infotrac.

Stanworth, Michelle. 1984. "Women and Class Analysis: A Reply to John Goldthorpe." *Sociology* 18: 159–70.

Stefancic, Jean, and Richard Delgado, eds. 1996. *No Mercy: How Conservative Think Tanks and Foundations Changed America's Social Agenda.* Philadelphia: Temple University Press.

Stowe, David W. 1996. "Uncolored People: The Rise of Whiteness Studies." *Lingua Franca* (September–October), 68–77.

Strongman, K. T., and J. Woosley. 1967. "Stereotyped Reactions to Regional Accents." *British Journal of Social and Clinical Psychology* 6: 164–7.

Sullivan, Andrew. 1999. "London Fog." *New Republic*, vol. 220, no. 24 (14 June), 24–9. Available from: Proquest.

Surel, Jeannine. 1989. "John Bull." In *Patriotism: The Making and Unmaking of British National Identity, Volume III. National Fictions*, ed. Raphael Samuel. London and New York: Routledge.

"Surfacing: Merchandising." 1994. *New York Times* (13 March), sec. 9, 3. Available from: Lexis-Nexis.

Swidler, Ann. 1986. "Culture in Action: Symbols and Strategies." *American Sociological Review* 51: 273–86.

Taitz, Sonia. 1999. "Film: The Spy Who Came in from the Cool Is a Bit of a Yankee." *New York Times* (6 June), sec. 2, 13. Available from: Lexis-Nexis.

Tajfel, Henri. 1974. "Social Identity and Intergroup Behaviour." *Social Science Information* 13: 65–93.

Tajfel, Henri, and J. C. Turner. 1979. "An Integrative Theory of Intergroup Conflict." In *The Social Psychology of Intergroup Relations*, ed. S. Worchel and W. G. Austin. Monterey, Calif.: Brooks-Cole.

———. 1986. "The Social Identity Theory of Intergroup Behaviour." In *Psychology of Intergroup Relations*, ed. S. Worchel and W. G. Austin. Chicago: Nelson-Hall.

Tatalovich, Raymond. 1995. *Nativism Reborn? The Official English Language Movement and the American States*. Lexington: The University Press of Kentucky.

Taylor, Donald M., John N. Bassili, and Frances E. Aboud. 1973. "Dimensions of Ethnic Identity: An Example from Quebec." *Journal of Social Psychology* 89: 185–92.

Taylor, Peter J. 1991. "The English and Their Englishness: 'A Curiously Mysterious, Elusive and Little Understood People.'" *Scottish Geographical Magazine*, vol. 107, no. 3, 146–61.

Thompson, Becky. 1999. "Subverting Racism from Within: Linking White Identity to Activism." In *Becoming and Unbecoming White: Owning and Disowning a Racial Identity*, ed. Christine Clark and James O'Donnell. Westport, Conn., and London: Bergin and Garvey.

Thompson, John B. 1990. *Ideology and Modern Culture*. Stanford, Calif.: Stanford University Press.

Thorne, Barrie. 1993. *Gender Play: Girls and Boys in School*. New Brunswick, N.J.: Rutgers University Press.

Tilly, Charles, ed. 1975. *The Formation of National States in Western Europe*. Princeton, N.J.: Princeton University Press.

Trudgill, Peter. 1983. *On Dialect: Social and Geographical Perspectives*. New York and London: New York University Press.

———. 1984. *Language in the British Isles*. Cambridge: Cambridge University Press.

———. 1986. *Dialects in Contact*. Oxford: Basil Blackwell.

———. 1990. *The Dialects of England*. Oxford: Basil Blackwell.

Trudgill, Peter, and Jean Hannah. 1994 (1982). *International English: A Guide to Varieties of Standard English*. London and New York: Edward Arnold.

Turney, Jon. 1993. "An Intellectual Loss That Must Be Stemmed." *New Scientist*, vol. 140, no. 1903 (11 December), 48–9. Available from: Infotrac.

UKgoods.com. 2001. "British Food and Groceries for Expatriates and Anglophiles." Available from: <http://www.ukgoods.com>.

United Nations Economic Commission for Europe. 2001. "Trends in Europe and North America." In UNECE Statistical Yearbook. Available from: <http://www.unece.org/stats/trend/gbr.htm>; <http://www.unece/org/stats/trend/ita.htm>.

Wales, Katie. 1994. "Royalese: The Rise and Fall of 'The Queen's English.'" English Today, vol. 10, no. 3 (39): 3–10.

Walvin, James. 1975. The People's Game: A Social History of British Football. London: Allen Lane.

Ware, Vron. 1992. Beyond the Pale: White Women, Racism and History. London and New York: Verso.

———. 1997. "Island Racism: Gender, Place and White Power." Pp. 283–310 in Displacing Whiteness: Essays in Social and Cultural Criticism, ed. Ruth Frankenberg. Durham, N.C., and London: Duke University Press.

Warner, Marina. 1985. Monuments and Maidens. New York: Atheneum.

Waters, Mary. 1990. Ethnic Options: Choosing Identities in America. Berkeley and Los Angeles: University of California Press.

———. 1998. "Optional Ethnicities: For Whites Only?" In Race, Class and Gender: An Anthology, ed. Margaret L. Andersen and Patricia Hill Collins. Belmont, Calif.: Wadsworth Publishing.

———. 1999. "Explaining the Comfort Factor: West Indian Immigrants Confront American Race Relations." Pp. 63–96 in The Cultural Territories of Race: Black and White Boundaries, ed. Michèle Lamont. Chicago, London, New York: University of Chicago Press and Russell Sage Foundation.

Watson, George. 1989. "Letter from Cambridge: Britain and the Brain Gain." The Hudson Review vol. 42, no. 2 (Summer), 182–9. Available from: Infotrac.

Weigert, Andrew, J. Smith, and Dennis W. Teitge. 1986. Society and Identity: Toward a Sociological Psychology. Cambridge: Cambridge University Press.

Wells, J. C. 1982. Accents of English I. Cambridge: Cambridge University Press.

West, Candace, and Sarah Fenstermaker. 1995. "Doing Difference." Gender and Society 9, no. 1: 8–37.

West, Candace, and Don H. Zimmerman. 1987. "Doing Gender." Gender and Society 1, no. 2: 125–51.

Weston, Kath. 1993. "Do Clothes Make the Woman?" Genders 17: 1–21.

Wheatcroft, Geoffrey. 1990. "Le Vice Americain." New Republic, vol. 11 (12 March), 46. Available from: Dialog Web.

Widdicombe, Sue, and Robin Wooffitt. 1995. The Language of Youth Subcultures: Social Identity in Action. New York and London: Harvester Wheatsheaf.

Williams, Patricia. 1991. The Alchemy of Race and Rights: Diary of a Law Professor. Cambridge, Mass., and London: Harvard University Press.

Williams, Richard. 1990. Hierarchical Structures and Social Value. Oxford: Oxford University Press.

Willis, Paul. 1979 (1977). Learning to Labour: How Working Class Kids Get Working Class Jobs. Farnborough, Hants.: Saxon House, Teakfield.

———. 1990. Common Culture: Symbolic Work at Play in Everyday Cultures of the Young. Boulder, Colo.: Westview Press.

WING (Women, Immigration, and Nationality Group). 1985. *World's Apart: Women under Immigration and Nationality Law.* London and Sydney: Pluto Press.

Winks, Robin W. 1998. "The Brits Who Do Not Induce—Nor Disturb—His Slumbers." *The Globe* (Boston) (25 January), F2. Available from: Lexis-Nexis.

Wolf, Matt. 1995. "Who Will Be the Next Ralph Fiennes, the Next Hugh Grant?" *New York Times* (1 January), sec. 2, 9. Available from: Lexis-Nexis.

Wordsworth, William. 1986. "I Travelled Among Unknown Men." In M. H. Abrams, ed., *Norton Anthology of English Literature*, 5th ed. New York: W. W. Norton.

Wright, Erik Olin. 1996. "Varieties of Marxist Conceptions of Class Structure." Pp. 388–432 in *Class: Critical Concepts. Volume IV*, ed. John Scott. London and New York: Routledge.

———. 1997. *Class Counts: Comparative Studies in Class Analysis.* Cambridge: Cambridge University Press.

Wright, Louis B. 1940. *The First Gentlemen of Virginia: Intellectual Qualities of the Early Colonial Ruling Class.* Charlottesville, Va.: Dominion Books.

Wright, Patrick. 1985. *On Living in an Old Country: The National Past in Contemporary Britain.* London: Verso.

Zelinsky, Wilbur. 1988. *Nation into State.* Chapel Hill: University of North Carolina Press.

Zerubavel, Yael. 1994. "The Death of Memory and the Memory of Death: Masada and the Holocaust as Historical Metaphors." *Representations* 45: 72–100.

Index

Accent(s): American, English reactions to, 121–22, 127–28; Americanized, 119, 128, 247n. 43; desire to maintain, social-identity theory on, 248n. 55; English (*see* Accent[s], English); French, American reactions to, 120; and identity construction, 248n. 51

Accent(s), English, 108–40; American reactions to, 86, 119–22; Anglophilic responses to, 119–22; categorization based on, 112–13; changes in, attitudes toward, 139; as class indicator, 65–66, 111–15, 241n. 6; cockney, 88, 133; as cultural capital, 121; de-emphasizing, 135–36; educational background and, 112, 113; flexibility of, 115–16, 123, 124; focus on, objections to, 134–37; and humor, 129, 130, 134; and identity work, 108–9, 110; length of time in U.S. and, 118–19, 247n. 43; manipulation of, 109, 123, 130; and national identity, 113, 124–25; as performance, 132–34; playing up, 122–25, 133, 134; and privilege, 83, 84, 85; regional, 111–14; RP (Received Pronunciation), 111–14, 133, 241n. 6, 245n. 16; and self-esteem, 109, 110, 124, 126–27, 128, 130; and superiority complex, 118, 127, 130, 133; symbolism of, 139; unconscious and unintentional uses of, 130–32; use in advertising, 80; work involved in, 123–25, 138, 139

Accountability: for Anglophilia, 82–84, 85, 90, 91, 107, 123, 212; and identity construction, 207–10, 222; for miscommunication, 126; for privilege, 61, 107

Advertising, use of English accents in, 80

Affirmative action, 180

African Americans: vs. black immigrants, 120; vs. black people in England, 176–77

Alienation, experience of, 96, 97

All Creatures Great and Small (TV show), 23

American English vs. English English: accommodation of, 119, 246n. 42–247n. 42; fluidity of movement between, 115; linguistic pitfalls in, 117–18, 125

Americans: accents of, English reactions to, 121–22, 127–28; accountability for Anglophilia, 82–84, 85, 90, 91, 107, 123, 212; attitudes toward national identity, criticism of, 47–50; class assumptions of, 88–89; contrast with English people, 59–60; cultural insularity of, 155; and English humor, ability to understand, 105; and ethnicity, criticism of emphasis on, 171, 173; inferiority complex of, 85–87, 106; interactions with, and identity construction, 210–12; masculinity of, 158–59; national pride of, 44, 48; racism of, criticism of, 72, 73; and regional identity, inability to relate to, 88–89; and sarcasm, supposed lack of, 101–2; stereotypes about, 39–40, 41, 42. *See also* United States

Anderson, Benedict, 141, 142

Anglophilia, 77–91; accents and, 119–22; accountability for, 82–84, 85, 90, 91, 107, 123, 212; class and, 78, 120; critiques of, 87, 91; as cultural capital, 82; definition of, 106; distancing from, 55; historical evidence of, 77–78; influence on English immigrants, 128–29; manifestations of, 78–80; and privilege, 13, 70, 71, 82–84, 120–21, 211–12; psychological benefits of, 127; race and, 78, 120; responding to, 80–81, 85–91, 216; theories about, 81–82

Anonymity, immigration and, 64, 65, 114; vs. celebrity status, 87–88, 89

Anthias, Floya, 14

Anti-immigrant sentiment, in U.S., 71; criticism of, 73; and racism, 166

Are You Being Served (TV program), 101

Arrogance, English: criticism of, 160; imperial legacy and, 146–47

Assimilation, issue of, 191–92

BBC English. *See* RP

The Beatles, and image of England, 30–31